"Goodwin's monograph goes above and beyond simple institutional histories of tribal colleges and universities by offering historical and intellectual contexts that led to their founding, growth, and development. His work gives attention and primacy to Native intellectual voices of the early and middle twentieth century by focusing on individuals whose names and work we are familiar with, but not perhaps in the context of higher education. Finally, Goodwin brings renewed attention to the intellectual activism that went alongside the Red Power Movement of the 1960s."

—MAJEL BOXER, *Journal of Arizona History*

"*Without Destroying Ourselves* is an exceptional addition to the Indigenous Education series alongside other works on American Indian experiences in settler colonial education."

—TEAGAN DREYER, *South Dakota History*

"Goodwin's sympathetic and insightful history underscores the importance of tribal colleges and universities as intellectual spaces that are educating, decolonizing, and sustaining the tribal communities they serve. This book fills a gaping void in American Indian historiography and will undoubtedly transform how scholars think about Indian education."

—BRADLEY SHREVE, editor of *Tribal College Journal of American Indian Higher Education*

"In the face of white colonialism, Native American leaders have long had to wrestle with the timeless question: How can we change without destroying ourselves? As John A. Goodwin demonstrates in this deeply researched and thoughtful study, answering this question has always been at the heart of Native intellectuals' efforts to create a model of higher education both by and for Indians. To understand the multiple struggles they encountered in this journey—a journey in which the issues of power and purpose were central—this study is must-reading."

—DAVID WALLACE ADAMS, author of *Education for Extinction: American Indians and the Boarding School Experience, 1875–1928*

WITHOUT DESTROYING OURSELVES

Indigenous Education

SERIES EDITORS

Margaret Connell Szasz
University of New Mexico

John W. Tippeconnic III
Pennsylvania State University

WITHOUT DESTROYING OURSELVES

A Century of Native Intellectual Activism
for Higher Education

John A. Goodwin

University of Nebraska Press
LINCOLN

∞

First Nebraska paperback printing: 2026

For customers in the EU with safety/GPSR concerns, contact:
gpsr@mare-nostrum.co.uk
Mare Nostrum Group BV
Mauritskade 21D
1091 GC Amsterdam
The Netherlands

Library of Congress Cataloging-in-Publication Data
Names: Goodwin, John A., author.
Title: Without destroying ourselves: a century of native intellectual activism for higher education / John A. Goodwin.
Other titles: Century of native intellectual activism for higher education
Description: Lincoln: University of Nebraska Press, 2022. | Series: Indigenous education series | Includes bibliographical references and index.
Identifiers: LCCN 2021042947
ISBN 9781496215611 (hardback)
ISBN 9781496244994 (paperback)
ISBN 9781496231031 (epub)
ISBN 9781496231048 (pdf)
Subjects: LCSH: Indians of North America—Education (Higher) | Indian universities and colleges—United States—History. | Indians of North America—Intellectual life. | Cloud, Henry Roe, 1885–1950—Influence. | Indian activists—United States. | Indian intellectuals—United States. | Educational change—United States. | BISAC: SOCIAL SCIENCE / Ethnic Studies / American / Native American Studies | EDUCATION / History
Classification: LCC E97.55 .G66 2022 | DDC 973.04/97—dc23
LC record available at https://lccn.loc.gov/2021042947

Set in Adobe Garamond Pro by Mikala R. Kolander.

For my father, who has drawn on his own experience as an educator and a "one-time intellectual" to offer me his advice and—more important—his humor.

And for my mother, who was an inspiration to all who knew her.

CONTENTS

ILLUSTRATIONS

ACKNOWLEDGMENTS

While I accept any errors or omissions in this document as my own, I understand that the successful completion of this project is due to a large and supportive network, beginning with my advisory committee at Arizona State University. Dr. Donald Fixico has always shown confidence in me, even when it felt unwarranted. I have benefited greatly from his wealth of experience during our discussions, and from his willingness to challenge me with the important questions and ideas that must be addressed when writing Native American history. Dr. Katherine Osburn has provided an admirable example of the energy and enthusiasm needed to approach both research and teaching, and her positivity as well as her pragmatic feedback have been welcome in this long process. Dr. K. Tsianina Lomawaima has similarly shown support for my ideas and research explorations, and has been invaluable in guiding those explorations and in consistently pushing me to strengthen my arguments. I can truly say I have been blessed to work closely with these three individuals.

Several others at asu were also instrumental in my progress. Dr. Paul Hirt was an astute and careful critic of my early research, and I still greatly appreciate his influence on my writing process. Dr. Bryan Brayboy was supportive in discussing the overall scope of my project, and offered advice for pursuing research funds. I wish to acknowledge the asu School of Historical, Philosophical, and Religious Studies, the asu Graduate and Professional Student Association, and the asu Graduate College for a combination of funds that supported my research process. Without these resources, I could not have conducted the far-reaching and in-depth research that has been vital to this project.

In my research, I have benefited from the support of many historians, archivists, librarians, and others whose knowledge and experience saved me countless hours and led me to the resources necessary to complete this work. Though many scholars have been far more generous than I could have ever expected, my email correspondence and discussions on the phone with Dr. Wayne Stein were particularly encouraging. His own work has been a constant resource for me, and his willingness to assist a young historian whom he had never met will always be appreciated. In a similar way, Dr. Renya Ramirez, through both correspondence and her numerous publications, provided key guidance during the revision process for the manuscript.

For their vital assistance during the various stages of the research process, I acknowledge Dr. Bradley Shreve at *Tribal College Journal*; Dr. Herman A. Peterson at the Diné College Libraries; Rachel Menyuk at the National Museum of the American Indian Cultural Resources Center; Nancy Brown-Martinez and Cindy Abel Morris at the University of New Mexico's Center for Southwest Research; Joyce Burner at the National Archives in Kansas City; and Sara Gunasekara at the UC Davis Special Collections. I also received generous support and advice from the staff members of the entire library system at Arizona State University, especially the Labriola National American Indian Data Center; the National Archives in Washington DC; the Spencer Research Library at the University of Kansas; the Sterling Library Manuscripts and Archives at Yale University; the National Archives of the Presbyterian Church; and the Haskell Indian Nations University Cultural Center.

Thank you as well to the readers who provided feedback on my manuscript proposal to the University of Nebraska Press. Those comments provided detailed questions and suggestions that were essential in pushing me to continually reconsider some of the most important issues addressed in the book.

Finally, I thank the many family members, friends, and colleagues who encouraged me in this long process and provided support and necessary distraction. I could never fully express how important this network has been for me, but I carry a deep appreciation for all of you—you know who you are. To my little Connie: you already love your books, and reading with you brings me so much joy. Someday I hope you get at least an ounce of joy from opening this book and seeing your name in print. I say a special thank you to my wife, Rachel, above all for your patience. You weren't my wife when this work started for me, and yet you still decided to say yes. That was a big leap of faith for you, and I think about it every day. Thank you. I love you.

WITHOUT DESTROYING OURSELVES

Introduction

How Can We Change without Destroying Ourselves?

On a bright spring day in April 1971, Navajo educators, medicine men, and tribal officials gathered near Tsaile, Arizona, to bless and break the ground at what would become the central campus of Navajo Community College (NCC—now Diné College).[1] The school was sanctioned by the Navajo Tribal Council, run by a Navajo board of regents, and dedicated to a mission in higher education that placed Indigenous issues at the center—rather than the periphery—of the curriculum.[2] Though NCC had been in operation for two years, the groundbreaking ceremony in 1971 confirmed the fledgling school as a distinctly Navajo entity. It was operating as a perfect example of what reservation residents had begun to call *Diné Bi'Olta* (the people's school, or the Navajo school).[3] As the campus site near Tsaile took shape, its carefully selected construction materials visually mimicked the rugged beauty of the surrounding mesas and mountains, and even represented some of the foundational aspects of Navajo creation stories.[4] In this process, the new campus became a protected space for Native identity within an educational landscape that had for so long been hostile to expressions of Native culture. As the first tribally controlled reservation college in the United States, Navajo Community College brought on a new era in American higher education. Thus it holds a distinct place in American history and in the history of Indigenous education.

While it stood out for its uniquely Navajo characteristics, NCC was also the spearhead of a much broader and interconnected movement to bring about other tangible sites of Native American self-determination in higher education. Seizing on the federal government's espoused turn away from aggressive termination policy, half a dozen tribal colleges and universities (TCUs) became candidates for permanent accreditation by the end of the 1970s and were driven by educators, students, and other activists who sought to cement education as a cornerstone of Native American self-determination. They explicitly asked themselves, "How can we change *without destroying ourselves?*"[5] The question arose as a thought exercise—a practical problem to solve rather than a hopeless lament. It was born out of a moment of opportunity, when Native people throughout America were searching for cracks in governmental bureaucracies in which they could plant the seeds of their own Indigenous agendas.

Today, dozens of these schools continue to carry out educational missions that weave together multiple related goals—at once tribally driven and connected to broader discourses and trends throughout Native America. In this way TCUs serve as examples of "Native hubs" in the sense that Renya Ramirez (Ho-Chunk) and others have used the term—as both physical and intellectual spaces, often within dominant American power structures, yet supporting efforts to reify and support Indigenous identity and community and to advance Native activism in a variety of fields.[6]

Up to now, few histories have explored the unique characteristics of tribal colleges and universities and the curricular and community missions they undertake, and those that exist often focus sharply on one tribe rather than the broader intellectual movements on which the institutions were built.[7] Wayne Stein (Turtle Mountain Chippewa), a long-time TCU administrator and advocate, has been one of the few scholars to explore the history of American Indian–controlled education—and specifically TCUs—as a central topic in book-length form.[8] His framing of the topic rests largely on the various legislative acts that provided funding, which, he persuasively argues, is the constant concern of the colleges. This focus gives clarity to the sequence of milestone moments for TCUs. And yet it provides less analysis of the intellectual arguments surrounding the fundamental idea of Native control and the deep historical roots of those arguments. Indeed,

Stein himself has suggested a need for delving deeper into this intellectual history, pointing out that "no one has fully explored the reasons for [tribal colleges'] genesis and continued existence."[9] Even since the publication of his assessment in the 1990s, few major projects have examined the topic in detail.[10]

A central aspect of my initial motivation in writing this history was thus to fill a scholarly gap by giving proper attention to the early tribal college movement as an important cornerstone of the overall fight for self-determination. But as the materials for this work came together, I was also struck by the degree to which TCUs harnessed specific elements of Native intellectual activism that originated well before the particular policy arguments between advocates of termination and self-determination. Furthermore, the arguments surrounding the early TCUs were developed in an activist discourse that stretched beyond the campuses and reservations, into a variety of Native hubs around the country. As a result, this work will not simply outline a case study of modern TCUs. Instead I argue that these schools are just one creative manifestation of a deep and resilient Native intellectual effort, built over the past century and meant to fundamentally reshape the relationship between American higher education and Indigenous people.

The motivation for locating this activist effort within education is clear. In some form, institutions of education have always conveyed (or denied) practical and symbolic power to students. As such, they have always been key battlegrounds in settler colonialism. In the modern United States of the past century, however, this relationship between education and power in society has become especially formalized and rigid in a way that is still recognized and accepted today.[11] As Native American tribes and individuals confront this reality, they are informed by a fraught history of contact and collision with the dominant models in American education—models that were often explicitly meant to destroy Indigenous culture.

So how, then, does this deeper history impact the contemporary actions of TCUs' supporters and other participants in Native intellectual spaces? How have Native activists attempted to address the pitfalls and restrictions in their relationships with American higher education and its attendant power and resources, and how have they learned from and built on previous efforts?

Exploring these questions, I seek to illuminate a key development in Native American history specifically, but also one that illustrates more broadly the complex relationship between modern power structures of settler colonialism and the Indigenous responses to those structures. As Renya Ramirez has written, history is full of moments when this relationship creates an intellectual "thicket" for Native people, who have repeatedly sought to pursue successful living on their own terms, even as they are forced to engage with entangling colonial systems.[12] In studying the thickets that crop up in this story, I employ a methodology influenced by cultural and intellectual history in the context of colonialism. Scholars in these fields insist on looking closely at moments of ambiguity in terms of identity, power, and meaning, and consider a wide array of sources as potentially illuminating.[13] In particular, I rely as often as possible on a source base built by Native leaders themselves—diverse collections of journals, newsletters, speeches, personal correspondence, oral histories, and other published and unpublished sources that reveal how the central themes of a movement for Native control in higher education were developed, shared, and revised over the course of many decades. While this movement was at times seemingly overpowered by bureaucratic and cultural pressures, I hope to capture its threads of continuity as clearly as possible by remaining closely attuned to the Native individuals and groups who took part in it, and by displaying them in their own words.

My effort to privilege Native voices will by no means ignore the power of colonial structures and societies. Violent disruptions and damages to colonized peoples are always a central part of the broader story of colonialism, and should never be forgotten. My work, however, does not in great measure add to the rich body of literature that describes the initial processes of extending colonial power over Native people. I will shed light instead on a long-term, continuous, and resilient thread of Native intellectual activism that emerges within and as a response to that context of collision.

Relying on the work of Manley Begay Jr. (Navajo) and others, I see this Indigenous response as vital to the shaping of culture.[14] In my work, discussions of culture are not undertaken to examine Native beliefs and practices in an ethnohistorical or anthropological sense. Rather, I focus on these moments of ambiguity and struggle because they reveal Native efforts to adapt, restructure, and utilize available materials to protect and advance their beliefs and practices. Native activist efforts within modern settler colonialism—rather than Native culture per se—are thus my subject of inquiry.

My focus on a form of Native intellectualism that emerged in an interaction with modern American institutions and pressures is not to imply that older or more guarded bodies of Native knowledge are nonintellectual or nonactivist. Rather, I am simply most interested in the interactions and adaptations that take place at the meeting points between America's dominant institutions of power and its marginalized peoples.

In particular, I focus on Native activists' articulation and pursuit of the belief that they deserved greater access to and control of institutions of higher education and leadership training in modern America. An "institution" in this case should not be viewed as inflexible or rigid. As the example of the Navajo Community College campus site near Tsaile, Arizona, illustrates, something as seemingly straightforward as a construction project for a new campus site could creatively reify a shared culture and history in profound ways. Furthermore, an institution could just as likely take on more flexible forms such as an intellectual seminar, a temporary government program, or a variety of other kinds of organization. Part of the genius of Indigenous activism has always been the creativity to employ institutional frameworks compatible with and recognizable to the world of settler colonialism, all the while protecting and advancing Native-driven goals. This history is no different.

Specifically, I begin with Henry Roe Cloud (Ho-Chunk) and his American Indian Institute, a preparatory school for American Indian boys founded in Wichita, Kansas, in 1915.[15] Purposefully taking in students from around the country, Cloud and his similarly motivated wife, Elizabeth Bender Cloud (Ojibwe), built a form of higher education specifically geared toward the expansion of Native intellectual leadership nationwide. Eventually, Cloud also became the first Native superintendent of Haskell Institute, in Lawrence, Kansas—one of the largest and most influential of the government-run boarding schools for American Indians. At Haskell in the 1930s, he broadcast his vision for Native-driven higher education and leadership on a larger scale, even as he struggled to exert creativity in the face of the bureaucracy that drove the school.

Cloud's Christianity and his deep training in American academia influenced his leadership style, in some ways giving the impression that he accepted wholesale the white American models of schooling for Native people. On closer examination, however, Cloud repeatedly employed the rhetorical tools and platforms of the colonial power as an inroad to his most consistent passion—supporting the potentially untapped strength of adaptable Native intellectualism and leadership in a way that could still endorse Indigenous expressions of identity. Renya Ramirez, Cloud's granddaughter, has admitted that he wove together a complex body of work that can be difficult to decipher. Through careful study and the incorporation of an intimate body of family knowledge, however, she has argued that he also relied heavily on his Ho-Chunk tribal training throughout his career, often in ways that overlapped with what white Americans considered their own "work ethic" and thus went undetected at the time.[16] This willingness by Native leaders to strategically practice adaptability in terms of the influences they relied on and the messages they delivered would remain a hallmark of the activism that I piece together in this history.

While tribal groups had of course always sought to control and refine their own complex forms of education, the Clouds' efforts stand out as the most significant for this project, which examines not only the interaction between Native intellectual activists and the dominant systems of higher education in America but also the long-term impact and continued relevance of that activism.[17] The Clouds' establishment of Native-driven higher education at the American Indian Institute in 1915 is the most notable such effort in the postallotment era of Native history, when the land bases, economic opportunities, and political power of tribes had been pushed to some of their lowest limits in American history.[18] The General Allotment Act of 1887, whatever the intentions of its sponsors, had accelerated a process of Native American land loss that continued well into the twentieth century. It also coincided with an effort by many off-reservation boarding schools to pulverize tribal identity and assimilate Native students into a white American model of citizenship.[19] In response, the Clouds ran the American Indian Institute in direct opposition to that model and the government power behind it. In so doing, they and their supporters disseminated a particular form of Native intellectual activism that sought to build and protect a more fluid and adaptive notion of Indigenous citizenship in modern America.[20] They positioned higher education and leadership training as a central pillar of that effort, and the threads of their vision far outlasted their own lives.

Henry Roe Cloud's work came at a crucial time in the history of American higher education. In his own schooling experiences, he observed that institutional higher education was becoming an increasingly important part of the American perception of model citizenship and personal empowerment. As historian John Thelin has pointed out, the connection between higher education and earning power, social status, and overall prestige in America became firmly cemented during the latter part of the nineteenth century and the early part of the twentieth.[21]

Though he understood well this development and sought to tap into its empowering aspects, Cloud sought not straightforward assimilation to a white American model but flexible adaptation for Native people to protect their tribal and broader Indigenous identities and communities—even as they gained a greater foothold in modern American power structures. This crucial and explicit distinction between *assimilation* and *adaptation* in Cloud's work would foreshadow the efforts of subsequent generations of Native activists in American education, who sought greater representation and empowerment while privileging tribal goals. Cloud persistently pursued the expansion of higher education "by and for" Native people, with the expressed purpose of building and maintaining an influential body of Native professionals and intellectual leaders.[22]

The momentum of the arguments behind Cloud's work in higher education would eventually be stunted by the politics of the federal government and the Bureau of Indian Affairs, and by the implementation of American Indian termination and assimilationist policies after World War II. Still, even while segments of Congress attempted to terminate the unique tribal status and identities of Native Americans, the core of Cloud's intellectual vision for Native leadership remained intact in a nationwide Native discourse in postwar America.

Much of this continuity was due to the determination of Elizabeth Bender Cloud, who had served for significant stretches as an administrator for the American Indian Institute in her own right. After Henry's death in 1950, she carried forward key principles of the American Indian Institute's educational mission into arenas involving higher education but also broader forms of community leadership and government.[23] Together with Elizabeth, other notable activists like D'Arcy McNickle (Salish Kootenai) echoed the focus on Native intellectual leaders *as Native people*, as well as a broader argument for greater tribal self-government.[24]

Eventually, McNickle too focused more explicitly on carving out Native hubs within American higher education, directing the Workshop on American Indian Affairs in Boulder, Colorado, in the late 1950s and early 1960s. The workshop's intense sessions produced a range of reactions among the students who attended, but overall they acted as a "vehicle for intellectual self-determination" as a new generation of Native intellectual activists arose.[25] The workshops directly influenced many of the founders of the National Indian Youth Council, who from 1961 onward compiled research on Native American education and supported a movement toward greater Native control in schooling and other public services.[26] At the same time, prolific writer Jack Forbes (Powhatan-Renapé, Delaware-Lenape) emerged as one of the strongest voices in resurrecting the call for Native-run institutions of higher education to build and maintain a body of intellectual leaders in the way that Henry Roe Cloud had envisioned.[27]

Not all influential Native intellectuals bought into the movement for tribal control in schooling. Some, like outspoken writer Rupert Costo (Cahuilla), feared that it would effectively reintroduce "segregation" in schooling.[28] Forbes, McNickle, and numerous others, however, viewed Native people's appropriation of American institutions as a form of self-determination and empowerment within American society, not as an undesirable exclusion or alienation from it. They continued to build a national conversation that was fueled by growing networks of Native leaders throughout the country. This nationwide discourse formed an articulate critique of the status quo in American education for Native students, and culminated with tribal communities seizing opportunities for tangible, community-driven projects in the 1960s and 1970s, including the growth of the first tribal colleges and universities. Activists at the national and tribal level demonstrated clearly that Native control of higher education presented an exciting opportunity to boost students' success—both in the context of mainstream American education and economics as well as in the realm of Native cultural identification and tribally centered notions of successful living.

While focusing intently on this vibrant intellectual discourse, this history will also illustrate how the argument for Native control in higher education was implemented on the ground level. Navajo Community College serves as the primary example in this effort, largely because of its relatively rich source base and its role as the first of the tribal colleges. Detailing the efforts of Navajo Community College to meet challenges in funding, curricular

construction, and accreditation contributes to a greater understanding of the actual day-to-day work of tribal colleges, especially in the early years of the TCU movement. At the same time,
supplementary sources from the other tribal colleges reempha-
size the broader implications of the movement for Native control in higher education on a national level.

With that national context in mind, I also examine Haskell
Indian Junior College (now Haskell Indian Nations University),
in Lawrence, Kansas, and Deganawidah-Quetzalcoatl University (D-Q University or DQU), in Davis, California, as key off-
reservation complements to the reservation-based tribal colleges.
Focusing on the transition at Haskell from a secondary and vocational boarding school toward a college model in the early 1970s
helps reveal the broad nature of a movement in higher education
that impacted not only various tribes but the Bureau of Indian
Affairs as well. While the majority of this history addresses the
period before full accreditation and permanent funding of TCUs
in the late 1970s, I also incorporate recent material to reflect on
how the original intellectual underpinnings explicated here remain
intact and relevant today.

Furthermore, the cases of Haskell and DQU raise difficult questions about the relationship between tribal colleges, the federal
government, and Native American self-determination. Specifically, what gains had been made for Native leadership at Haskell
from the days of Henry Roe Cloud, and what bureaucratic challenges and restrictions still remained in the 1970s and beyond?
How do the forms of Native activism developed at the pantribal
DQU or the government-run Haskell engage with or exist apart
from the nation-building efforts at TCUs that serve reservations
and their specific tribal communities? Finally, does a form of
self-determination in higher education that involves appropriating American models and government programs actually provide
opportunities for true Native empowerment, or does it simply
push Native people into a new thicket of settler colonialism?

Fortunately, Indigenous scholars such as Glen Coulthard (Yel-
lowknives Dene), Robert Warrior (Osage), and a host of others

continually press these kinds of fundamental questions today. But these questions do not diminish the work done by the activists studied here. As Warrior writes, "Native studies benefits from living within the tension between . . . varied positions," and activists like the Clouds, McNickle, Forbes, and others intentionally and persistently contributed to similarly difficult conversations in their own time.[29] Jack Forbes, for instance, as an outspoken proponent of self-determination, doggedly challenged both the American government and the espoused Native American self-determinationists in the 1960s and 1970s.[30] Studying Forbes's university project at DQU provides a glimpse into the potential that he and other Native activists saw in transcending tribal and even national boundaries to link together intellectual inquiry, professional training, and grassroots Indigenous activism.

Overall, this story traces how, in multiple stages throughout much of the twentieth century, an array of Native activists and organizations wove a tapestry of intellectual discourse that recalled and reiterated Henry Roe Cloud's central motifs. These people appropriated existing forums in person and in print to broadcast their goals while also creating their own institutional platforms and sites of publication to enhance their rhetorical power. They built from a foundation of tribal and Indigenous culture, history, and identity while also emphasizing forms of intellectual and professional training that could meet and adapt to the unique challenges facing Native people in modern America. Despite the need—in constantly shifting webs of bureaucracy and discourse—to rework and reshape the presentation of these goals, the activists studied here carried them through with remarkable continuity.

In many cases, such as the daily struggle to organize and fund the earliest tribal colleges and universities, the activist struggles of people like Henry Roe and Elizabeth Bender Cloud in the prewar era seem distant. But continuity in strategic philosophy and purpose remains evident in the mission statements that tribal colleges and universities developed in the 1960s, 1970s, and beyond. Many TCUs continue to espouse these same goals. They pursue the dual purposes of preserving and protecting Native history and culture while enabling Native students to become more successful and impactful in arenas of mainstream American intellectual, professional, and political life. Despite clear and formidable challenges, the emergence of this approach in a philosophical discourse and eventually in practice at Native-driven institutions has made a significant impact on access to and control of higher education.

This overall effort from the time of Cloud to today is a form of what I have been calling "Native intellectual activism." While the period covered in this history witnessed many forms of activism, I use the term "Native intellectual activism" to draw attention to the specific combination of principles—higher learning and leadership "by and for" Native people—espoused by individuals from Cloud to those active today. I also employ this term because the thread of activism I study was and is still oriented toward the continual growth of Native intellectualism through both old and new forms of higher education. It involves action that is political but also specifically educational, and thus it rests on the input of Native intellectuals on the national level but also on local educators, tribal administrators, government officials, and students themselves. In this inclusive conception of Native activism, I borrow from historian Daniel Cobb, who states that "convening summer workshops for college students, organizing youth councils, giving testimony at congressional hearings, authoring books and editorials, and manipulating the system from within" should all be considered forms of activism.[31] Activism, in other words, is more than the use of ostentatious tactics aimed at garnering publicity.

My examination of this history is also influenced by scholars who have uncovered similar American stories—stories of marginalized actors seeking to carve out their own protected spaces and platforms in the dominant discourses shaping American life. Gail Bederman, for example, describes ideological concepts of civilization, race, and gender in nineteenth- and twentieth-century America as "coercive" and yet "internally contradictory."[32] While the contradictions and fallacies of oppressive discourses "frequently give them a tenacious power," they also present opportunities for action, where oppressed individuals or groups can turn a seemingly dominant structure against itself for the benefit of the marginalized.[33]

In *Citizen Indians*, Lucy Maddox borrows from Bederman and applies a similar framework to studying the influential members of the Society of American Indians—including Henry Roe Cloud.[34] Robert Warrior's *Tribal Secrets* also serves as an important model for approaching Native history with a focus on early, underappreciated intellectual figures and how they addressed American culture and power structures.[35]

Maddox notes that some of the most successful Native intellectuals were those who deftly appropriated and manipulated the dominant white American discourses and rhetorical tools available to them. She highlights a certain performative aspect in the lives of Native public leaders that could become uncomfortable but also useful. As Renya Ramirez's work illustrates, this framework applies directly to Henry Roe Cloud, who utilized his stature as a Yale graduate and Christian minister to pitch ideas of Native-driven higher education and positive portrayals of Native culture to influential white audiences.[36] The leaders and organizations that subsequently built on Cloud's ideas necessarily employed similar tactics. They embraced government programs and funding when those resources addressed the needs of Native people but often shifted their energies away from those channels and sought to invent new ones when supportive momentum stalled.[37] By borrowing from Bederman, Maddox, Ramirez, and other scholars who work in a similar vein, I can indirectly utilize some of intellectual history's foundational theoretical writers, while remaining grounded in the specific historical context of Native education and activism in modern America.

Regarding the individuals and historical topics I study, secondary literature lacks unifying works to bring Henry Roe Cloud, Elizabeth Bender Cloud, and their contemporaries into a conversation on the founding of TCUs and the arguments on which they were built.[38] Furthermore, this historical scholarship is often isolated from contemporary work in American Indian studies.[39] I seek to demonstrate that the disparate threads of this scholarship must be tied together, from the Clouds to the birth of TCUs to contemporary models of Native-driven education as part of larger projects of self-determination. In so doing, my project can address a gap in the literature and illustrate that the goals of tribal colleges and universities are part of a longer Native intellectual and activist tradition that remains relevant today.

While my work can never achieve the level of personal depth and beauty that Ramirez is able to build into her family-tribal history of the Clouds, my array of research and my conclusions largely dovetail with and advance—rather than repeat—her story. Many of the leaders highlighted here were eager to have their ideas shared and debated by both Native and non-Native advocates throughout the country, and their rhetorical efforts and personal communications provide a rich source base. For instance, Henry Roe Cloud took care to share his thoughts on Native American education with his students in school newspapers. But he went much farther by utilizing a variety of publications to broadcast his ideas throughout the country, all the while engaging in extensive correspondence with Native and non-Native advocates. D'Arcy McNickle and Elizabeth Bender Cloud utilized their positions within the Bureau of Indian Affairs as well as nongovernment organizations to embody Henry's vision of Native leadership and to maintain a visible activist presence after his departure from the educational spotlight. A later generation of Native educational leaders like Jack Forbes and the founders of the National Indian Youth Council worked with mainstream American educational and political systems while also carrying on their own discourse in Native hubs. Harnessing and redirecting the power of newsletters, journals, books, and other rhetorical tools—often by creating their own publications and printing centers—became a hallmark of this intellectual activism, and helped preserve the Native voices that contributed to it.

Perhaps no one appreciated the power of these rhetorical tools more than Henry Roe Cloud himself. In September 1933, as he began his first school year as superintendent of Haskell Institute, Cloud had already taken over as editor of the *Indian Leader*, the school's newspaper. He wasted no time in expressing with plain language the significance of the white American audience in Native life—whether it came in the form of the federal government or the public at large. "The Indian race is on trial," he asserted.[40] "Those Indians who have been put in positions of responsibility here at Haskell Institute are on trial . . . [and] the student body is also on trial."[41] Rather than shrink from this scrutiny, however, Cloud accepted the challenge and charged his Native students to do the same.

For those familiar with the struggles that Native individuals and communities still face in education, economics, and politics, the voices I highlight in this history will sometimes appear overly optimistic. It is not my goal to conceal the difficulties and the barriers that exist in this history, or to argue that the implementation of Native-driven institutions of higher education has been universally successful. But it is one of my fundamental goals to capture this discourse's Native voices in their own words, in their own time, and in doing so to reveal the enthusiastic, tenacious, and truly inventive nature of this vein of activism. When Henry Roe Cloud suggested that the "Indian race" was "on trial," he did not expect that reality to disappear quickly or easily, but neither did he accept it as a reason for despair. Instead, he reimagined the "trial" metaphor as a chance to acquit oneself with skill and determination, to succeed on a visible platform. After all, he argued, "it is high time that [the] foremost men and women of the Indian race should be recognized and given an *opportunity* to bear responsibility and exercise authority," and he was not about to let that opportunity pass him by.[42]

I write a history of this activism knowing that many of its most ambitious visions have still not fully materialized but also knowing that its central intellectual and philosophical characteristics remain intact, and still possess potential for empowerment. I write this history believing that the energy that boils to the surface in the words of these activists came not from naiveté or shortsightedness but from a willingness to see opportunity within struggle, and from a deep appreciation of the motivating potential, the worthiness, and the lasting resilience of a shared idea for change.

ONE

By and for Indians

Henry Roe Cloud and Early Twentieth-Century Activism
for Native-Driven Higher Education

The past century has seen the development and implementation of an argument for greater Indigenous access to and control of higher education in the United States. Tribal colleges and universities (TCUs) represent one of the clearest manifestations of that intellectual effort. These schools serve as tangible markers of a shift toward Native American self-determination in the latter part of the twentieth century, and as continuations of a much deeper tradition of Native activists attempting to harness modern institutions of colonial power for their own needs and goals.

While the first tribal college was not established until the late 1960s, this intellectual history stretches back much farther. Looking closely at the life of Henry Roe Cloud and the work he pursued reveals how he engaged the most powerful systems of American education and government, in an attempt to carve out a visible platform for his particular form of Native intellectual activism. His crucial distinction between straightforward *assimilation* to white society and *adaptation* as a conscious strategy for young Native leaders encouraged greater representation and empowerment within American society while privileging tribal goals. Henry's wife Elizabeth Bender Cloud became instrumental in the pursuit of that activist leadership in her own right. Together, their decades-long work in this vein would leave a significant and resilient core of intellectual inspiration for the later movement toward TCUs and other forms of Native-driven higher education in America.

Why Henry Roe Cloud?

In 1915 Henry Roe Cloud founded the Roe Indian Institute (later the American Indian Institute), envisioning the school as a national, pantribal center for intellectual leadership training among Native students. Cloud at this time was just emerging from his own outstanding academic career, and his institute served as a center of higher education dedicated to academic and professional life beyond the common vocational programs offered to Native students at the time. Cloud sought to expand Native Americans' opportunities in higher education by focusing on levels of academic study that translated to intellectual leadership, rather than purely vocational training that translated to a permanent working-class status. Crucially, however, this notion of intellectual leadership was also grounded in Indigenous culture, identity, and communities—including the study of tribal histories, languages, governments, and contemporary socioeconomic challenges.[1]

While Cloud was certainly not the first Native figure who sought greater opportunities for leadership through American schooling, there are several reasons he serves as a focal point and a foundation of this history. First, this history is primarily concerned with a set of intellectual principles within Native American higher education that were eventually endorsed and cemented in the founding of tribal colleges and universities in the 1960s onward. Perhaps the clearest expression of TCUs' intellectual argument has been the affirmation that Native people in the United States deserved greater access to and control of their own pathways in higher education than had been available before the twentieth century. Just as important, TCUs are built on the argument that Native-driven institutions of higher education can maintain a level of adaptation to modern American power structures while still actively building and preserving Indigenous expressions of identity. Henry Roe Cloud, more than any other Native leader of his era, directed his efforts according to these simple yet profound ideas. Through his words and deeds at the American Indian Institute, Haskell Institute, and elsewhere from 1915 onward, Cloud would outline a vision for Native American higher education and leadership that shows remarkable continuity with the goals and mission statements of TCUs to this day. Moreover, his demonstration in a variety of public arenas of an overall concept of Native activism has exemplified a key thread in Indigenous intellectual responses to modern American power structures over the past century.

As illustrated in previous studies, Cloud's era was one of Progressive reform not just for elite white Americans but for a variety of segments of society. The founding of the Society of American Indians (SAI) in 1911 represents a milestone moment in the modern Native response to American settler colonialism and its ramifications.[2] The organization, which included many of the era's best-known Indigenous intellectuals and professionals, took a novel stance for the era in preventing non-Native members from holding voting power within the organization.

But even among notable Native reformers such as Charles Eastman (Dakota), Arthur C. Parker (Seneca), Zitkala-Sa (Dakota), and Laura Cornelius Kellogg (Oneida), Cloud stands out for his persistent dedication to reforming and restructuring American education in both the private and governmental arenas. Historian Hazel W. Hertzberg sees Cloud as exceedingly influential even when compared with his illustrious peers. "Of all the old [Society of American Indians] leaders," Hertzberg writes, "the man who most deeply affected the reformulation of Indian policy was probably Henry Roe Cloud."[3] Long before this posthumous praise, a commissioner of Indian affairs, John Collier, very plainly referred to Cloud as "the most important living Indian" in the early 1930s.[4]

Cloud was well positioned to carry out one of the first great attempts at reshaping the landscape of Native American higher education in the United States. He had experienced firsthand not only the boarding school system at Genoa Indian School in Nebraska but had gone on to become the first Native American graduate of Yale University. His training in theology further strengthened his intellectual credentials as well as his ability and willingness to articulate what he saw as the strengths of a Christian education. This aspect perhaps best represents the ambiguity of and tension surrounding an activist like Cloud, who constantly navigated a "thicket" of modern American discourses on race, gender, religion, "Civilization," and other real and imagined factors of identity.[5] While Cloud's Christian moral outlook remained with him throughout his decades-long efforts to altogether change the meaning of higher education for Indigenous people, he also strengthened and repeatedly broadcast his belief in the importance of Native expressions of identity. He was thus well trained and well known throughout both white and Indigenous circles of power, with a charismatic appeal and enough recognition to bridge that gap and accomplish what few other Native leaders of his era could have attempted.[6]

At the American Indian Institute as well as during his work within the federal government's Bureau of Indian Affairs (BIA), Cloud's efforts to reshape the educational landscape for Native Americans focused strongly on the concept of leadership. His expression of Native intellectual activism was dedicated to the expansion of a body of Native leaders beyond those very few who, like himself, had managed against the odds to gain access to the highest levels of American schooling. He worried about the relatively few chances for Native students to reach that elite academic status, and sought to expand opportunities in higher education and engrain a process of education for leadership among Native people. Overall, he wanted to institutionalize a sense of not only Native *access* to greater levels of education and training but also Native *control* of that training through leadership positions in educational and community networks.[7]

Cloud approached this great labor with a nuanced notion of the role of assimilation in the lives of Indigenous people. He was wary of aggressive assimilationist tactics, and while he often spoke of the importance of Christian teachings in the shaping of strong students, he often chose to emphasize basic principles like hard work, honesty, and dedication, which were not only compatible with but often integral to his sense of Ho-Chunk teachings

By and for Indians

as well.[8] Moreover, Cloud consistently expressed his fears about overzealous assimilation and his pride in expressions of Indigenous and tribal identity. He was decades ahead of his time in the ways that he encouraged students to strengthen their knowledge of tribal histories, languages, and cultures while simultaneously preparing for strategic uses of mainstream American educational, political, and economic systems.[9]

Together, these characteristics reveal Henry Roe Cloud as a crucial force in developing an early critique of the existing American system of education for Native people as well as a dedicated effort to reform and reshape that system. He wanted to transform a system of schooling from a trajectory limited by basic grade school and vocational training into one that truly opened up all of modern America's educational, political, and professional institutions of power to Native people and communities. His public recognition, along with his persuasive charisma and his tireless dedication to his cause, enabled him to garner enough support to demonstrate in some ways his vision for this changed landscape of Native American higher education.

Over time, monetary and bureaucratic challenges left Cloud's efforts frustrated and stunted by the eve of World War II. And yet his fundamental principles would be carried forward, resurrected, and reshaped in the postwar period. Even as the intellectual backbone of the tribal college movement developed and gained support in the 1960s, 1970s, and beyond, it would show remarkable continuity with the early twentieth-century work of Henry Roe Cloud.

While Henry's wife, Elizabeth Bender Cloud, has gone largely unmentioned up to this point, it must be acknowledged that she was also instrumental in this activist effort. As the early part of this history is largely concerned with clearly articulating Henry Roe Cloud's form of Native intellectual activism, it will be useful to focus first on the rich story of his writings, speeches, correspondence, and actions before discussing in more detail how Elizabeth aided, complemented, and advanced that effort in her own right.

To properly understand Cloud's form of intellectual activism and his growth as a leading figure of educational reform, it is instructive to study his experience with American schooling. In this process, it is crucial to accept culture and identity as fluid and changing over time through constant negotiations, rather than being static and permanent.[10]

The scholarship on the experience of Indigenous students in boarding schools and other settler colonial educational models is rich, including many works that emphasize forms of resistance and the maintenance of tribal identities throughout the process.[11] That larger narrative is not the primary focus of this work, but it does provide a fundamental context for Henry Roe Cloud's personal journey and in turn for the activism studied here. Though his academic training in this framework of settler colonial institutions tested him in ways that are difficult to comprehend today, Cloud was remarkably able to navigate the American educational system with a strong sense of his Ho-Chunk identity intact, all the while constructing his own framework for his efforts as an educational reformer.

By the time he laid out the key aspects of his vision for Native American education in an essay titled "Education of the American Indian" in 1914, Henry Roe Cloud had experienced firsthand the full range of schooling possible for Native students early in the twentieth century.[12] Like so many Native children of his generation, Cloud (then called Wo-Na-Xi-Lay-Hunka) was taken from his reservation home at a young age to attend a government-run boarding school. In his case, Genoa Indian School in Nebraska provided the initial destination. After several years at Genoa and another industrial school in the 1890s, Cloud attended Santee Mission School, also in Nebraska, followed by a preparatory school in Mt. Harmon, Massachusetts, followed in turn by Yale University, and finally Auburn School of Theology in New York.

The Protestant Christian influence he encountered made a tremendous impact on his life, and his ability and willingness to preach remained a strong part of his character throughout his adult life.[13] Indeed, two of the most important relationships he developed during his years as a student were with the Reverend Walter and Mary Roe, who ministered to Native Christians and impressed Cloud with their "overflowing life of service for the Indian race."[14] The Roes took a great supporting interest in Cloud and his educational and career efforts. The bond was close enough that the Roes, who had lost a child of their own, informally adopted Cloud as their son, and young Henry folded their surname into his own.[15] Even after Walter Roe's death in 1913, Mary Roe and Henry Roe Cloud maintained close contact and shared an overlapping interest in Native education.[16]

In Cloud's progression from boarding school to Ivy League to Christian seminary, it is tempting to see a clear path of assimilation, from an impoverished childhood on the reservation to eventual inclusion in the elite levels of mainstream American education. Cloud, like many Native intellectual leaders of his time, even embraced the appearance of a contemporary American professional. He routinely wore a suit and tie in public, kept his dark hair short, and sported a well-trimmed mustache and glasses. One of his earliest influential writings, "From Wigwam to Pulpit," even seems to suggest a linear, assimilationist track in its title.

Scholars at times accept this assimilationist narrative wholesale, without a more nuanced inquiry. Jason Tetzloff, for example, in his 1996 dissertation on Cloud's career as an activist, states rather brusquely that Cloud "was committed to the goal of greater assimilation of the Indian into American society."[17] Tetzloff repeatedly stresses Cloud's Christian education and his preaching efforts as part of that push for greater assimilation, and argues that Cloud mirrored the sentiments of the rest of the Society of American Indians in this outlook.

The rather simple conclusion that the activist used a "strong assimilationist" approach in his reform efforts, however, detracts from a deeper understanding of Cloud's complex approach to assimilation and Native American identity—which will be explored in more depth in this chapter.[18] Moreover, this label of "strong assimilationist" in reference to a group like the SAI can grossly oversimplify not only the multifaceted pressures surrounding an entire body of the era's Indigenous intellectuals but also the strategic responses they marshalled in response to those pressures. As Gregory Smithers details in his study of the SAI's early publications, the use of the term "assimilation" among activists during that era could often mean simply bringing Native people and their communities into a more equitable and formal relationship with the dominant American systems of power, without compromising tribal and Native expressions of identity.[19] Smithers's careful study of the SAI's early writings aligns with what Renya Ramirez sees in Henry Roe Cloud's work as an effort to build from both tribal and white American educations to create "Indigenous intellectual weapons" in defense of "cultural citizenship" for Native people.[20] In other words, Cloud believed that access to full citizenship and its attendant sources of power within the nation-state should not require the compromising or erasure of Indigenous culture or tribal belonging.

As further illustrated by these and similar close readings of the era, Native leaders who did align in their efforts were still confronted with the dominant white American discourses on race, gender, and culture. As best they could, they "deliberately adopted, manipulated, and transformed the means already available to them for addressing white audiences."[21] This does not mean that leaders like Cloud or the others necessarily compromised their personal beliefs for the sake of appealing to white audiences, but they were undoubtedly aware that a certain level of performance played a necessary role in their lives as public intellectuals and activists.

Regarding Cloud specifically, the "assimilationist" label fails to provide any real insight, as it not only oversimplifies his personal experience but directly clashes with some of his own descriptions of his vision for Native American education and leadership. It is thus more instructive to examine Cloud's experiences in American schools, noting the ways in which he chose to *deviate* from their straightforward assimilationist tactics and maintain expressions of Native identity when he had the opportunity to do so. As he transitioned from standout student to charismatic educator and activist, he was able to use his leadership positions to construct a more nuanced approach to the era's aggressive calls for assimilation as he sought to transform the relationship between Native students and American schooling.

One key instance in which Cloud expressed his ideas for reshaping that relationship occurred in 1914 when he published his essay "Education of the American Indian." Poised perfectly between his long career as a student and his future career as an educational reformer, Cloud outlined the intellectual argument for what would become his American Indian Institute (AII), the prep school for Native students that he would direct for nearly two decades. The essay directly addressed numerous influential "friends of the Indian" at Lake Mohonk but was circulated more widely via the *Quarterly Journal of the Society of American Indians* as well.[22] By closely reading this and other early texts related to the American Indian Institute's founding, we can glean some of the key beliefs that guided Cloud's efforts to achieve greater Native access to and control of higher education and positions of leadership in the ensuing decades.

In his 1914 essay, Cloud assessed the broad scope of Native American education in the early twentieth century and discussed how the nature of that entire system impacted Native populations socially, politically, and economically. One of the strongest influences evident in his perspective was his own experience at the Genoa Indian School. Cloud's attendance at Genoa in the 1890s occurred at a time when the most powerful men in federal Indian policy hailed assimilationist schooling as the quickest and most logical way to aid Native populations and bring individual students into the fold as productive members of the American republic.

As an example, Thomas J. Morgan, the commissioner of the Bureau of Indian Affairs from 1889 to 1893, employed an authoritative voice on the consequences of Native tribal living that reflected the deeply biased racial and cultural discourses of the era. Morgan praised the work of Captain Richard H. Pratt, whose military-style education for Native students at Carlisle Indian School became a model of the boarding school era. In his own vision for the ideal educational approach toward Native students, Commissioner Morgan wrote that schooling of Native American children should occur as early in life as possible, not only for the more rapid "disintegration of the tribes" but so that "habits of industry and love of learning . . . [could take] the place of indolence and indifference."[23] Advancing this colonizer's trope in which "Civilization" towered above the "indolence" of Indigenous life, Morgan optimistically concluded that "in a single generation," the entire body of Native students could be "brought into intimate relationship with the highest type of American rural life."[24]

Cloud, however, understood how a government boarding school operated in the real world. He made this clear in "Education of the American Indian" when he wrote of the apparent disconnect between the ideals of boarding schools' vocational training and the reality of the work that students performed. In schools like Genoa, students spent approximately half of their day in vocational training that was ostensibly directed toward the learning of a productive trade.[25] But this system was also used to reduce the running costs of the schools, which often resulted in students performing repetitive and menial tasks rather than acquiring a true craft.

In contrast to Morgan's blanket assessment of tribal living, Cloud's Ho-Chunk upbringing had instilled in him a sense of the value of useful labor, and ironically it was the government-run school that represented a roadblock to the cultivation of a work ethic.[26] As he expressed it, "I worked two years turning a washing machine . . . [and] such work is not educative. It begets a hatred for work, especially where there is no pay for such labor."[27] While Cloud praised the value of truly instructive vocational training in preparing students for meeting the needs of modern American capitalism, he also worried about the "dangers" that the American economy posed for any unprepared worker. Thus, what Commissioner Morgan saw as a boarding school system that produced "honorable, useful, happy citizens of a great republic, sharing on equal terms in all its blessings," Cloud instead understood as one that groomed students for a tedious life of labor as members of the underclass.[28]

In Cloud's eyes, the failings of the boarding schools' vocational programs were only exacerbated by the relatively low level of academic training these schools accomplished. Even in 1914, surrounded by the rhetoric of rapid assimilation and the inevitability of the disappearance of tribal culture, Cloud seemed to understand more clearly than his contemporaries that Native American identity would continue to endure, both on and off the reservation.[29] Indeed, a full two decades before the repudiation of the allotment policy through the 1934 Indian Reorganization Act, he spoke of reservation lands not as an antiquated system of the past but as a key component of a future that should necessarily play into a Native student's learning: "[the student] must study the physical environment and topography of his particular reservation, for these in large measure control the fortunes of his people."[30] The futures of Native communities, he reasoned, would depend heavily on leaders whose training prepared them to meet all the challenges that mainstream white Americans faced, *in addition to* the unique challenges that impacted Native people. The Native leaders charged with meeting this "two-fold" dilemma needed to "be more than grammar-school men. They must be trained to grapple with these economic, educational, [and] political" dynamics as they overlapped in their lives.[31]

In examining the challenges facing Native people, Cloud diverged from the common chorus of the assimilationist voices. The most enthusiastic of these, such as Commissioner Morgan, attempted to sweep away the economic and social problems of Native communities "in a single generation" of tribal disintegration, while Cloud envisioned instead a concept of Native American "adaptation."[32] As hinted above, I view the purposeful distinction made between these two terms to be vital to Cloud's entire vision of Native intellectual activism in modern America. The ability to *adapt* to dynamic challenges—*while remaining true to one's fundamental identity*—rather than simply *assimilate* to a vague notion of Americanism would remain a crucial aspect of Cloud's message to future leaders as he embarked on his career as an educator.

For Henry Roe Cloud, the ability to adapt as a leader required a level of intellectual training that the boarding school system simply did not meet. Remarking on the level of schooling provided to most Native students, he argued that "if every person . . . had only an eighth-grade education with which to wrestle with the problems of life and the Nation, this country would be in a bad way."[33] Put simply, even if the government boarding school system *did* fully accomplish its goals of a grammar school education and a part-time vocational training, it would fall short of providing the leadership training that Cloud saw as necessary in twentieth-century America.

Rather than rest with a critique of the boarding school system or a vision of reforming it alone, Cloud expanded his scope to assess how poor training early on prevented Native students from reaching higher levels of schooling that were ostensibly open to them. "This system," he argued of the government's schooling for Native students, "is resulting in an absolute block upon the entrance of our ablest young people into the . . . colleges of the land."[34] As the first Native American to graduate from Yale University, he acutely understood the dearth of Native students at the highest levels of American education. He flatly refuted the notion that any inherent intellectual failings were to blame, asserting that "the difficulty lies in the system rather than in the race."[35] Having achieved postgraduate degrees from both Yale and the Auburn School of Theology, he knew that to white audience members and readers he must represent an obvious illustration of this point.

Building from his critique of the contemporary system of schooling for Native students, Cloud concluded "Education of the American Indian" by briefly outlining his own vision for an institution that could succeed in places where that old system had failed. By providing a rigorous training in academic as well as skilled vocational pursuits, he optimistically hoped to bring about the growth of a new body of Native leaders who could address the unique needs of their tribal communities and of Native people through-

By and for Indians

out the United States. Rather than seek to reinvent the grammar school or children's boarding school, Cloud attacked the evident gap between Native American populations and higher education. His proposed school would act as a preparatory school for those students seeking higher learning and for those who wanted to gain enough training to return as leaders to modern reservation communities.

The American Indian Institute as a New Platform for Native American Higher Education

In 1915 Henry Roe Cloud began to put his vision into action when he and Mary Roe founded the American Indian Institute in Wichita, Kansas. "Feeling that the United States government was unable for many reasons to more than partially care for" Native students' needs, Cloud sought to operate entirely free from government funding and oversight.[36] As an alternative, Cloud hoped to rely on a backbone of Christian and philanthropic organizational donations.

As Renya Ramirez carefully traces, Cloud's Christian teaching did not diminish his activism in defense of tribal cultures and their pragmatic resources. For example, by the time of his 1914 proposal for the American Indian Institute, if not sooner, he had begun to openly avow activist stances such as the protection of tribes' trust status in defense of government efforts to exert authority over their lands.[37] Thus, as Cloud stressed the importance of a Christian education at his proposed institution, he did so in ways that emphasized values held by a broad swath of the American people, regardless of religious affiliation. He repeatedly spoke of the role of "self-support" and "self-denial" as moral qualities that paid positive dividends in American economic and social structures, but he did not mention specific religious teachings or denominational leanings. Indeed, early documents related to Cloud's proposed school explicitly spelled out the desire to maintain a nondenominational approach, "thus allowing a broad appeal to Christian and philanthropic interests."[38] In the early years of what would become the American Indian Institute, Cloud's own

Christian education and beliefs certainly impacted the way the school constructed its curriculum and activities. But the nondenominational approach allowed him to garner support from a diverse range of individuals and organizations outside the AII, all the while privileging his goals of leadership training and "the promotion of higher education among" his Native students.[39] And while he continued to link a broad Christian worldview to commonly held American economic and social values, Cloud simultaneously emphasized the importance of leaders *as Native people.* In this way, he eschewed the simplistic forms of identity-erasing *assimilation* common to his era and instead preached a sense of *adaptability* that reserved room for Native languages, cultures, and identities in the face of settler colonialism. A variety of sources from Cloud's educational career demonstrate how he maintained and emphasized this important distinction throughout his years as an intellectual activist, beginning with his first major efforts to advance Native access and control in American higher education.

At the American Indian Institute, Cloud directed his attention not at the American university per se but at the relationship between the American university and the country's Indigenous population. He understood that the existing education system perpetuated a gap between Native students and positions of influence and leadership in American society. He sought to address that gap by creating a new form of higher education—a prep school designed and run by Native administrators to meet the unique needs of Native students and their communities. Overall, Cloud's work at the American Indian Institute became a constant struggle to maintain the levels of energy and financial support necessary to develop a fledgling academic institution outside the established structures of government-sponsored schooling. Yet that work brought about a lasting impact on the education system while demonstrating a commitment to both expanded access and expanded control for Native people in higher education.

Multiple contextual factors led Cloud to address the void of Native American preparatory schooling rather than to attempt an ambitious reinvention of the university model itself. First, his own experience in American higher education was undeniably difficult but also successful. Not only was he able to excel in that model, but he did so while maintaining his Native language and his ability to operate successfully as a leader among his Ho-Chunk people and as an advocate for other tribes as well.[40] It is reasonable to assume that he envisioned similarly successful experiences for other Native students. Thus Cloud focused not on barriers or negative aspects *within* the university but on the issue of access to that level. As he wrote in "Education of the American Indian," he observed "an absolute block upon the entrance" of students into colleges and universities in the first place.[41]

The educational climate of the era also likely impacted Cloud's strategy. Early in the twentieth century, Americans within academia had already begun to worry that a broadly focused college system was becoming overextended.[42] Rather than support general higher educational efforts through new universities, academics and donors turned to "the vision that advanced scholarship in selected topics might best be promoted by establishing special institutes that would attract scholars from across the nation."[43] This description fit Cloud's school remarkably well, as the American Indian Institute dedicated itself to a particular kind of student with a particular set of goals and needs, while seeking students from throughout the country.

Cloud had in fact chosen Wichita, Kansas, as a "strategic position" for his school largely because of its relative ease of access "from all parts of the United States," and he soon drew students from as far away as Alaska.[44] The American Indian Institute thus arose according to the model that it did because of a specific need that Cloud perceived, and it addressed that need in a way that translated to the contemporary system of American higher education while seeking to fundamentally change how that system served the Native American population.

A closer look at the context of early twentieth-century American education reveals just how perceptive Cloud was of the precarious position of Native students, and just how vital his school would be in addressing the United States' failure to provide those students with adequate routes to higher education. As Cloud had experienced, higher education was not unreachable for Native students, but neither was it part of a recognizable, institutionalized path. At the same time, a massive trend in American schooling threatened to further separate students in the mainstream education system from their Native American counterparts. Just as the American Indian Institute began its work in 1915, the United States stood in the midst of a rapid boost in high school enrollment, with the percentage of fourteen- to seventeen-year-olds enrolled in high school more than doubling from 1910 to 1920.[45] Cloud understood that this trend was largely bypassing Indian country, and he sought to use similar quantitative data to make the dire need of his school more evident to potential supporters. In this context, he viewed his American Indian Institute not as one of many possible trajectories to higher education but as a unique and crucially important platform within higher education itself.[46]

While Cloud sought to improve Native access to higher education and positions of leadership, he also set out a clear demonstration of Native *control* in higher education. Relying on a wide range of individual and organizational donors to meet the costs of running his school and acquiring the necessary facilities, he showed a preference, however, for Native educators and staff, who directly oversaw the American Indian Institute's curricular mission throughout its history.[47] Students enrolling at the AII thus entered a true Native hub, encountering first-hand examples of Native intellectual leadership on a daily basis.

Despite the need to constantly travel for fundraising efforts, Cloud maintained a close eye on the school's direction, striking a balance between the unique perspectives of Native students and the overall demands of modern America. For instance, because few of his students could afford tuition, he structured the coursework in a way that allowed them to work for approximately two hours per day and receive compensation toward tuition and books, part of his emphasis on "self-help" training that he viewed as especially useful for Native students.[48] By keeping this workload low and compensating students, however, he offered a system that differed from his own tedious government boarding school experience and more closely approximated the experience of working part-time to pay for college tuition.[49]

He also sought to maintain a set of courses that "correspond[ed] to the . . . curriculum of academies for which full credit is given as an entrance course in any up-to-date college or university."[50] During the first several years of operation, the AII rented classrooms at the nearby Fairmount College in Wichita.[51] Courses included "Geometry; Botany; American History . . . English; Zoology . . . German, Latin . . . Algebra, Ancient History . . . and a course in Agriculture under one of the college professors."[52] In this way, Cloud structured a diverse and rigorous academic backbone that he knew would translate to the elite levels of American academic systems.

In both the depth and breadth of this instruction, Cloud signaled his ambitious goals for his students, and he viewed the initial results with great satisfaction. While the school began with fewer than ten students, and while the First World War also hampered enrollment early on, Cloud remained faithfully optimistic. After the first several years, he wrote with pride that his "vision has been fruitful, and the four classes which have been graduated from this institution already have provided twelve students in institutions of higher learning."[53] In his updates to donors and potential supporters, he regularly celebrated not only the general advancement of graduates to colleges and universities but also a diverse range of individual students' successes, from "electrical engineer" to "medical missionaries to their own people."[54] In these examples Cloud's understanding of Indigenous leadership is displayed as a concept that involved a broad spectrum of abilities and vocations. He saw the AII as a center for training Native students to acquire a high level of adaptability to meet the challenges of a wide range of callings.

As discussed above, the balance that Cloud sought in his school's curricular mission is easily misinterpreted in hindsight. His emphasis on a Protestant Christian education is sometimes interpreted as an assimilationist threat to Indigenous culture and religion. As one example, he utilized the American Indian Institute's newspaper, the *Indian Outlook*, to occasionally voice his concerns over the use of peyote in religious ceremonies, referring to these ceremonies as "outworn social customs."[55] But to conclude more broadly that such a concern constituted a desire to rid his students of their tribal or Native identities would be a mistake. As Thomas Maroukis has detailed, peyote and Peyotism were not well understood by the general public at the time, and yet the substance became a target in the dominant Progressive-era discourse as an intoxicant that should be criminalized as such.[56] The intense debates even caused major fault lines among the Society of American Indians, with "extreme accusations made at conferences, in publications, and in correspondence."[57] This was also the era when zeal for the prohibition of alcohol was at its height, and Cloud's rhetoric on peyote makes more sense when placed within that context. His comments on peyote in the *Indian Outlook*, for example, focused on principles of self-discipline and the avoidance of distractions rather than particular religious teachings. In other words, peyote for Cloud was a threat to his vision of leadership training because of what he viewed as its intoxicating nature, and because it thus represented a potentially dangerous block on students "be[ing] in a condition to work as they should."[58]

Cloud's criticism of Peyotism, then, should not blind us to his explicit desire to cultivate Native American knowledge, identification, and pride among his students. As Renya Ramirez has carefully detailed, Cloud adopted Christianity in a way that fit within his own tribal identity, and he sought the same type of experience for others.[59] Thus, while he employed the *Indian Outlook* to print an article decrying peyote, he also printed several pieces extolling Native American "morals, characteristics, art and traditions" as "a permanent enrichment to [America's] composite civilization."[60] In his correspondence, as well, Cloud stressed the AII's mission of enabling students to "preserve their Native arts," while staff and students at the school manifested that effort in an annual powwow and other ceremonies.[61]

Cloud's attempts to privilege Indigenous identity also included positive portrayals of Native American groups and individuals both past and present. The *Indian Outlook* printed articles on important Indigenous historical contributions to areas ranging from agriculture to music, while also running a reprint of a series titled "Some Indian Leaders, Past and Present."[62]

One of the featured "present" leaders, Robert Paul Chaat, was a graduate of the American Indian Institute who went on to embody the kind of adaptable Native leadership that Cloud hoped to cultivate. Through the eyes of Chaat's grandson, Comanche author Paul Chaat Smith, we see how quickly the dominant cultural understandings of "Indian" and "white" identity could become obscured, upended, and inadequate. Smith observes that according to one common portrayal of the Native American experience, "Grandpa Chaat should have [become] a self-hating, colonized oppressor" because of his experience—like Cloud—with aggressively assimilationist education early in his life and because of his Christian training.[63] But—again like his predecessor and mentor Cloud—he instead became a recognized authority in Native communities, as both a Christian and a Comanche. "He carried out the duties of a spiritual leader . . . [and] offered unconditional love" without apparent conflicts of identity or affiliation.[64] Smith concludes simply but insightfully, "Grandpa Chaat was a Christian, but he led a church full of Comanches who sang Comanche hymns."[65] In navigating the personal and collective difficulties posed by these apparent contradictions and acting as a Native leader, Chaat became an excellent example of what Henry Roe Cloud envisioned for graduates of the American Indian Institute.

The focus on adaptable Native leadership in Cloud's writing and editing at the AII also touched on concrete realities facing the infrastructures and economies of Native American communities. For example, he hoped that a dramatic rethinking of the relationship between farming and education could inspire young Native students to become leading agricultural experts on their reservations. Rather than "schools where their best education only teaches Indians to do things by rote . . . or spend their time waiting for instructions," Cloud envisioned a more comprehensive education system for Native students that blended higher academic training and comprehensive agricultural education.[66] He thus saw the reservation economy not as an afterthought but as a complex system that held obvious challenges but also potential for great improvement. In this discussion, Cloud characteristically employed the key word *adapt*—a subtle but important distinction from *assimilate*, and one that he would continue to make throughout his career.[67]

His correspondence, together with the *Indian Outlook*, reveal in one sense a strong Christian mindset and a distinct intolerance for what he viewed as vices and flaws that posed a threat to a mature work ethic. And yet these writings also run contrary to the assimilationist narrative, revealing an explicit desire to provide students with positive examples not just of leadership but of *Native* leadership. Cloud presented these ideas to students not simply as a way of preserving a memory of the past while assimilating to American society. Instead, these ideas were part of a call to build on a foundation of pride, to *adapt* to the challenges presented by modern American life, and to address the contemporary and future needs of Native American people and their communities.

While he viewed positively the American Indian Institute's qualitative success, Cloud was eager to expand, take on more students, and make a more substantial quantitative impact. He repeatedly printed "The Plan for the Future" and the "Budget of Immediate Needs" in the *Indian Outlook*, brief write-ups that outlined the goal of expansion to 125 or even 200 students.[68] With these goals in mind from the outset, he directed much of his energy toward the ever-present task of fundraising. Mary Roe remained a supporter in this effort, helping Cloud attain by 1921 support from the National Society of the Daughters of the American Revolution (DAR).[69] For much of the school's history, Cloud would continue to piece together donations that trickled in from various chapters of the DAR across the country. Still, some of these donations amounted to as little as five dollars, and while Cloud took care to acknowledge and respond to each gift, he clearly felt frustration at the gap between the espoused moral support and the practical financial support that his efforts garnered.[70] With the school running on a budget of roughly $1,500 per month by the 1922–23 academic year, the small gifts of voluntary organizations could come as a blessing but were also unreliable.[71] The American Indian Institute was therefore constantly in perilous financial straits and repeatedly forced to rely on the generosity of individual members of the school's board of trustees or those who knew Cloud and his work intimately.[72] In these conditions, large-scale expansion proved impossible. The AII maintained a maximum enrollment of approximately forty students for the majority of its existence.[73]

By the late 1920s, Cloud remained as convinced as ever of the positive impact of his work but sought to leave behind the draining task of traveling the country, grasping for fragmentary donations. He managed to negotiate an arrangement for the Presbyterian Board of National Missions to gradually take over ownership and funding of the American Indian Institute. He viewed this as an important step in the school's history, as it finally established the sense of permanence and security that he viewed as both a sign of vindication for his work and a necessity for any future expansion.[74] His excitement was palpable in his letters to his closest colleagues on the board of trustees and to Mary Roe. "For the first time in my life," he wrote, "I shall be able to throw my life and personality into the administration of this Institution, its teaching and its influence. . . . I shall not be harassed day and night with money problems, big bills to pay and no money in sight. What a joy and a relief it will be!"[75]

Unfortunately, the transfer was slow to develop, and in 1931 Cloud accepted a field representative position within the Bureau of Indian Affairs, hoping to expand his form of Native intellectual activism to a broader platform. In the late 1920s and into the 1930s, the Bureau of Indian Affairs began to more seriously address the failings of its education system, which Cloud had so notably worked to overcome since 1915. It made sense for an increasingly reform-minded BIA to seek out the activist's expertise and energetic leadership, and it also made sense for Cloud himself to seize an opportunity that might allow him to cultivate his vision on an expanded scale.

In his absence, Elizabeth Bender Cloud took over many of the responsibilities involving the administration and budget of the American Indian Institute. This arrangement had long been solidified during Henry's many speaking and fundraising tours, and it displayed the trust that he and Elizabeth shared in one another's leadership.[76] Years later, one of the Clouds' daughters, Anne Woesha Cloud North, would recall that her parents had preached to their children the imperative of embracing higher education and active leadership, regardless of gender.[77] Moreover, Elizabeth seemed to be consciously building on a long tradition of Ojibwe women as leaders, which "did not seem to present a problem for Ojibwe people, but only for whites."[78] Indeed, the Clouds' views were not shared by the more conservative Presbyterian Board, which eventually arranged for Mr. Henry P. Douglas to take over as superintendent. In this change, the institute followed white American social and professional norms, securing a male head to oversee a school for young men. But it crucially lost Elizabeth's experience and familiarity with the institute's mission, not to mention an Indigenous activist perspective at the helm. In the ensuing years, the AII's imperative as a unique platform in Native higher education faded away, and the school became a boarding house for Native students who attended local high schools and colleges in Wichita.[79]

As he prepared to leave the American Indian Institute in 1931, Cloud had experienced a decade and a half of the excitement, hope, and frustration that came with his ambitious undertaking. Though the school had never managed to expand its numbers as he had hoped, and though the Great Depression battered Americans of all colors, he maintained his optimism and his determination. He referred to the academic year in 1931 as "one of the best years we have ever had," and went on to praise a young Cherokee teacher for his leadership at the school.[80] Ever the advocate for Native leadership, Cloud was undoubtedly proud that his school had demonstrated this leadership at the administrative, faculty, and student level.

With the American Indian Institute, Cloud had successfully expanded Native American access to higher education while simultaneously demonstrating the potential for Native control of that effort. He had molded an institution that reflected his desire to address the needs of Native students and their communities in ways that government schools had failed, while also aligning the academic curriculum with the standards of American higher education. In these efforts, he had employed a strong Protestant Christian framework to strictly jettison any social and cultural influences that threatened the pursuit of higher knowledge and training. And yet his writings reflected his desire to build a sense of pride in Native identity and a sense of responsibility to tribal communities. His idea of leadership at the American Indian Institute was thus not a mold into which students must assimilate but a set of principles and skills through which they could attain a level of adaptability necessary for meeting the challenges of modern Native American life in the United States.

Expanding the Message through a Government Platform

Well before he joined the Bureau of Indian Affairs in 1931, Henry Roe Cloud had already been working to reform its education policy. Clearly, his work at the American Indian Institute from 1915 onward represented one strategy for addressing what he saw as the government's failures regarding Native students. He had explicitly argued just as much in his "Education of the American Indian" essay from 1914. But in the late 1920s he took advantage of another opportunity to more directly influence the BIA's programs. In 1926 and 1927, Cloud served as the only Native American member on the survey team for the monumental investigation of federal Indian policy that became known as the Meriam Report. Because of the report's influence on government policy, and because of the vital nature of his personal contribution to it, the project helped cement Cloud's position as a leading expert on Native American education in the United States.[81]

From this key moment onward, Cloud briefly stood out as the most influential voice on the problems of the government's relationship with Native individuals and communities. Just a few years after the release of the Meriam Report, Cloud became the first Native American superintendent of one of the BIA's largest educational centers—Haskell Institute in Lawrence, Kansas. Whereas he had previously operated entirely outside the government's system in his attempts to address the BIA's educational shortcomings, he now worked within that very system to expand the impact of his vision. His time in government service was fraught with challenges just as significant as those he had faced in the private arena. Still, as the most notable voice in Native American education, he explicitly maintained his dedication to expanding Native people's access to and control of higher education and leadership training. If only for a brief time, he successfully broadcast that vision on the largest platform available to him. Furthermore, he maintained that Native students, when equipped with the proper tools, would become leaders adaptable enough to meet not only the challenges common to all members of twentieth-century American society but also the challenges facing Indigenous people in particular.

For Cloud, working on the Meriam Report represented a major opportunity to maintain his position at the American Indian Institute while also advancing his goals of educational reform in a way that would make a direct influence in the governmental arena. In its published form as *The Problem of Indian Administration*, the Meriam Report was a massive document that over the course of eight hundred pages addressed nearly all aspects of Native Americans' relationship with the United States government, including "educational, industrial, social and medical activities . . . property rights and general economic conditions."[82] Cloud's position on the ten-person survey team was listed as "Indian adviser," but his contribution went far beyond that of a passive adviser. In no area was the importance of his role clearer than in the survey of the federal government's schooling for Native students, where education professor W. Carson Ryan Jr. served as the specialist. For while Ryan had gained vast experience carrying out educational surveys and making recommendations for improvement, Cloud was the only survey team member with experience not only as a student in the BIA's program but as an administrator and educator in a Native American school.[83] Throughout the course of the survey team's investigations and in the writing of the document itself, no one contributed more work than Cloud. Not only did he make as many visits to BIA agencies as any other member, but he also took up residence near Washington DC for the summer of 1927 to remain intimately involved in crafting the report's overall message and specific recommendations.[84]

The Meriam Report's section on government-run schools highlighted many of the same frustrations that Cloud had identified over a decade earlier in "Education of the American Indian." As that essay had done, the Meriam Report focused heavily on the shortcomings of the BIA's industrial and vocational education. For instance, the report concluded that "an institutional scheme which stresses production rather than genuine vocational training, an almost complete absence of qualified teachers, and a lack of the necessary guidance, placement, and follow-up machinery, make the vocational program of the boarding schools relatively ineffective."[85] Specifically, the survey team doubted that the training received in government-run schools went "far enough to enable the student to become a skilled workman even after a reasonable period of experience. This is one of the gravest faults of the system."[86]

The report repeatedly stressed the needs for greater funding and higher teaching standards in order to employ more qualified instructors in the BIA's system, and in no area was this problem of greater concern than in the effort to improve access to higher education. As the writers of the report pointed out, "the first requisite for an 'accredited' high school . . . is that the teachers shall be graduates of standard four-year colleges with some professional preparation in education courses. So far as can be ascertained, no government Indian school meets this minimum requirement."[87] In these circumstances, the leap to higher education remained daunting because colleges would simply not accept students without adequate preparation in an accredited secondary school. Cloud's personal voice became especially clear in this passage, as the report went on in the same paragraph to list the American Indian Institute as one school successfully addressing the problem of access to higher education for Native students. Elsewhere, Cloud again relied on his experience to include specific examples of how Native students could quickly rise in higher education and positions of leadership. For instance, he provided the illustration that "graduates of the American Indian Institute . . . representing fifteen tribes . . . have in the past four years done successful work in higher institutions of learning in eight states."[88]

Cloud's experience working on the Meriam Report not only confirmed his earlier views of the BIA's education system but also strengthened his resolve to maintain and expand his own work. Though he expressed frustration at the apparent lack of success in many of the government's efforts, he remained as committed as ever to the goal of increasing Native access to higher education and positions of leadership. "I have just completed a survey of the general conditions of the Indian race all over the United States," he wrote in early 1928, "and I have come back with the positive conviction that a great deal of . . . work must yet be done."[89] While the American Indian Institute represented a key piece of that work, Cloud also expressed the opinion that a "half century" or more would pass before the fundamental conditions hampering Native American educational and economic pursuits could be ameliorated.

This long-term outlook, combined with the reality that the BIA still represented the most massive instrument of dialogue between Native communities and the mainstream power structures of American society, may have convinced Cloud that operating solely in the private arena was not enough. After all, the common criticism in the Meriam Report had not been the BIA's motives but that the bureau stood in need of more qualified, capable leaders. Cloud, dedicated and experienced as he was in the pursuit of higher learning, undoubtedly saw himself as one such leader. Thus, by the early 1930s, as the American Indian Institute

By and for Indians

proved unable to expand beyond its usual forty students, Cloud sought to take advantage of the BIA's resources and institutional structure to make a more extensive impact. When he was offered a position within the bureau as a field representative in the fall of 1931, he accepted.[90]

In this position from 1931 to 1933, Cloud traveled widely, investigating problematic relations between the BIA and reservation communities. Because the work varied with the assignment, it is difficult to pick out a clear expression of his developing thoughts on education in particular. One of his most important tasks, however, required an investigation of potential fraud involving Haskell Institute's athletics program. Founded in 1884, Haskell had become the most influential BIA school—with nationwide name recognition and over nine hundred students—by the time Cloud visited as part of the Meriam Report team in the late 1920s. The school had begun working as a potential bridge to address the gap that Cloud had identified between Native students and higher education, and yet like myriad American institutions of the era it had also become known for questionable academic and fundraising practices related to its football program.[91] Cloud's investigation as a field representative convinced him that a change in leadership would be necessary if the school was to truly serve its evolving purpose as an extension to higher education rather than as a thinly veiled powerhouse enrolling "athletes of the most dubious kind."[92] He got his wish for a change in leadership when the newly appointed commissioner of Indian Affairs, John Collier, quickly sent Cloud back to Haskell as superintendent in 1933.

As he did so often in his career, Cloud approached his work at Haskell Institute with optimism and energy. The importance of his new post was partially reflected in the numerous letters that flooded his desk in the opening months of the 1933–34 school year.[93] News of his appointment had spread across the country, and people in a wide variety of positions and circumstances wrote to wish him the best. One Native educator expressed his conviction that Cloud would guide students to greater "higher educational opportunities" and continue to inspire strong leadership to "Indians all over the United States."[94] Unfortunately, this optimism regarding Haskell's future was soon held in check by the impact of distressing forces outside Cloud's control.

In the midst of the Great Depression and the massive government shakeup that ensued after 1932, the Bureau of Indian Affairs had by the time of Cloud's arrival at Haskell already begun the process of shuttering several off-reservation boarding schools. In the summer of 1933, Commissioner Collier wrote that the BIA was "practically forced to shut down no less than ten boarding schools, and in every case, without exception, the resistance is intense."[95] One of the first moves regarding Haskell was to cut the school's enrollment from nine hundred to six hundred students, and to cut the faculty accordingly.[96] Furthermore, the bureau sought to reconfigure the school's entire curriculum and mission. "Haskell's future, to be justified at all," wrote Collier, "must be as a specifically vocational institution reaching into the advanced grades."[97] The reductions to the student body, the faculty, and the budget—not to mention the hardline directives regarding the curriculum—represented immediate hindrances on Cloud's ambitions. These events were set in motion before he arrived to take up his new post in Lawrence, leaving him hamstrung and with the feeling of simply "keeping [his] head above water."[98]

Despite these immediate challenges, Cloud soon regained his usual resilient voice and felt compelled to argue for the virtue of the school's very existence, just as he had been forced to do at the American Indian Institute. As early as the fall of 1933, Cloud was writing Collier to convey what he saw as the precarious nature of the school's future. On the one hand, he expressed his confidence in the students and in the institutional groundwork at Haskell, painting a picture of great potential that needed only to be nurtured and inspired. At the same time, he argued, the school could grow stronger and maximize that potential only with the full and continuing support of the BIA. At times, Cloud sensed that support was lacking. For instance, he attempted to arrange multiple visits to educational conferences and meetings with college officials in order to elevate Haskell's profile, bring the institution into an established dialogue with American higher education, and glean knowledge from educators at the next level. But as these trips fell through because of a lack of funding, his frustration became clear.[99]

By the summer of 1934, he took a more direct approach in laying out his case to Collier and other officials, and his letters illustrate once again his ability to pursue his goals of Native intellectual activism while grappling with American political discourses and powerful individuals. Budget cuts and the curtailment of enrollment, he argued, left Haskell unable "to do a creditable educational work," much less excel as a national center of Native leadership and higher learning.[100] Cloud plainly expressed the opinion that if the school was destined to shut down completely, it would do better to carry out its last few years on a full budget rather than limp along with restrictions that "penalized" faculty and administrators so heavily that "we cannot ourselves maintain our own self-respect."[101] In a separate letter to W. Carson Ryan, his one-time colleague on the Meriam Report, Cloud challenged Ryan to use all his influence in the BIA's educational division to make Haskell an exception to the policy of closing federal boarding schools.[102] Cloud argued that Haskell could "do a most outstanding and creditable piece of work for our Indians" by "getting out a *Native and national leadership*," but only if given proper support from the BIA.[103] He referenced a statement Ryan had previously made about the future of Haskell depending heavily on the work of its superintendent. Obviously feeling he had done everything he could to lead the school through difficult circumstances, Cloud closed by appealing to Ryan's personal character and asking him to return the favor: "I believe in you and I believe that you are a man of your word. . . . I am counting on your word to be good."[104]

Within a few months, Cloud finally received a sign of support. As Haskell celebrated its fiftieth anniversary in November 1934, Commissioner Collier paid a personal visit to the school. Delivering a speech to some three thousand students and visitors, Collier emphasized the unique position of Haskell in the

BIA's plans, stating that "the only reason our department sent so valuable a man as Dr. Henry Roe Cloud . . . here as head of the school recently was because we do emphatically believe that Haskell has a future."[105] Beyond the particular praise for Cloud—"the most important living Indian"—Collier outlined his thinking on the overall and long-term goals for Haskell.[106] "For many years to come," he argued, "we will continue to need institutions where young Indians can be given intensive training for leadership," with ample room for "self-expression [and] the retention of [one's] own culture and spiritual life."[107] Cloud had finally received the assurance of bureaucratic support that he had so desired, and he immediately wrote Collier to express his gratitude for the reaffirming visit.[108] But Collier's words had done more than simply address the rumors swirling around the school's future. His portrayal of Haskell's mission clearly echoed Cloud's own educational vision. He described a vision of academic and leadership training that translated to the dominant trends in American society as well as to Native contexts—a vision that recalled directly the work Cloud had pursued for nearly twenty years.

Capped as it was by the commissioner's address in front of three thousand onlookers at the school's fiftieth-anniversary celebration, this yearlong narrative surrounding Haskell's uncertain future carried a high level of drama. Throughout the process, Cloud was consistently willing to stand up to BIA officials to demonstrate his vision of Native intellectual leadership and seek the perpetuation of that leadership among a younger generation. Over time, Cloud's persistence in this regard would eventually become central to his demotion within the BIA by the end of the decade. But that persistence was also vital in the everyday grind necessary to broadcast his vision for Haskell as a national center of Native leadership training.

Nowhere did Cloud's vision come through more clearly than in the pages of the *Indian Leader*, Haskell's school newspaper. He immediately took over as the paper's editor, not only soliciting articles from readers across the country but also publishing his own editorial pieces. In his first issue of the *Leader*, Cloud included a biographical write-up of himself and employed quotes from a previous speech in which he had implored students to take their cues from the tangible examples of Native leadership before them. "We who are Indians on the faculty [and] staff," he wrote, "have made up our minds that we will not disappoint the Washington Office in this great trust which they have reposed in us. I believe that you, the student body, are going to see to it that you also will not disappoint."[109]

Cloud soon expanded on his central theme by reprinting a running series simply titled "Indian Leadership." While this series was credited to a journalist from Iowa, it hammered home many of the key arguments that had been part of Cloud's educational program for two decades. One key aspect of this series was that as it illustrated useful work habits and advice for future Native leaders, it also encompassed a wide range of positive characteristics. In one installment of the twelve-part series, the author emphasized "the first requirement of Indian leadership: To plan, to build, to achieve the glory, nobility, and the individual satisfaction of leadership, one must develop a pride in one's own race."[110] Native American identity was thus held up not as merely a positive embellishment to one's personality but as the very bedrock of a Native leader's character. Subsequent articles in the "Indian Leadership" series suggested the maintenance of tribal music, dance, and art as methods for discovering the personal joy of one's culture and history. The series as a whole, however, did not portray Native identity as a hobby or something to be acquired simply by studying past histories. Indeed, the articles frequently stressed the importance of building positive relationships with and learning from contemporary Native leaders among one's own tribe and on a national scale.[111]

Beyond this series, Cloud further illustrated his vision of Native leadership by working to ensure that the school's paper portrayed a variety of tribal and Native American identities. Like the "Indian Leadership" series, Cloud employed examples relating to both historical and contemporary circumstances. He frequently reprinted articles focusing on a number of "beautiful" creation stories and other aspects of tribal histories, and printed a speech of his in which he supported the preservation of these histories "as a means of instilling in the young Indian a pride in his race."[112] In another instance, Cloud reprinted an article on a new Cherokee museum project where administration was held "in the hands of Indians."[113] The project involved white American educators as well, but it provided Cloud with a tangible example of Native students engaging in a form of adaptable leadership and intellectual activism, even at the community level. He could display for his students that in the hands of ambitious Indigenous leaders, an institutional model that may have traditionally served narratives of settler colonialism could now privilege tribal perspectives and identities.[114]

In other ways as well, Cloud's guidance at Haskell suggested that both past and present were key aspects of the identity of a Native leader. As part of the focus on current issues, he repeatedly included brief writeups of the activities of former students, pointing out that many had contributed during the Great Depression by supervising relief efforts within Native communities. And while the curriculum at Haskell entered a general shift toward more vocational training, Cloud consistently ensured that students were made aware of developing opportunities for higher education in colleges and universities.[115]

In his direction of the *Indian Leader*, Cloud employed a variety of portrayals of Native leadership to advocate and inspire greater access for his students both to higher learning and to positions of power in tribal communities and nationwide organizations. Having been severely hamstrung in areas of curricular development and outreach, Cloud seized on the newspaper as a valuable rhetorical tool, and used it as a Native-driven platform for broadcasting his ideas. This effort in many ways was a continuation of what he had begun at his American Indian Institute in 1915. Only after years of work, however, did Cloud's complete vision of Native American higher education and leadership reach its clearest expression.

Native leadership, he informed his readers, began with a pride in one's tribal and Indigenous connections. This pride was built through a personal knowledge of creation stories and histories of past leaders, as well as the maintenance of tribal dances, music, and art. It was strengthened by pursuing a high level of education and training, by learning from modern-day Native leaders, and by serving tribal communities and national organizations. Through all these steps, students and burgeoning leaders could attain a level of adaptability that was explicitly "distinguished from assimilation."[116] Twentieth-century Native leadership for Cloud thus began with a strong sense of Native American identity and was fulfilled through a dedication to addressing the unique set of circumstances facing Native communities and individuals.

Maintaining a Native Activist Voice within the Bureau of Indian Affairs

As it turned out, Henry Roe Cloud's tenure as Haskell's superintendent ended after just two school years. While Commissioner Collier had expressed his great confidence in Cloud's leadership abilities, he sought to direct those abilities elsewhere, in support of the Indian Reorganization Act (IRA) of 1934.[117] The IRA sought to support and restructure tribal governments, to formalize the relationship between those governments and the United States, and to aid various forms of development for Native communities. Collier could rely on Cloud's rapport among Native communities and his charismatic speaking ability to rally support for the law as it was being debated around the country.

For his part, Cloud was optimistic that the legislation could empower local Native leaders and their governments, and he expressed his willingness to "stand shoulder to shoulder to fight" for it along with its allies.[118] Despite some compromises that weakened the IRA's final form, Cloud saw it as a potentially valuable tool in protecting an adaptable form of identity and cultural citizenship for Native people in the United States.[119] In the early years after the law's passing, it made sense that he would agree to support Collier in his effort to ensure that as many tribes as possible embraced the implementation of this "Indian New Deal."[120]

While his removal from Haskell's leadership role stalled his particular educational mission, this decision by Collier to boost the IRA did not initially dampen Cloud's resolve. He was unwavering in his overall commitment to Native intellectual activism and leadership, even as his role within the BIA changed.

Unfortunately, the implementation of the Indian Reorganization Act became an unfulfilling process for Cloud and many Native leaders across the country. Cloud was immediately disappointed in the final law's modest provisions for Native students' higher education, which he had characteristically argued needed an ambitious commitment from the U.S. government.[121] Just as frustrating was the IRA's heavy-handed implementation of uniform governmental structures at the expense of greater tribal creativity and independence. As Cloud witnessed these practical shortcomings developing over time, he risked his own career trajectory by maintaining an outspoken and articulate voice of criticism, rather than act as a token Native American mouthpiece for the Collier program.

His persistence in raising concerns about the IRA and the BIA in general created serious tension within the bureau and brought about career consequences, including a demotion and a substantial pay cut.[122] He was relegated in 1940 to an agent's position at the Umatilla Agency in Oregon, a move he interpreted as an attempt to force his resignation. As a man who had once realistically considered the possibility of ascending to become the commissioner of Indian Affairs, it was undoubtedly galling to be exiled from the national visibility and influence of the BIA's highest levels of power.[123] Still, in choosing to accept the position at Umatilla, and in carrying out the duties of that position until his death in 1950, he demonstrated on a daily basis a sense of Native resilience—a commitment to Native people and their communities that he had always preached among his students. At Umatilla, both Henry Roe Cloud and Elizabeth Bender Cloud made the most of his position. Henry simultaneously emphasized the importance of Native languages and traditions while supporting tribal resource rights as crucial to success in modern America,

By and for Indians

and Elizabeth proactively encouraged women's leadership roles and educational advancement.[124]

While Cloud might have felt that his national impact could have been much greater in the last fifteen years of his life, this does not detract from what he accomplished in the previous twenty. His work at the American Indian Institute from 1915 onward addressed a devastating disconnect between the espoused belief that colleges and universities stood open to Native students and the reality created by an inadequate BIA school system. Though small in size, the American Indian Institute addressed a clear need by expanding Native American access to higher education, while also demonstrating Native control within the school's administration and faculty. As the school's founder and director, Cloud also made clear his belief that Native students must prepare to meet the demands of modern American society without succumbing to straightforward assimilation or the erasure of Indigenous culture. He sought to cultivate and strengthen Native identity rather than pulverize it—a fundamental departure from the assimilationists of the early twentieth century.

Subsequently, in his contributions to the influential Meriam Report and his service as superintendent of Haskell Institute, Cloud expanded his ideas to a larger platform and sought to more directly influence the resources and actions of the Bureau of Indian Affairs for the better. He argued strenuously for the future of Haskell as a national center of Native American education, and even while the curriculum shifted against his ideals, he was able to refine his intellectual conception of Native education into one that focused sharply on the concept of leadership.

At Haskell he laid out his most fundamental principles, demonstrating Native intellectual leadership not only to his students on campus but to readers across the country. His principles for Native leadership relied on a solid base of cultural pride, grounded in tribal histories but also developed through an understanding of the contemporary challenges common to all Native American people. When Cloud was pulled away from Haskell to back the Indian Reorganization Act, he took the opportunity to further demonstrate his own ideal of leadership by advocating for Native people, supporting the idea of increased Native representation in BIA leadership and in tribal administration. Even at the end of his career, Cloud's commitment to reservation administration in Oregon lived up to his own educational blueprint, which had always included service to local Native communities.

The general momentum of the intellectual arguments behind Cloud's work would eventually be stunted by the preoccupations of World War II and challenged by the intense implementation of American Indian termination policies thereafter. But his particular thread of Native intellectual activism remained. By the time the discourse leading to the tribal college movement began materializing in the 1960s and beyond, this seemingly distant educational vision was resurrected and reinvigorated with remarkable continuity. The argument for attacking contemporary Native American issues from a strong base of Indigenous identity echoed Cloud's own voice, as did the more general call to expand Native access to and control of higher education.

It seems fitting, then, to conclude the discussion of Henry Roe Cloud's impact with an example of how his voice carried on long after his life. Leaders of the tribal college movement in the 1960s and 1970s made a habit of employing the phrase "by and for"—as in education by and for Native Americans, or publications by and for Navajos.[125] Not only did Cloud's educational mission support this phrase, but he in fact helped bring it into its common usage. With Cloud at the helm of the *Indian Leader*, the paper advertised itself as a publication "by and for Indians."[126] While this simple phrase itself may seem inconsequential, it represented a fundamental worldview for people like Cloud. Its deeper meaning and the decades-long activist effort that he dedicated to that meaning were crucial contributions in his own era and have clearly remained relevant to Native people ever since.

TWO

A New Spirit of Leadership

Carrying the Threads of Cloud's Vision

As Henry Roe Cloud's prominence in the national discourse on Native American policy waned in the 1940s, the nature of that discourse shifted. John Collier, as commissioner of Indian Affairs from 1933 to 1945, pushed hard to carry out the provisions of the Indian Reorganization Act of 1934 (IRA).[1] Collier's fascination with communal societies and his belief in the positive elements of Native American culture had informed his support for the legislation. He and other advocates of the IRA sought to aid material developments concerning health, education, and economics, while increasing the level of community control and self-government exerted by Native people. But the act had fallen short of the ambitions of Cloud and many other Native leaders when it came to its concrete implementation, with the government's oversight of tribal governing structures a major example.

For Cloud, the final terms of the IRA were also weak in the area of higher education for Native students. While the act provided modest opportunities for student loans, Cloud considered loans a half-hearted substitute for the more impactful direct scholarship aid that he had envisioned.[2] Furthermore, the brief language concerning education within the IRA explicitly directed that funds be put toward students in "vocational and trade schools," indicating the persistence of narrow-minded expectations for Indigenous students to remain in the laboring class.[3] During the early development of the bill, Cloud had hoped the IRA could be a revolutionary catalyst for his goal of reforming the entire relationship between Native students, higher education, and positions of leadership, but in the end the educational provisions of the legislation remained peripheral and unimaginative.

Moreover, any vision for expanding Native community control under the Indian New Deal did not receive lasting support. In the era immediately following World War II, as Republicans in Congress began to attack much of the government infrastructure of President Franklin Roosevelt's New Deal, a handful of senators from western states began a renewed push for the termination of Native American tribes' trust status with the federal government.[4] In this context, a focus on higher education became overshadowed among Native activists by the immediate concerns about the very nature of Native peoples' status in America.

Still, a new generation of Native intellectuals made Cloud's essential argument for increased empowerment and leadership a centerpiece of their activist mission to defeat terminationist policies. Some of the people responsible for carrying out these efforts worked on paths that overlapped with Cloud's only briefly. D'Arcy McNickle, for example, rose as a key Native leader in the Bureau of Indian Affairs (BIA) just as Cloud's influence within the bureau diminished. Others, especially Cloud's wife, Elizabeth Bender Cloud, obviously held deep personal and professional connections to Henry Roe Cloud and his work, advancing forms of activism that built on his own vision while also addressing the context of the IRA and termination.

Over time, McNickle and Bender Cloud did return their focus to higher education as a centerpiece of the effort to promote Native intellectual leadership in both local and national contexts. Their determination to navigate the threat of termination with much of their original goals and influences intact sheds light on the resiliency of the intellectual tradition that Henry Roe Cloud and his allies sought to develop and disseminate. Eventually, the efforts of McNickle and Bender Cloud were supplemented by a separate but similarly inspired activist trajectory, embodied most strongly by Jack Forbes. Forbes did not share the same immediate link to Cloud, but his mission to inspire a national body of young Native leaders through a particular form of higher education borrowed from Cloud's approach and echoed with remarkable continuity his work at the American Indian Institute and Haskell. Thus, even as new generations of Native leaders like Forbes lacked personal connections to Cloud, they were able to access the deeper tradition of intellectual activism exemplified by his work, build on its ideas, and adapt them to new circumstances. As D'Arcy McNickle once remarked, "Ideas . . . have a way of living, whatever forces may be ranged against them. An idea cannot be crushed like an eggshell."[5]

Continuity of Native Intellectualism through American Political Transitions

Even in the midst of their work to support the passage and implementation of the Indian Reorganization Act in the 1930s, Henry Roe Cloud and commissioner of Indian Affairs John Collier perceived the potential threat of termination. Cloud, Collier, and other reformers were always aware that at any time, a significant number of influential people within the federal government viewed the trust status of Native American tribes as impractical and inefficient, and would seek to eliminate that relationship. Changes in this aspect of federal Indian policy in U.S. history have often been described as a "pendulum," swinging back and forth between the protection of Native sovereignty and, as with termination, the erosion of that sovereignty.[6] While this metaphor may provide a useful introduction to the topic, it is hardly instructive for a sustained historical examination. Rather, like many key political or philosophical debates, the struggle over the status of Native people and their tribal entities in the United States has been a constant battle. America's New Deal era was no exception. Indeed, as early as 1935, with the Indian Reorganization Act having passed just months before, Collier warned that segments of Congress would soon regroup in an effort to officially "abandon" the reorganization effort.[7] In 1938, when D'Arcy McNickle wrote for the BIA publication *Indians at Work*, he praised the early results of Indian reorganization but again lamented "a tendency in Congress" to use those same positive results as an argument for accelerating the IRA's demise and withdrawing federal support.[8] At every turn, he hinted, forces in Congress would push for the termination of the U.S. government's legal responsibility to provide services to Native people and to work on an equitable level with tribes.

Deeply concerned about these persistent terminationist tendencies, Collier exerted a heavy personal influence over the effort to protect the Indian New Deal. A key piece of his strategy was an increase in the number of Native individuals working within the BIA and advocating for the IRA. As other historians have previously discussed, Collier, in his attempt to sell the IRA to reservation communities, began seeking pliable young Native voices as an alternative to the nationally renowned and outspoken Henry Roe Cloud.[9] This new group of leaders, however, would share much of Cloud's activist spirit and initiative.

Historian Frederick Hoxie has argued that the influence of the IRA was an unmistakable victory for many ambitious Native activists of the time, although this victory was not always equally shared by Native communities and did not always materialize in ways that Collier or other government officials had envisioned.[10] Robert Yellowtail (Crow), who became superintendent of the Crow Agency in 1934, represents a clear example of this generation of activists who owed at least some of their growing influence to Collier's efforts, and yet were unafraid to pursue Native-driven goals that may not have directly aligned with the commissioner's vision.

Like Henry Roe Cloud, Yellowtail understood activist approaches to Native American policy as necessarily complex and contradictory. As superintendent, he campaigned for the IRA but did not allow his tribe's failure to approve the legislation to detract from his outspoken attempts to garner federal support for his agency and for the rights of his tribal members. He, like Cloud, simultaneously advocated for greater federal commitment to aiding tribes as well as greater tribal autonomy in terms of governance and community leadership.[11] With or without the implementation of the Indian Reorganization Act, Yellowtail understood treaty rights as a basic piece of tribal autonomy and authority, and for

A New Spirit of Leadership

that reason would eventually become a staunch opponent of termination in the postwar period.[12]

While Yellowtail's years of work fighting for greater tribal sovereignty and leadership made him a local embodiment of the era's Native activism, it was D'Arcy McNickle who quickly gained greater influence in John Collier's BIA. Yellowtail's efforts were often entrenched in divisive reservation politics.[13] By contrast, McNickle's more eclectic background and experience—not to mention his well-known writing ability—were desirable traits for Collier's pushing of the IRA to a nationwide audience.[14] McNickle also shared the look of a government man of twentieth-century America. Like Cloud, he wore glasses and a well-trimmed mustache, and was often seen in a full suit and tie. His serious countenance, however, was also complemented by a charismatic sense of humor and a wry smile. Despite fitting the model of what Collier wanted in a BIA man, McNickle—again like Cloud—was also willing and able to broadcast his own form of Native intellectual activism, regardless of whether that occurred within the context of the BIA's official reorganization program.

McNickle rose to prominence in the national discourse on American Indian affairs in the 1930s as a writer and a BIA official, and this rise occurred just as John Collier ushered Henry Roe Cloud to the outer margins of influence in the bureau.[15] As one of Collier's most trusted advocates within the BIA, McNickle addressed the entire spectrum of federal Indian policy in his work. This approach initially could have prevented him from focusing on a single issue in the way that Cloud had done with higher education at the American Indian Institute. And yet McNickle's prolific work as a writer and a leader of various national organizations helps us understand that his form of activism did in fact share and build on some of the most important foundations of Cloud's effort to develop greater Native access to and control of leadership positions in the dominant systems of American education and politics.

McNickle's character was partially shaped by many of the same experiences that other Native activists of the early twentieth century had faced. He attended federal boarding school as well as a mission school, and went on to experience life at one of the most prestigious institutions in Western education.[16] While Henry Roe Cloud became the first Native American to graduate from Yale University, however, McNickle's brief time at Oxford University was intensely frustrating and did not leave him with the same lasting network that Cloud's education had.[17] Moreover, while Cloud drew on his theological training throughout his career as a Christian educator, McNickle was more likely to criticize the role of missionaries in Native life.[18] Despite these differences in how they emerged from Anglo-American higher education and training, McNickle and Cloud shared much in how they approached the most crucial questions regarding Native peoples' status in the United States. By the time McNickle began asserting his influence in John Collier's BIA, it was clear that he shared many of the basic pillars of Cloud's approach to Native intellectual activism and leadership.

Perhaps the most crucial characteristic the two shared was their outlook on the topic of assimilation. Cloud's work has been somewhat misunderstood in this regard because, on the surface, his Christian preaching and his emphasis on schooling that aligned with the dominant institutions of white American society may seem assimilationist.[19] On closer examination, however, we understand through Cloud's own words and actions that he advocated a type of "adaptation" for individual Native leaders as well as "opportunities [for] organized effort" for Native people collectively.[20] The path to Native American leadership for Cloud was rooted in history and cultural traditions, was concerned with the empowerment of individual Native professionals as well as reservation communities, and was explicitly "distinguished from assimilation."[21]

In a similar way, McNickle became an influential and captivating Native voice in his era precisely because he fixed attention on the potential alienation and the difficult negotiations faced by Native people in assimilationist institutions and settler colonial settings.[22] McNickle's writings from the very outset of his career

A New Spirit of Leadership

express a concern over a simplistic, assimilationist approach to the "Indian problem." In a 1937 piece for the BIA publication *Indians at Work*, McNickle laid out his frustrations with the persistence of presumptuous assimilationist rhetoric that permeated literature about Native people. He argued that the central problem of this rhetoric stemmed from pervasive ethnocentrism, "thinking of Indians as emerging from savagery and being hastened on the road to salvation."[23] In separate pieces over the span of the next several years, McNickle reiterated his harsh criticism of straightforward assimilationist policy.[24] The proper alternative, he asserted, was an approach that acknowledged the strength of Native cultural practices in the face of a long history of attacks, that supported Indigenous languages alongside the practical use of English, and that gave Native Americans the power to make "adaptations" to the challenges of modern life in the United States—"as they found agreeable."[25] In these writings, we see remarkable continuity in the ways that McNickle and Cloud understood the fundamental issues regarding Native people and their communities, as well as the basic principles on which they hoped to support the growth of Native leadership nationwide.

While Cloud's focus on leadership centered most intensely on American higher education and Native students, McNickle's early work was more directly tied to the context of the Indian New Deal sought by John Collier's BIA. Because of the ambitious nature of reorganization and its focus on multiple aspects of tribal organization, McNickle considered leadership in the broad context of self-government, imagining education as one of the many aspects therein. Still, as McNickle studied and wrote on the impact of the IRA, he repeatedly stressed the importance of developing Native leadership through education and training in a variety of fields.

As McNickle saw it, the importance of the Indian Reorganization Act was not the initiative that the federal government showed in passing the legislation but the initiative that the law would allow to flourish within Native communities. "It isn't enough to have a law on the statute books," he wrote.[26] "The law must operate in the lives of men and women before it begins to have meaning."[27]

That meaning—the law's impact as seen in "an array of human facts," as McNickle put it—was just "coming into being" in the late 1930s. The need to support it fully—both within the federal government and within the communities it impacted—would remain critical for years.

As Cloud had sought to cultivate highly adaptable students who worked from strengths in both Native and non-Native forms of leadership training, so McNickle saw the future of Native self-government as necessarily relying on multiple skill sets and bodies of knowledge. As early as 1941 he wrote of his concern regarding the possible loss of Native languages.[28] He understood the value of elders' local leadership in many Native communities, and called on both the BIA and those communities themselves to support the proper training of younger generations in their Native tongues. He saw language as an obvious bedrock of identity but also a practical and necessary tool for accessing all segments of community authority and leadership. In his analysis of the issue, McNickle characteristically pointed to the need for the BIA to contribute as much as possible to a solution while also insisting that Native people themselves seize an opportunity to better train their own emerging leaders. Unfortunately, this piece appeared just days before the Japanese attack on Pearl Harbor, which pulled the United States—including tens of thousands of Native Americans—into World War II. Beyond this particular issue, however, McNickle continued to articulate a similar stance on myriad forms of leadership training, consistently arguing for significant and prolonged support from the BIA while also conveying the importance of Native communities employing their own people and ideas in the effort to self-govern.[29]

The common outlook that Cloud and McNickle shared regarding the damaging impact of forced assimilation—as well as the value of a resilient Native leadership that was built on a flexible range of identities and skill sets—led them both to support the initial push for the Indian Reorganization Act in the 1930s. They understood John Collier's program as a crucial step toward halting the eroding effects that policies like the 1887 General Allot-

A New Spirit of Leadership

ment Act had had on tribes' land bases, socioeconomic well-being, and political power.[30] Still, both men were confident in their own abilities and their own visions for cultivating greater Native leadership locally and nationally. As Collier's efforts enhanced the breathing space for these visions, Cloud and McNickle seized the opportunity but showed they were unwilling to simply act as "good Indian" mouthpieces for the BIA.

Cloud had sought an explicit separation from the government's Native American boarding school system in his establishment of the American Indian Institute, but his willingness to speak his mind regarding his frustrations with the direction of the BIA carried over to his service under Collier as well. In his rhetorical fight for continuing Haskell Institute's mission of training adaptable young Native leaders, Cloud had stated bluntly that he trusted his own conception of Native American education and his own "procedure" in carrying out his mission. "It does not matter so much to me whether I am in the government service or out of it," he wrote.[31] "I am not laboring for the perpetuity of my own job" but rather for the sake of the educational vision that Haskell represented.[32] Clearly Cloud considered his primary goal the development of a national body of Native intellectual leaders, regardless of how directly the federal government supported that goal.

McNickle, at least under Collier, was less likely to so definitively separate his own perspective from the mission of the BIA. Yet, in how he chose to write on Native American issues for the bureau, he did show his willingness to go beyond a straightforward endorsement of the Indian Reorganization Act. In one of his earliest pieces for the BIA periodical *Indians at Work*, in fact, McNickle chose not to address the IRA or any specific federal policy by name.[33] Rather, he spoke of the historical roots of Native American landlessness and poverty, and the connection between that history and the federal government's responsibility to address those issues. Taking it a step further, he singled out a group of Native people on the U.S.-Canadian border near Great Falls, Montana—a group that lacked official tribal recognition from either the United States or Canada. By choosing to focus on a group of people without federal recognition, McNickle revealed his desire to advocate for a greater federal commitment to the basic concerns of Indigenous people, regardless of the official terms of reorganization.

McNickle's understanding of the fundamental issues facing Native people in modern America, as well as his commitment to address those issues through an expansion of Native intellectual leadership, aligned him in many ways with the perspective of Henry Roe Cloud. So, too, did his willingness to adhere to his understanding of the issues' principles rather than to the limits of a particular policy or regime. While he recognized the value of the "promise" provided by the Indian New Deal, McNickle eventually came to view the act in the same way that Cloud had, as a "compromise measure" that did not go far enough in giving tribes "a degree of control" vis-à-vis "the federal employees assigned to their reservations as administrators."[34] By the 1940s, if not from the very beginning of his career, McNickle was explicitly asserting tribes' right to self-govern, regardless of whether they had endorsed the IRA.

This commitment to principle would push McNickle to steadily distance himself from the federal government in the postwar period, a time when the bureau began to support the interests of those members of Congress who most aggressively pushed for termination and rapid assimilation. Eventually, that separation from the Bureau of Indian Affairs would allow McNickle to take greater personal control over implementing his own vision for the development of a generation of Native intellectual leaders who could impact policy in local reservation communities as well as on a national scale.

Separation between Native Intellectual Activism and the Federal Government

The postwar era brought a steady separation between the Bureau of Indian Affairs and the leading Native activists in the United States. John Collier left his position as commissioner of Indian affairs in 1945, World War II came to an end, and in the ensuing years many members of Congress began to rally against the bulked-up government bureaucracy that President Roosevelt's New Deal had constructed. In this atmosphere, a handful of vocal members of Congress—led by Senator Arthur Watkins from Utah—drew particular attention to the trust status of Native American tribes, seeking to dismantle the government structures and services that supported that status.[35] D'Arcy McNickle, who spent several years attempting to combat this pressure from his position within the BIA, was simultaneously at the forefront of an effort to organize apart from the bureau. The National Congress of American Indians (NCAI) became perhaps the strongest example of this effort.

In 1944 McNickle and other prominent Native activists both within and outside the BIA began seriously considering the need for a national organization that could voice concerns about federal Indian policy and present a unified front in defense of Native Americans' rights.[36] Perhaps sensing the end of his own era amid a political push away from the New Deal, John Collier encouraged these early exploratory meetings involving some of the employees under his direction.[37] Collier's powerful influence in his twelve years as commissioner had no doubt allowed a greater sense of responsibility and freedom of expression among these Native leaders.

McNickle and the other founders of the NCAI did, however, recognize the importance of keeping the organization a true representation of Native American interests and thus free from government control. Soon after its founding, the group passed resolutions that prevented active bureau employees from holding positions as officers within the NCAI.[38] This effort to develop the organization as a Native-driven entity called to mind the Society of American Indians' rules preventing non-Native members from holding voting power in that organization. There were even prominent members such as Arthur C. Parker and Zitkala-Sa who represented a direct link between the NCAI and the deeper tradition of intellectual activism in the SAI.[39] Like the SAI, the NCAI's members included men and women from dozens of tribes, and were arguably even more representative than the previous generation's organization in terms of connections to diverse reservation interests. Robert Yellowtail, for example, became an early member of the NCAI but remained deeply involved in local reservation government.

Despite its eclectic makeup, the new organization sought to succeed where the SAI had failed in arriving at a unified understanding of its purpose. At their first convention in 1944, the original NCAI members adopted a constitution that addressed Native American empowerment in a broad sense. The organization's central goals were to "secure the rights and benefits to which [Native Americans] are entitled under the laws of the United States . . . to enlighten the public toward a better understanding of the Indian race; to preserve cultural values . . . to preserve rights under Indian treaties . . . and to otherwise promote the common welfare" of Native people.[40] This broad scope was part of the constitution's strength, because it conveyed the interconnectedness between cultural, political, and socioeconomic welfare. It also transcended the limits of the era's most immediate political battles concerning the role of the BIA or the implementation of any particular policy by stressing historical treaties as the basis for the contemporary rights and sovereignty of Native people. These arguments may seem simple, but it is important to note how quickly Native activists organized on a national scale to capitalize on the breathing space that the Indian New Deal had provided. While the Indian Reorganization Act of 1934 was properly hailed as a landmark policy for its repudiation of allotment and its support of reservation governments, within ten years the activists organizing the NCAI were already attempting to transcend the constraints of the IRA and preparing to defend Native rights even more broadly, despite the ominous cloud of termination on the horizon.

While he continued working actively within the Bureau of Indian Affairs until 1952, D'Arcy McNickle's leadership in the NCAI was evident from the beginning.[41] When he met with President Truman's Committee on Civil Rights in 1947, he spoke as a representative of the NCAI, not the BIA.[42] Throughout his statements to the committee, McNickle employed this subtle distinction to clearly define a Native position on federal policy and

A New Spirit of Leadership

to explain the role of the NCAI as the preeminent Native-driven effort to defend Native Americans' rights. It was important to McNickle to point out the perspective of the NCAI as an "organization made up entirely of persons of Indian blood."[43]

In speaking from that perspective, McNickle generally deemphasized the role of the BIA and instead underscored some harmful misunderstandings in the relationship between tribes and the federal government. He saw Native people under attack on two fronts. First, he characterized terminationist momentum as emanating from a misguided effort to "emancipate" Native people from tribal life; by contrast, McNickle argued that abolishing reservations would in fact be "emancipating the Indian away from [what] little property he has left."[44] He also illustrated that paradoxically, Native people's tribal identification was often turned against them as justification for denying voting rights, veteran's benefits, or other civil services.[45] In the face of such fundamental erosions of Indigenous peoples' rights on multiple fronts, McNickle saw the BIA as overwhelmed. By downplaying the BIA and instead speaking as an NCAI leader, he strove for an impact that reached well beyond the scope of the bureau, hoping to influence President Truman and his entire administration as directly as possible. "We believe," he stated, "that the President could give Indians a great deal of help merely by informing his [cabinet] of the legal status of Indians, why they have [that] status . . . and what ought to be the attitude of the Federal Government with respect to their status and their rights."[46]

McNickle may have been ahead of his time in seeking such a concrete defense of Native Americans' rights from the president in 1947. Even the President's Committee on Civil Rights was hesitant on whether it was their duty to address systemic violations of Native people's legal status, as opposed to everyday violations of their civil rights based solely on racial discrimination.[47] Still, McNickle's willingness to argue for Native people as an NCAI leader in a way that transcended his role in the BIA was an early sign of developments to come.

By 1950, with the introduction of Dillon S. Myer as commissioner of Indian Affairs, the BIA's alignment with the Congressional push toward termination appeared firm.[48] Myer's most significant previous experience had occurred during the Japanese internment effort as part of the War Relocation Authority, where he gained little knowledge of Native American policy but showed hints of his general belief in the benefits of cultural assimilation.[49] As for his administrative style, he had no intentions of becoming the figurehead of a bold policy in the way that John Collier had. Instead, he sought to organize the BIA as an efficient tool for carrying out the policy that Congress set forth. By 1953 that policy was explicitly laid out in House Concurrent Resolution 108 and Public Law 280, which respectively advocated the elimination of the federal government's responsibility to uphold tribes' special trust status, and the implementation of state jurisdiction over tribes.[50]

During this period, McNickle took on an active role in the NCAI that allowed him to bring about the types of Native community action that he had advocated in vain during his long tenure with the bureau. Over time, his efforts to cultivate and maintain Native intellectual leadership on a local and national level would begin to embody the educational vision that Henry Roe Cloud had laid out decades earlier.

Renewed Push for Native Leadership
Platforms in the Termination Era

While McNickle's work in the Bureau of Indian Affairs had allowed him to address in a broad sense the fundamental issues impacting Native people throughout the country, it had also left him frustrated by the apparent lack of commitment to building significant programs to aid reservation communities. He had never witnessed what he had hoped would be the BIA's sustained impact in terms of developing and empowering tribal leadership and supporting economic development.[51] By the early 1950s, the "promise" of the Indian New Deal was not only incomplete but in immediate danger. In this context, McNickle moved beyond his attempt to institute change within and through the government and instead sought to inspire that change among Native people more directly, through both local and nationwide organization.

The vehicle for this direct impact became an action-oriented wing of the NCAI called American Indian Development (AID). In 1950 and 1951, McNickle developed AID and became its director, hoping to raise money for nongovernment programs that could inspire tribes "to build up their communities through their own efforts" and attain "real control over their destinies."[52] Within the first year of full operation, AID was administering three separate information-gathering and educational programs in Utah, Oklahoma, and Arizona.[53] While McNickle and his staff members relied on their valuable experiences to assist tribes in organizing to address their perceived needs, special emphasis was placed on developing locally grown activism and leadership.[54]

From the outset, Elizabeth Bender Cloud joined forces with McNickle as assistant director of AID.[55] After Henry's death in 1950, Elizabeth had taken on a more public leadership role of her own. In addition to her role with AID, she acted as chair of the Indian Affairs Division of the General Federation of Women's Clubs.[56] This position allowed her to share with a wide, reform-minded audience her perspective on Native American issues and connect with a broad supportive network in the private sector—similar to the network her husband had relied on when seeking funding for the American Indian Institute. While these particular leadership roles came to her rather late in life, her abilities had been apparent much earlier. During Henry's frequent absences from the American Indian Institute, she had shown her willingness to take over the administrative and financial duties and bear "the brunt of the work" for extended periods.[57] Now, years later, she seized on the ambition and energy of McNickle's AID program and infused it with an articulate dedication to the type of education and training for Native intellectual leadership that her late husband had always pursued. Her abilities as an organizational leader and a writer seemed to match her appearance. Even in her sixties, her shoulders and facial features projected strength but were paired with a warm and disarming smile.[58]

As with Henry, Elizabeth's diverse body of work throughout her career has been a challenge to categorize.[59] Even Renya Ramirez, an anthropologist and the Clouds' granddaughter, has readily admitted moments when Bender Cloud's own writings seem to adopt "painful settler-colonial assumptions" belying the conceptions of gender, race, and "Civilization" in early twentieth-century America.[60] And yet Bender Cloud deftly handled and manipulated the powerful rhetoric of "Indian assimilation" and termination while consistently reiterating themes of Native-driven leadership.[61] As with Henry's stance on assimilation versus adaptation, the nuances in Elizabeth's work must be highlighted rather than smoothed over in an attempt to categorize her neatly as "by and large assimilationist."[62] Those nuances, rather than anomalies, are vital illustrations of strategic choices on her part regarding how to exert influence as a Native leader within incredibly restrictive discourses. In her case, the context of Indian termination provides perhaps the clearest indication of these strategic choices. For instance, in reports for AID she and McNickle embodied NCAI's unity in openly criticizing the push for termination, writing that termination would place Native people in "the unhappy position of possibly being held liable for the sins of their benefactors."[63] But she was also able to subtly modify the delivery of that message for different rhetorical platforms.

When Bender Cloud addressed a predominantly non-Native audience through the publications of the General Federation of Women's Clubs, she chose a more cautious approach. For example, she admitted that the dominant discourse on Native American assimilation may have stemmed from the "sincere efforts" of non-Native people, but she emphasized that "Native leadership is convinced that the American Indian must accomplish his own *self-determination* and growth on a new frontier of development. Indians must themselves through their own efforts chart the course of their future."[64] As she continued, she chose not to criticize the notion of assimilation directly. Rather than emphasize negative aspects of forced assimilation that white readers may have always accepted, she laid out a positive vision of the future as one in which Native American individuals and their communities persisted, with "Indian leadership directed to the end of self-support and self-government" in Native communities.[65] That leadership, she insisted, must be spurred on by funding for the types of programs that AID was enacting, as well as for broader "scholarship aid for ambitious boys and girls who are now ready for higher educational training, but who have not the extra funds" to take on the tuition.[66]

In this way, Elizabeth Bender Cloud displayed her understanding of the powerful discourse surrounding termination and assimilation, while attempting to push that power in a direction that she saw as more beneficial to Native people. She sought to appeal to the "sincere efforts" of a non-Native audience and direct that positive energy toward a practical end that could empower Native people "for social, political, economic, and citizenship responsibilities" in their own communities.[67]

The first manifestation of this effort through AID was a series of local workshops near reservation communities, which began in 1951 and developed throughout the decade. While the long-term material impact of these workshops was difficult to measure, Bender Cloud early on noted that "a new spirit of leadership [was] awakening."[68] For the directors of AID in the first years of the workshops, the most crucial impact was a momentous shift away from bureaucratic dictation and toward an approach to the concerns and needs of Native communities that grew from the inside out. "The solving of Indian problems," McNickle and Bender Cloud wrote, "is a question of starting with people, at the place where they are."[69] They repeatedly stressed the desire of AID to distance itself from the paternalistic stance that had for so long characterized the federal government, and instead to encourage communities to assess their own needs and establish their own goals. Ultimately, the strategy from AID was "to counsel and advise, but . . . not attempt to manage the affairs of a community."[70] This must have been a difficult exercise in patience for AID's directors and staff, who clearly felt a sense of urgency in the face of termination.

Still, the experiences of both D'Arcy McNickle and Elizabeth Bender Cloud had led them to believe that the particular form of Native leadership they were cultivating was perfectly suited for addressing the challenges of their time. At the American Indian Institute and later in her own activism, Bender Cloud had participated in an effort that acknowledged the power of modern American systems of education, economics, and politics but simultaneously promoted Native leaders' use of those systems *as Native people* who could in turn advocate *for Native people* in particular.[71] In his own right, McNickle's career by the 1950s had long displayed a sense of continuity with this theme. Just as the Clouds had, McNickle advocated the maintenance of Native cultures, languages, and lands, as well as a high level of "adaptation" to the powerful modern forces of American law and politics.[72] And by the late 1950s and early 1960s, McNickle became deeply involved in a new effort that even more closely aligned with the Clouds' original vision of intellectual activism through higher education.

Beginning in the late 1950s, McNickle became interested in an opportunity to reach students in a way that promised to go beyond individual communities and to promote the growth of a nationwide body of Native intellectual activists. Founded in 1956 as simply the Workshop on American Indian Affairs, this program brought together Native American undergraduate and graduate students from around the country for six-week summer seminars to educate students on the intersections between settler-colonial history and contemporary Native issues.[73] Although higher education opportunities for Native students were undoubtedly greater in the 1950s than in the era of Henry Roe Cloud's American Indian Institute, the workshop was designed with a similar mission—to act as a pantribal Native hub within the larger landscape of American higher education. Like the AII, the workshop operated as a flexible platform for exploring specific issues of Native life in modern America but was also recognized as a credit-bearing program by mainstream colleges and universities.[74]

The workshop began at Colorado College and was originally run by University of Chicago anthropologists, including Sol Tax,

Rosalie Wax, and Robert K. "Bob" Thomas (Cherokee). It soon found a home at the University of Colorado in Boulder, where McNickle had lived since the formation of AID.[75] In the first years, he acted as a guest speaker and close observer of the workshop, and by 1960 he was intimately involved in its planning and execution.[76] McNickle gave the workshop greater stability and continuity by ensuring in 1960 that it became a centerpiece of AID's program, administered directly by that organization rather than through a more temporary and sporadic ad hoc committee.[77]

The workshop's overall mission was honed under McNickle to focus, like AID's earlier programs, on self-actualization of Native leadership in practical ways: to "help Indian students find meaning and purpose in college work," and to promote among them a better understanding of "subject matter that touches their lives and has meaning."[78] McNickle and the other directors had noted that despite the higher levels of enrollment over time, many Native students experienced persistent difficulties in American higher education, and the workshop hoped to confront those difficulties as directly as possible. Native students, they observed, often felt marginalized not only because of the pressures of cultural stereotypes in the education system but because of prejudices that the students themselves had come to harbor as well.[79]

Cherokee instructor Bob Thomas was perhaps the most influential force on the early workshop, eliciting intense and sometimes emotional responses from the students because of his steadfast defense of Native cultures in the face of assimilationist arguments.[80] Rosalie Wax, who acted as an instructor and director and wrote an extensive report on the early years, noted that many students were confused and frustrated by Thomas's perspective, possibly because they had encountered in American schools the view that rapid assimilation was the only positive course for Native Americans.[81] In the end, this energy—even when born out of confusion or frustration—became a centerpiece of the workshop and was viewed as an essential aspect of the intense program. Not only were students gaining a better knowledge of "Indian legislation; tribal histories; reservation planning; [and] the administration of law and order in Indian communities," but they were also undergoing a self-examination in terms of their identities as Native people and activists in a challenging modern world.[82] In these tense but enlightening seminars, Thomas, McNickle, and the other directors hoped to inspire young Native students to garner the benefits of mainstream American higher education in order to work toward not only Native-driven socioeconomic goals but also a fundamentally "better view of themselves, of their abilities, of their place in the future."[83]

It must be acknowledged that these workshopped explorations of Indigenous identity were not universally endorsed by Native activists. Vine Deloria Jr.'s *Custer Died for Your Sins* delivered a remarkably cutting critique in 1969. Deloria railed against the "workshop orgy [developing] during the summers," a collection of programs he viewed as repetitive and overly theoretical exercises directed by "anthropologists and other friends."[84] Deloria's use of the term "friend" in this critique calls to mind the generations of white Americans calling themselves "friends of the Indian," who had long attempted to rectify the "Indian problem." In previous eras, those efforts had included policies such as the Dawes Act, which resulted in the loss of tens of millions of acres of Indigenous landholdings through allotment and accompanied the massive attempt at cultural assimilation exemplified in the boarding school system. In the 1950s and 1960s, Deloria saw the workshops as similarly damaging, despite being oriented around the supposed protection of Native identity rather than its erasure. Even with the focus now placed on protections of Indigenous culture, he insisted that the anthropological obsession over abstract problems like "authenticity" and biculturalism added to the already difficult paths facing maturing young students, and even suggested that the workshops contributed to the abuse of alcohol among attendees.[85]

For Deloria, theoretical obsessions could suppress, rather than cultivate, young Native leadership. He issued a call for a renewed focus on the practical rather than the abstract problems of settler colonialism. "Regardless of theory," he bluntly reasoned, "the Pyramid Lake Paiutes and the Gila River Pima Maricopas are poor because they have been systematically cheated out of their water rights," and "the Plains Indians have an inadequate land base . . . because of land sales. Straddling worlds is irrelevant to straddling small pieces of land and trying to earn a living."[86]

In this critique, however, Deloria's interpretation actually aligns well with Henry Roe Cloud's earlier intellectual activism at the American Indian Institute and Haskell Institute.[87] Cloud had studied and come to understand as well as anyone the history of settler colonialism from an Indigenous perspective, dating back to the first days of white settlement.[88] From 1915 to the 1930s and beyond, he pushed young Native students to build on but also beyond the tribal identities that were rooted in that historical experience, toward attacking the practical issues that existed in their contemporary communities. As examples, he employed rhetorical platforms to highlight tribal control of history-telling institutions at the same time that he praised former students who assisted Native communities during the Great Depression and promoted more innovative agricultural education that would translate to the conditions of reservation communities.[89]

Moreover, in the case of the Boulder Workshops, Bob Thomas emerged as an outstanding exception to Deloria's overall disdain for anthropology's treatment of Indigenous people. Indeed, Thomas was a significant influence on Deloria's development as a Native intellectual activist, and undoubtedly agreed with significant portions of Deloria's critique.[90] Thomas blamed American school systems for perpetuating false dilemmas that grouped Indigenous people into poverty-stricken "traditional Indians" on the one hand and counterfeit imitators of white American culture on the other.[91] He felt these dilemmas threatened to needlessly alienate Native college students from their communities, and he wanted the workshop students instead to find solidarity across tribal and generational lines, working together toward a proactive, intellectual approach to the modern ramifications of settler colonialism. Many attendees—while undoubtedly exposed to the tangle of theoretical discussions referenced by Deloria—did emerge energized to tackle concrete problems and make positive, tangible impacts for tribal communities.[92]

As one key example, several workshop attendees went on to become the leaders and founders of several regional councils and eventually the National Indian Youth Council (NIYC), organizations that would prove crucial to expanding a national discourse on Native American self-determination and the theme of empowering Native leaders within the education system.[93] Mel Thom (Paiute), Clyde Warrior (Ponca), Herb Blatchford (Navajo), and Bernadine Eschief (Shoshone), among others, represented this strong link between the Boulder Workshop and the ensuing wave of intellectual activism represented by the NIYC.[94] As the 1960s progressed, the philosophical underpinnings and goals of the workshop would also resonate in the founding missions of tribal colleges and universities.

McNickle and the other promoters of the workshop at the dawn of the 1960s sensed the growing impact of their endeavor, viewing it as a pivotal "new idea in Indian education."[95] The program's influence on emerging young leaders was unmistakable. But in their enthusiastic focus on the future, the directors' claims of a "new idea" in education may have overlooked just how closely they worked toward the same fundamental principles of an activist effort begun years before. Indeed, Henry Roe Cloud had labored for two decades to bring together promising students from across the country, to improve the relationship between American higher education and those Native students, to give their education greater meaning, and to demonstrate and further inspire "a Native and national leadership."[96] Whereas Cloud had felt compelled to address a serious gap between Native students and the American higher education system, the organizers of the summer workshop in Boulder were able to build on the momentum generated by the fact that in the late 1950s, young Native students began entering colleges and universities with greater regularity. Rather than see it stall, McNickle and the workshop organizers sought to direct that momentum into a burgeoning movement, and both instructors and students perceived a sense of urgency in the moment. As Ute student Joan Noble expressed of the formation of NIYC, "there seems to be the leadership needed in these people. Let us not let it die in our hands."[97]

But they were not alone, even in their own time. In the late 1950s, Jack Forbes had already begun developing his own vision for Native American higher education that even more directly drew on the example of Henry Roe Cloud's approach to Native intellectual activism.

Reimagining a National Center of Native-Driven Higher Education

There was not just one model of Native activism in the twentieth century. Even within the particular vein of activism studied here—which concerned itself with the control of and access to education and Native leadership development—the styles and backgrounds of the individuals involved varied. Activists sometimes served as community leaders on the reservation level, and at other times worked toward broad pantribal organization. As the examples of the Clouds and McNickle have shown, these areas of focus could overlap. Still, certain shared characteristics have stood out. One key trait shared by the activists studied here was an ability to understand and utilize the power of racial and cultural discourses of the time. The Clouds and McNickle all displayed in their writings the ability to address the concerns of both Native people and non-Native advocates of their work. They drew on their experiences with the dominant systems of Anglo-American education and politics while attempting to move and reshape those systems in ways they saw as more beneficial for Native people with Native identities. They maintained a balanced perspective that viewed leadership as the product of multiple sources of learning, and as something concerned with both local action and broader organization.

Jack Forbes shared these traits. Born in 1934, he was certainly of a different generation than the others highlighted here.[98] When Elizabeth Bender Cloud and D'Arcy McNickle first outlined their frustrations with termination and their ambitions to develop Native leadership programs through AID, Forbes was just a teenager.[99]

But this context did not escape him, and he would soon become one of its central voices and actors. As a young adult, pictures of his clean-cut face, soft eyes, and faint smile belied his sharp rhetorical voice. He advanced quickly through the American higher education system, earning his master's degree at age twenty-two and a PhD in history and anthropology from the University of Southern California at twenty-five.[100] He was also clearly perceptive of cultural and racial discrimination from an early age, not only in its details but in how it operated on a grand scale. He wrote as a teenager about his personal observations of and misgivings regarding racial segregation in the South, but also contextualized those personal and anecdotal experiences as part of a systemic problem.[101]

Before he completed his formal education, Forbes was already displaying his activist spirit. In 1957 he wrote directly to the U.S. secretary of the interior to express his concerns regarding the direction of postwar American Indian policy.[102] Though he wrote prolifically throughout his life, this one letter captures the seed of what motivated Forbes as a Native activist. In it, he railed against the postwar policy of Indian relocation, which sought to accelerate Native American movement away from reservations and toward jobs and homes in urban areas. Forbes, who observed the impact of this program in Los Angeles, argued that it did little other than push Native people into "sub-standard or slum sections" of major cities.[103] He targeted the relocation program specifically but understood it as just one piece in a long and deliberate policy of breaking down tribal communities and identities. He referred to the Indian New Deal of the 1930s as the one notable exception in a general effort "to white-wash the Indian, destroy his religion and force him to become a copy of the European-American."[104] Despite his clear anger and frustration, Forbes showed his ability to carefully delineate the multiple levels of his argument. Native Americans, he asserted, were under attack not only in terms of their basic right to practice their cultures but also in terms of their particular legal rights to their homes and lands that were anchored in the treaty process.[105]

A New Spirit of Leadership

Forbes made this type of direct activist action a decided strategy. In 1960, with the election of John F. Kennedy to the White House, Forbes attempted to utilize the administrative turnover as an opening for inspiring a turn away from termination and forced assimilation, with education as a primary focus. He aggressively pursued a variety of strategies for influencing policy makers, regularly sending letters and proposals to members of Congress and eventually corresponding directly with members of the president's cabinet—including Vice President Lyndon Johnson.[106] Like Cloud and McNickle, Forbes showed in his activist efforts an interest in how the long course of settler-colonial history intersected with contemporary Native political and legal issues, and he expressed a willingness to throw himself into the effort to "re-construct" the entire approach to how those issues were taught.[107] As this effort developed, it quickly became an articulate and creative mission that aligned closely with the work carried out by Henry Roe Cloud early in the twentieth century.

Much like Cloud, Forbes was an educator who viewed the promise of a growing Native intellectual activism as a movement that required a fundamental change in how Native students experienced the mainstream system of education.[108] He also understandably saw education as interwoven with all other aspects of social and economic well-being. In what was becoming a frustrated refrain for Native American activists by 1960, Forbes viewed the essential perspective of the Bureau of Indian Affairs and the schools they provided as one that "obsessed [over] the idea of 'Anglo-izing' the Indian."[109]

In one of his first communications with the Kennedy administration, Forbes outlined in detail his assessment of the problems stemming from this assimilationist stance, as well as potential alternatives. He understood the obsession with assimilation as a "tragic failure" that only exacerbated the social and economic problems of Native communities by replacing any positive sense of self with a makeshift copy of American working-class identity.[110] In schools motivated by assimilationist goals, Forbes argued, Native students were soaked in a worldview of American exceptionalism that not only degraded Indigenous cultural practices but excluded their entire perspective from the "historic community."[111] In other words, students felt the need either to assimilate or to identify with a "lost people."[112] In this problematic position, he argued, they struggled to become leaders "for their own people [or] for society in general."[113]

Forbes focused on alternatives that began not with the ostensible practicality of basic vocational training or "modernization" but with an acknowledgment of the contributions of Indigenous cultures to American society. As Cloud had done in publications such as the *Indian Leader* decades before, Forbes described positive endorsements of Native culture and identity as the *foundation of*—rather than simply an adornment to—a student's growth and success.[114] In a letter to a colleague in 1961, Forbes suggested that "a pride in, and knowledge of, the Native American heritage" would not only "improve the social-psychological attitudes of Indian students [but of] Indian people in general."[115] He did not settle, though, for making suggestions and appealing to various members of the academic and political power structures. These appeals were only one part of his strategy. Like Cloud, Forbes began to focus on higher education and Native leadership, organizing his own effort to directly cultivate the change he sought. In 1960 and 1961 this effort grew into an extensive proposal for a pantribal American Indian University.[116]

As hinted at above, the relationship between Native students and American higher education had already changed significantly between the founding of Cloud's American Indian Institute in 1915 and the development of Forbes's proposal in the early 1960s. In a broad sense, the American infrastructure of colleges and universities had swollen considerably, with a higher percentage of the general population attending and graduating from these institutions.[117]

For Native American people in particular, the change had been even more profound. The direct efforts of Cloud and other educators had begun to expose and address the disconnect between Native students and higher education in America, and had better prepared students to successfully bridge that gap. By the 1950s, as McNickle and the directors of the Workshop on American Indian Affairs had noted, the nature of the problem had shifted but it had not disappeared. While there no longer existed the same "absolute block upon the entrance of [the] ablest young [Native] people into the schools and colleges of the land" that Cloud had observed, there remained in McNickle's and Forbes's eyes a cultural disconnect between educational institutions, Native students, and their communities.[118] Native students in postwar American higher education encountered a general lack of perspectives emanating from Indigenous communities, to the point that many students failed to understand how that education could relate to their own reservation population.

This cultural disconnect, Forbes perceived, was not simply an inconvenient aspect of a prejudiced system but a powerful and concrete obstacle between Native students and meaningful success in higher education and the related positions of power and leadership.[119] Facing this reality, his proposal for an American Indian University laid out a vision that aligned remarkably well with the work that Henry Roe Cloud had pursued in his two decades at the American Indian Institute and Haskell.

Forbes began his proposal with a simple premise. "One of the greatest problems facing the American Indian today," he wrote, "is the lack of trained leadership."[120] Native leadership for him represented a broad concept that depended in part on professional training in everything from "medicine [and] law . . . [to] economics and agriculture," and in part on a more subjective "sense of inner pride and security" that came from positive endorsements of Indigenous identity.[121] As he progressed through his ambitious university proposal, Forbes articulated a host of tangible strategies for a simultaneous approach to both of these aspects of Native leadership.

He began with teacher training, endorsing an explicit commitment to training "as many teachers of Indian ancestry as possible."[122] This step, he argued, would not simply increase the number of Native American professionals in the short term but also would

cultivate a more positive sense of identity for an entire generation of students. Native American teachers would simultaneously address several problems, in Forbes's eyes. For one, they
could begin to counteract generations of "an Anglo-interpreted
version of history, culture, [and] values" by teaching from a perspective that genuinely empathized with that of Native students
and their communities.[123] At the same time, however, the teachers would stand as tangible embodiments of adaptable leadership
by drawing on Native and non-Native teaching techniques and
languages. With this vision of teacher training as his first priority, Forbes hoped to lay the groundwork for a more positive sense
of identity among an entire generation of Native students who,
in turn, might contribute to a growing body of Native leaders
throughout the country.

Throughout his proposal, Forbes illustrated how his American Indian University could impact a host of Native individuals and their communities. He supplemented his endorsement
of bilingual education by proposing that his university might
organize research to help tribes develop written versions of their
languages, if they did not already have them. "Once a person is
literate in his native language," he argued, "it is much easier for
him to become literate in an unfamiliar tongue."[124] He went farther by suggesting that the university "would attempt to make
the whole nation its campus" by creating a variety of media in
both English and Native languages, broadcasting "new ways for
solving problems, how to develop tribal enterprises, what other
Indians are doing, and a multitude of other" possibilities.[125] Here
again, Forbes focused on the development of practical skills by
drawing on both Native and non-Native knowledge bases. Students would earn university degrees and credentials while actively
engaging Native communities and their particular needs. Not only
that; they would host conferences and lectures to bring together
tribal officials and organizers from across the country.[126] In this
way, Forbes envisioned his university as a vital pantribal hub and
rhetorical platform in what he hoped would be a growing movement of Native intellectual activism.

A New Spirit of Leadership

As he formalized his proposal for an American Indian University in 1961, Forbes viewed the relationship between Native people, the mainstream education system, and positions of leadership and power in American society much as Cloud had nearly five decades earlier. Forbes observed that the American education system did not properly serve Native students, especially in the realm of higher education. This problem, he argued, stemmed largely from an assimilationist mindset that continued to dominate American schooling—including and especially within the Bureau of Indian Affairs.[127] While the Workshop on American Indian Affairs in Boulder had become a testament to the growing number of Native students entering college and seeking meaningful impacts, Forbes was as keen as the workshop directors in noting that those students still faced serious identity challenges in American schools, contributing to lagging rates of graduation and professional success.[128] In Forbes's mind, a national center of higher education designed by and for Native people could help address that problem. At the same time, such a center would encourage its students and educators alike to approach a second and broader issue—the desire for a growing body of highly adaptable Native leaders to act on behalf of their local communities and defend the rights and sovereignty of Native American people in general.[129]

In his assessment of the challenges facing Native people in modern America, as well as in his efforts to approach those challenges through a particular type of education and leadership training, Forbes resurrected and reapplied Cloud's vision to "train into efficient leadership . . . young Indians from every tribe."[130] It is difficult to know whether he modeled his American Indian University proposal directly on Cloud's vision for the American Indian Institute, but the possibility certainly exists. Forbes was a voracious researcher on numerous aspects of Indigenous history, and among the thousands of pages of documents in his research materials are photocopies of Cloud's writings in the *Quarterly Journal of the Society of American Indians*, the same publication in which Cloud printed his proposal for the American Indian Institute.[131]

Regardless of whether Forbes consciously imitated the American Indian Institute in 1960 and 1961, it is clear that he was accessing and promoting a form of Native intellectual activism that Henry Roe Cloud had helped to develop and disseminate.

Forbes's envisioned American Indian University, like the American Indian Institute, would prize a balanced ideal of leadership—built on a foundation of Native identity and a knowledge of Indigenous history and culture, but also highly adaptable to and conversant in the aspects of mainstream American education, economics, and politics that impacted contemporary Native communities. In delineating the disciplines he considered vital, Forbes was of an open mind in the same way that Cloud had been. Students at the American Indian Institute in 1917 encountered everything from geometry to American history to agricultural education, as Cloud strove for an eclectic sense of leadership that was simultaneously rooted in the practical and the academic.[132] In the same vein, Forbes sought to address the renewed pressures on Native identity in his own time by "train[ing] Indian students for professional work of all kinds," but with an explicit desire to cultivate "a dynamic synthesis" of multiple ways of thinking and multiple bodies of knowledge.[133] "The American Indian University," he wrote, "should above all, be an Indian-controlled institution . . . an expression of the Indian community."[134]

Linking Eras of Native Intellectual Activism

A key purpose of this history is to link eras and threads of Native intellectual activism that have previously been studied separately. A more nuanced understanding of the era of federal termination for Native Americans is a crucial part of that effort. The pendulum metaphor, though intended to offer an explanation of how federal Indian policy has developed, has also encouraged an oversimplified understanding of the presence of Native activism. The metaphor suggests that in one era, Native activism grew through the work of individuals like Henry Roe Cloud and groups like the Society of American Indians, and through federal support in John Collier's Indian New Deal. In the next era, the narrative holds, a powerful swing of the pendulum toward termination wiped away those gains and the momentum of Native activism.

By focusing on the persistence of a line of Native intellectual activism represented by Henry Roe Cloud, the history uncovered here offers a different interpretation of the termination era. Certainly, this era saw direct threats to the tribal status of Native people, and renewed pressures for rapid cultural assimilation. But it also witnessed the persistence of the fundamental principles of Henry Roe Cloud's intellectual activism, and the bridging of one generation of Native leaders to another by key individuals like Elizabeth Bender Cloud and D'Arcy McNickle. Jack Forbes represented one of the new generation. He adapted Cloud's principles and methods to the contemporary context of the termination era, while also working in ways that spoke to the potential opportunities of the 1960s and beyond. In other words, the tradition of Native intellectual activism that Henry Roe Cloud, Elizabeth Bender Cloud, and others of the early twentieth century built and developed was not wiped away in one generation but was carried through a challenging period, adapted to changing circumstances, and reinvigorated by a new generation of activists.

While he operated in line with Henry Roe Cloud's older intellectual tradition, Jack Forbes also stood at the edge of a powerful movement that had not yet fully developed. Much changed in the days between Forbes's outline of his proposal to a colleague in the spring of 1961 and when he distributed its more formalized version to dozens of government officials and interested Native activists that fall. Sol Tax and D'Arcy McNickle had organized the American Indian Chicago Conference that summer, bringing together hundreds of Native attendees from dozens of tribes throughout the country. Soon after came the official formation of the National Indian Youth Council, supporting research into new tribal educational programs and fighting for the protection of a wide range of other Native rights. That same summer, the *Journal of American Indian Education* (*JAIE*) printed its first issues at Arizona State University, helping to link the work of a broad array of

researchers and Native leaders, and becoming an additional rhetorical platform in support of education *by* and *for* Native people.

The summer of 1961 thus represented an exciting moment in a
burgeoning national discourse on Native American issues. Native
control of and access to institutions of higher education became a
vital piece of that conversation. Forbes acted as a key voice in this
growing national conversation, corresponding with Tax, McNickle,
the leaders of NIYC, and tribal officials, while also having pieces of
his work published in the *JAIE* and other emerging Native-driven
publications. His vision of an American Indian University took
years of persistent work to develop, but its basic sentiment—a
pantribal hub of education and leadership training created *by* and
for Native people—stood as a central point of emphasis for many
Native educators and their advocates throughout the 1960s. As
they shared information, supported and published each other's
research, and in general linked together an emerging national discourse, they also began formalizing the fundamental arguments
for the creation of tribal colleges and universities as tangible new
sites of Native intellectual activism.

FIG. 1. Henry Roe Cloud poses near the site of the American Indian Institute, about 1916. Courtesy Columbia University Libraries.

FIG. 2. The inaugural class of the American Indian Institute poses
with visiting photographer Gustavus Lindquist, about 1916.
Courtesy Columbia University Libraries.

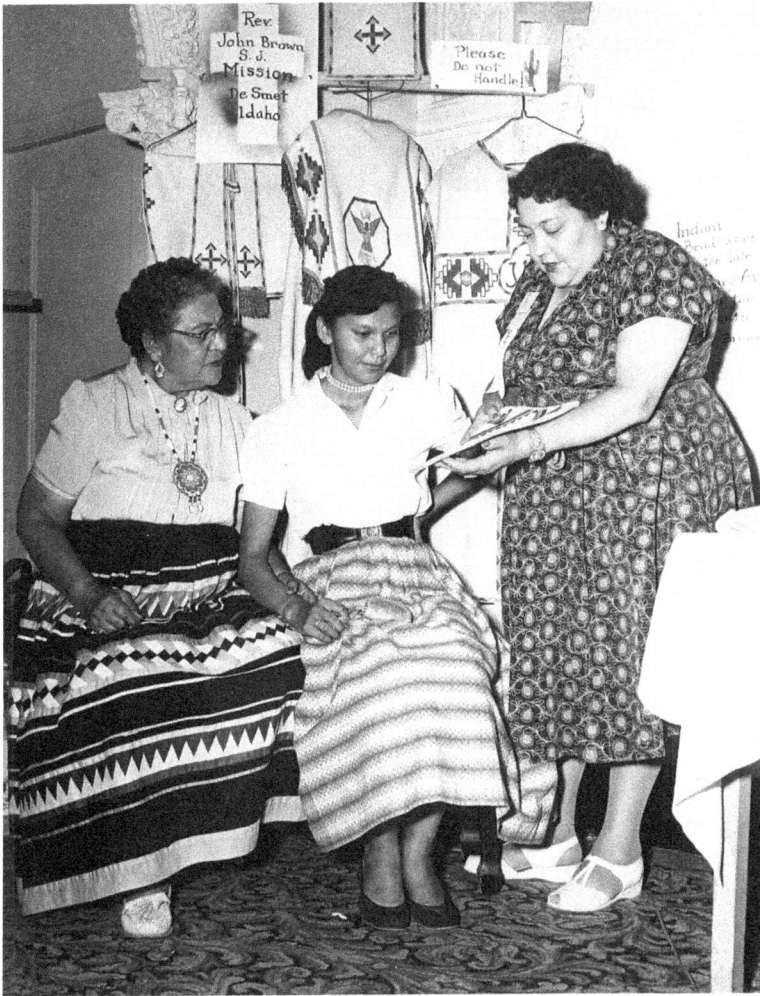

FIG. 3. Elizabeth Bender Cloud (*left*) views bead work, date unknown.
National Museum of the American Indian, Smithsonian Institution
(NMAI-010_pht_095_002).

FIG. 4. D'Arcy McNickle takes notes during the American Indian Chicago Conference, 1961. National Museum of the American Indian, Smithsonian Institution (NMAI-010_pht_070_002).

FIG. 5. Jack Forbes poses in a classroom, date unknown. Special Collections, University of California, Davis (AR-198 box 14, folder 8).

FIG. 6. Students of the Workshop on American Indian Affairs study a reading, with D'Arcy McNickle just visible at center left, date unknown. National Museum of the American Indian, Smithsonian Institution (NMAI-010_pht_131_002).

THREE

Indian-Controlled and Indian-Centered

*Driving Home the Argument for Native
Control in Higher Education*

In June of 1961, San Carlos Apache chairman Clarence Wesley provided the opening article of the inaugural edition of the *Journal of American Indian Education* (*JAIE*). His message was straightforward but powerful: "I realize the fact that there are people who talk about integration, assimilation, acculturation, first class citizenship, etc. But you know the American Indians have something different that was bestowed upon them by the grace of God, such as our songs, tribal dances, arts and crafts, our religion, games and stories. Some of these are fast disappearing and my question is: are we going to continue to lose these precious gifts through this process of education or becoming white men? Or should we continue to identify ourselves as Indians, which to me is no disgrace."[1] The brief passage sums up much of what mattered most to Wesley, the characteristics that placed him in a deeper intellectual conversation and body of activism laid out by the likes of Henry and Elizabeth Cloud, D'Arcy McNickle, and Jack Forbes. Like the others, Wesley sought to engage with and utilize the dominant systems of American education and politics while attempting to reshape those systems in ways he saw as beneficial for Native people with Native identities. He characterized these identities not as relics of the past but as foundations for living in the modern American world. He repudiated straightforward assimilation, maintaining a balanced perspective that viewed Native leadership as an adaptable product of multiple sources of knowledge, concerned with both local action and broader organization. His opening article for the *JAIE* thus built on a line of intellectual thought that had been forming within and between Native individuals and communities for generations. Yet the context of the early 1960s did present opportunities for shared activism that were unlike those of previous eras. During this era, students and educators throughout the country began demanding that American higher education better serve the needs of ethnic and racial minorities.[2] And Chairman Wesley, while a charismatic leader, represented just one of many voices in a growing national discourse on the particular relationship between Native students and the American education system.

In that same month of June 1961, Wesley would be one of over five hundred Native leaders from over ninety tribes to assemble for the American Indian Chicago Conference, organized by University of Chicago anthropologist Sol Tax, along with D'Arcy McNickle and the organizers of the Workshop on American Indian Affairs.[3] McNickle and his staff even chose to hold that summer's workshop in conjunction with the Chicago conference, rather than in Boulder. Out of the Chicago conference came the Declaration of Indian Purpose, a statement presented to President John F. Kennedy in 1962 that asserted Native peoples' right to "retain spiritual and cultural values" as well as the more proactive "right to choose our way of life."[4] The declaration's simple but assertive statements of Native rights held the key intellectual principles of the fight for Native American self-determination. This movement sought not only to halt the momentum of terminationist policies but to empower each tribe to "act as an emerging nation which buys and uses technical assistance from outsiders but retains control over all [its] programs."[5] Unfortunately, little federal action came about as a direct result of the declaration. Still, the presentation of this statement to the Kennedy administration and the Department of the Interior was an early sign of intent from a swelling body of Native intellectual activists who would become increasingly articulate, vocal, and creative in their action throughout the decade.

For the workshop's students in Chicago that summer, the spark of energy they felt was actually born out of an intense frustration with the older generation of tribal leaders that they had always looked up to. From the outset, Bob Thomas and D'Arcy McNickle perceived a tone in the structure and the direction of the conference's discussions that threatened a total breakdown of collaboration, and it disheartened many of the workshop's students.[6] They witnessed among the older reservation leaders a stance of "politicians," who sought to protect channels of communication and resources they could control without the input of other "radical" groups such as nonrecognized tribes and nonreservation urban activists. Moreover, the young attendees detected a tired refrain of deference to the federal government that, in the words of Clyde Warrior (Ponca), was "sickening."[7] In this context, the conference could never produce a perfectly unified vision that would match the ambitious goal of articulating "what Indians want for their future."[8]

Still, the frustrations of the conference were also complemented by an equally intense feeling of cohesion and resolve that grew among the workshop students as they processed and worked through this adversity. They formed a pantribal hub of their own that involved debating and drafting their own statements of purpose between sessions, planning for future organization and action, and in many ways transcending the structured forum of the Chicago conference. Despite the older representatives' wrangling over issues such as the relative importance of federal recognition, urban versus rural issues, and "progressive" versus "traditional" identity politics, the workshop attendees and some of their young allies built on the shared experience as a momentous starting point for further action in both local and national settings. Within weeks they formed the National Indian Youth Council (NIYC). This body built on the organizational network of previous regional councils. Originally founded in Gallup, New Mexico, the group quickly became truly collaborative and pervasive, pulling in many of the brightest young Native intellectuals from across the country, and aggressively pursuing improvements in Native American health care, economic opportunities, and especially education.[9]

The inaugural issue of the *Journal of American Indian Education*, the Chicago conference, and the founding of the National

Indian Youth Council marked the summer of 1961 as a watershed moment for a burgeoning national discourse on issues impacting Native people. Though much scholarship has been devoted to the public profile of Native activism in the form of "Red Power"—which would not reach its full heights until the formation of the militant American Indian Movement (AIM) in the late 1960s and early 1970s—the developments of the summer of 1961 indicate that an intellectual activist infrastructure was indeed developing much earlier.[10] Chairman Wesley's ponderings on Native identity in the inaugural issue of the *JAIE* represented just a small but insightful whisper in a conversation that would explode into life in the ensuing years. The vital balance espoused by the likes of the Clouds, McNickle, and Wesley—seeking to protect expressions of Indigenous identity while promoting an adaptable form of Native leadership—would not only influence the eclectic new generation of scholars and activists such as the National Indian Youth Council but also directly inform the mission statements and educational goals of the first tribal colleges and universities (TCUs) in the 1960s and 1970s. These schools would stand as some of the earliest tangible expressions of Native American self-determination, for while new federal economic support helped jump-start these institutions, they were Native-driven projects in philosophy and practice.[11]

Tribal colleges and universities also represented a vital extension of a type of Native intellectual activism that simultaneously endorsed national organization and local action. As historian Donald Fixico has suggested in the context of urban Native experiences, it would be a mistake to assume that the sense of pan-Indianism rising in postwar America would necessitate the erosion of particular tribal identities. Indeed, unifying behind an Indigenous activist mission through workshops or activist organizations could also bring an energizing opportunity to reaffirm "tribal identities with pride during the drastic changes" of the era.[12]

This concept had informed Henry Roe Cloud in his work at the American Indian Institute, where he had hoped to foster Native leadership on a national scale but also urged his students to better understand the needs and goals of their local, tribal communities.[13] It had been a hallmark of the work done by Elizabeth Bender Cloud and D'Arcy McNickle with the National Congress of American Indians and American Indian Development (AID) in the 1950s, and would now become a vital characteristic of the National Indian Youth Council and the tribal college movement.[14] As opportunities within the mass of federal bureaucracy occasionally opened up, advocates of TCUs organized quickly to share organizational strategies and lobby for support through accreditation and legislation. All the while, though, they oriented their curricular and community-based goals from a tribal perspective. As the argument for tribally controlled higher education gained strength in the 1960s and 1970s, the documents produced in this discourse underscored a two-pronged characteristic of the Native voice in this era. In a collective sense this voice was growing stronger and louder through an increasing use of publications and other rhetorical tools, while at the same time commitments to particular tribal projects and particular tribal visions of the educational landscape remained equally significant.

Developing a Critique of the Status Quo

Despite the exciting signs of a growing conversation on American ethnic and racial issues in the early 1960s, tangible change in terms of how these issues were addressed would require years of persistent work. For Native people who sought to protect their unique tribal status and to assert their identity in the face of termination, this persistence was especially important. Native-driven programs could not develop without a powerful and articulate critique of a status quo that was built on generations of settler colonialism.

In the development of their critique, Native and non-Native advocates of reform held education as a focal point for potential change. Tribal leaders, United States politicians, and even Bureau of Indian Affairs (BIA) workers consistently drew connecting lines between the quality of education and the overall health of Native people and their communities.[15] The reasons for this focus on education are numerous but not difficult to understand. Like most Americans, after all, Native people had carefully built their educational traditions through generations of practice. One Navajo educator wrote that "according to our forefathers, if we lose our own education, we would lose our true image. We cannot achieve our full potential unless we use our own . . . right to education which makes us unique people."[16] This reliance on tradition did not prevent efforts at reform. As early as the 1950s, Navajos called explicitly for greater access to American higher education and leadership training as a means to "supplant" non-Native professionals as lawyers, land managers, doctors, and nurses within their community, and as a way to improve economic conditions on the reservation.[17]

While debates about how to maintain appropriate forms of education and leadership training had always occurred in Indigenous communities facing settler colonialism, the discourse available for Native people from the summer of 1961 onward was unique—in its scale as well as its particular message. In their correspondence and numerous publications, outspoken Native activists and their advocates in the 1960s began to focus on schooling for Native Americans as a nationwide issue with systemic problems, relying on a disparate collection of tribal experiences and case studies but connecting them in ways that displayed a need for widespread reform. Throughout the decade, research spurred by these activists demonstrated a broken relationship between Native people and American schools, and paved the way for increasing the level of Native control over the broad goals and everyday methods of schools and other attendant institutions.

As indicated above, the *Journal of American Indian Education* became a key platform for laying out these arguments. From its first pages, the *JAIE* signaled the presence of vibrant voices in a debate over the problems, needs, and future directions of education for Native people. Clarence Wesley set the stage by explaining the conditions of his San Carlos Apache community before broadening his perspective to a national framework. "Too few of our Apache children are finishing high school. Too few of those who do . . . are going on to college or into some other professional training. When they do . . . too many fail to make the grade there."[18] In his straightforward writing, Wesley spoke for his community but soon went on to invoke the situation of Native people around the country, pointing out troubling trends that impacted a wide range of students as well as their larger social and economic networks. In public schools, he concluded, there was simply "no close relationship between the Indian parent and the school beyond that of a passive" one.[19]

Wesley's assessments did not single out one specific element of Native American schooling but viewed the entire system as an interconnected whole. As Henry Roe Cloud had done decades earlier in his essay "Education of the American Indian," Wesley deftly utilized the opening piece in the *JAIE* as a call to action on a national scale—painting a picture of the contemporary state of schooling for Native students, addressing a broad audience of interested and reform-minded observers, and rhetorically asking *where can we go from here?* In answering this question, identification and clarification of the problems were the first steps. While the *JAIE* provided an essential platform for broadcasting the conversation, practical work had to be carried out to provide concrete, evidence-based illustrations of the problems in American Indian education.

Though still in its infancy, the National Indian Youth Council served as a catalyst for pursuing that end by conducting original research projects, collecting and disseminating information on ongoing projects throughout the country, and publishing the results. As many of the NIYC's founding members built on their experiences in the Workshop on American Indian Affairs, they ambitiously sought to embody and "promote fellowship among Indian youth of different tribes . . . [and to] promote creative leadership among [Native] youth."[20] The workshop influences of leaders like D'Arcy McNickle were clear, as the founders of NIYC utilized their training in the mainstream systems of American higher education but also pledged to respect "traditional ways of living" and "the leadership of Indian elders."[21] Additionally, like Jack Forbes, they readily called out the terminationist policies of the BIA and the federal government overall as misguided, or, worse, as intentionally destructive to Native cultural practices.[22]

What might have been less clear even to the NIYC founders is how the type of leadership they sought to embody called to mind a vision laid out by previous Native intellectual activists in the early twentieth century. Much like the Clouds, they hoped to influence American Indian policy and Native community well-being on a grand scale, by drawing together and inspiring a diverse collection of young Native intellectual activists who believed that "the highest principles of citizenship" and the "strength of the American Indian heritage" were not mutually exclusive.[23] In fact, they argued, "the development of greater leadership [among] Indian youth" in modern America *depended on* "a sense of security" in Native identity and the "values and beliefs of [Native] ancestors."[24] The language of this mission statement showed not only the core principles of McNickle's influence but in turn a remarkable continuity with the Clouds' approach to education and leadership training in the early twentieth century at the American Indian Institute and at Haskell. Consciously or not, this deeper thread of Native intellectual activism would guide NIYC's members as they sought meaningful change in a wide range of issues—from economic development to the protection of citizenship rights like voting to the assertion of treaty-based rights as well.[25] Moreover, it would remain especially relevant in their frequent efforts to bring about a fundamental change in the relationship between Native students and American institutions of education.[26]

Part of the NIYC's strength was its willingness to collaborate openly. In its early years, the NIYC distributed many newsletters but also produced two larger publications to carry its voice to thousands of readers.[27] The journal *Aborigine* laid out the NIYC's organizational structure, mission statement, and much of the seminal correspondence of its founding members, while by 1963 *Americans before Columbus* (*ABC*) began publishing research-based articles.[28] These journals and correspondence reveal that the NIYC was, like Clarence Wesley, interested in viewing the educational landscape in a broad sense, fraught with deeply ingrained issues

Indian-Controlled and Indian-Centered

that stemmed from settler colonialism, were perpetuated in a host of modern institutions, and infected all levels from early childhood to higher education and job training.

This ambitious outlook toward systemic change produced a two-pronged effect that addressed the topic of Native intellectual leadership in both the short term and the long term. For example, the NIYC founders continued to dedicate themselves to building on the momentum of their own activist spirit by reaching out to fellow college-aged Native students—imploring them not only to "support tribal leadership" and "develop common goals" but also to "conduct [their] own research," and "build alternate solutions."[29] These words were more than empty rhetoric. The NIYC soon brought in hundreds of members and eventually became a sponsor of the United Scholarship Service, an organization that by 1964 dispersed over $100,000 in aid and counseling services to Native American and Hispanic college and secondary students.[30]

During the early 1960s the Workshop on American Indian Affairs also remained a crucial influence that connected the young members of the NIYC to a mature Native intellectual activism that had developed over the course of several decades. Under D'Arcy McNickle and AID, the workshop sharpened its focus on the relationship between young Native leaders, their tribal communities, and the larger American society in a way that harmonized with a long-developing intellectual movement. The workshop's recruiting materials utilized language that called to mind not only the voice of McNickle but that of Henry Roe Cloud before him—repeatedly stressing the specific concept of "adaptation" as opposed to assimilation, in an effort "to develop skills for using the social, political, legal and other resources" of American society, but in ways that maintained "an appreciation of [Native] culture" and "the values and aspirations of the Indian people."[31] In these ways, McNickle, the workshop instructors, and the students themselves could acknowledge the power of modern American institutions in education and government while openly working to repurpose those structures in ways that aided rather than attacked their tribal communities and unique missions.

In particular, the NIYC's leaders utilized their existing positions within the higher education system to organize meaningful research and community action projects that might ameliorate the disconnect between American schooling and Native students at all levels, starting as early as elementary school.[32] One of the most prominent figures in these efforts was Robert V. Dumont Jr. (Assiniboine), who served as one of the NIYC's early vice presidents and sat on the selection committee for the United Scholarship Service.[33] Just as important were his efforts to study schooling for Native American youth and to develop programs designed to improve the relationship between reservation communities and the administrators and teachers in their schools. Like Cloud, Dumont utilized his Ivy League training and influence to lead Native activist efforts on a national scale while also attempting to directly impact local Native communities.

By 1963 and 1964, Robert Dumont's research became a key part of the NIYC's efforts to pinpoint problems in the education system and highlight potential areas for dramatic, positive change. The journal *ABC* became instrumental for collecting studies by NIYC members as well as non-Native social scientists. Like the *JAIE*, *ABC*'s publication of these research efforts helped piece together an argument that illustrated the failures of the status quo in schooling for Native American students. These studies and the associated commentary by *ABC*'s writers described conditions for Native schoolchildren as inadequate for fostering success both in terms of qualitative observations of students' confidence and in measurable standards of achievement. For example, an Emory University study of Oglala Sioux youth in South Dakota schools detected "an appalling and frightening separation and lack of communication between teachers and students, school and community, administrators and teachers, and parents and the school."[34] Surveyors went farther by concluding that "teachers had only a superficial knowledge that their students were from a culture radically different from theirs."[35] In a separate study, Dumont arrived at similar conclusions. He argued that within the average reservation community, "education is synonymous with *school*," meaning a

Indian-Controlled and Indian-Centered

strong aversion by students because "school" connoted a rigid, foreign institution "totally unrelated to what happens in the home or the community where [they] grow up."[36]

Throughout the country, these kinds of observations struck a chord with many who studied schooling for Native American students. Nelson Lose, governor of the Gila River Pima-Maricopa Tribes in 1962, noticed a tension resulting from the assimilationist stance that seemed to permeate the messages from schools' authority figures, which "left the Indian [student] with a feeling that all the old is bad. [However,] it has also left him unconvinced that the new is good; therefore, he operates without [any] strong value system."[37] Through the *Journal of American Indian Education*, the publications of the NIYC, and other Native-produced sources, these types of comments displayed a widespread belief that the BIA and public schools had largely failed to rid themselves of assimilationist approaches that left Native students feeling alienated and reservation communities powerless. They showed the belief that Native students everywhere experienced a lack of adequate support as they attempted to achieve success according to the norms of the American education system. And, just as important, they revealed the perception that those schools hindered the development of success on tribal terms as well.

That these qualitative observations could be shared at all is important, especially because of their widespread expression throughout a nationwide discourse. But they also meant that Native American students struggled in measurable ways—ways that translated to their eventual social and economic prospects and, in turn, to the everyday conditions of their communities. Research of New Mexico public schools conducted in the early 1960s and published in the *JAIE* made this struggle exceptionally clear. Among eleventh and twelfth graders tested, Native American students were approximately five grade levels behind average in reading.[38] These numbers undoubtedly spoke to a language divide that could not be completely blamed on public schools or their teachers. Yet, in an environment with a high percentage of Native students, the schools showed a general lack of innovation in meeting the problems experienced by these students. Eighty percent of the teachers had no professional training in the teaching of reading skills, and this dearth of appropriate attention in the eyes of Native students and their families became another sign of "public schools fail[ing] to function equally well for all students."[39]

The Bureau of Indian Affairs, too, struggled with discouraging results in its schools. For many years, BIA schools had stood as powerful symbols of cultural assimilation and the attempted erasure of tribal identities. This status was due in large part to the legacy of the off-reservation boarding schools, which bore characteristics of their military influence well into the twentieth century—in their uniforms, their strict daily schedules, their limits on family visits, and their frequent reliance on the menial labor of students.[40] While the BIA in the 1960s attempted to distance itself from the culturally hegemonic stance of previous eras, officials such as Commissioner Philleo Nash admitted that progress was slow.[41] Many Native leaders who focused on educational improvement continued to see the BIA as inefficient and at times "hostile."[42]

The disconnect between Native students, communities, and their schools—along with the poor educational achievement that followed—meant high dropout rates throughout Indian country. Discouraging graduation and retention rates represented one of the most frequently expressed problems in the discourse of Native American education throughout the 1960s. Anthropologist Paul Kutsche studied Cherokee high schools and concluded that "the Cherokee feel [the] system does not now serve them in important ways, [as] the dropout data eloquently testify."[43] In Oglala schools of South Dakota, researchers found that because of a vast gulf between the ostensible authority represented by school officials and the actual social and cultural influences that students respected, "peer groups thrived with a fearful and frightening power strong enough to push students out of school."[44]

As the Boulder Workshop organizers and tribal officials around the country knew all too well, even when students did move on to college, success was elusive there as well. At the University of New Mexico in the early 1960s, education professors noted that approximately 75 percent of all Native American students dropped out before graduating.[45] As Clarence Wesley of the San Carlos Apache pointed out, the failure rate at the University of Arizona was very similar.[46] Dr. Robert "Bob" Roessel Jr., who worked for years toward greater control by Navajos over their education systems, estimated that Navajo dropout rates in higher education remained above 80 percent into the final years of the 1960s.[47] Again, the host of Native-driven publishing platforms growing in the 1960s became essential for demonstrating and affirming that these experiences were common among numerous tribes from all across the country, whose students encountered an array of mainstream American institutions of higher education. In this context, the successes of the workshop's students—many of whom became active in the NIYC—stood out as the exceptions to a discouraging and persistent trend that appeared to stem from systemic failures.

At first glance, the efforts of the NIYC and other intellectual leaders to view the education system with a broad lens seemed only to add to the discouragement felt by Native communities. After all, their research revealed that all levels of schooling throughout Indian country had similar problems—namely, the lack of meaningful connections between schools and their Native students and, thus, feelings of alienation, poor performance, and high dropout rates. And yet even the simple collaborations of research, writing, and debate that surrounded these disheartening conclusions contributed to a kind of positive momentum. Diverse voices became linked through research-centered publications like the *JAIE* and *ABC*—as well as broader editorial works like *Many Smokes* magazine and the publications of Rupert Costo—and offered multiple perspectives but also a growing sense of a shared conversation. While opinions varied on some of the pedagogical issues of the structure and day-to-day operation of schools, many interested Native leaders at the national and community level began to circle around a common set of fundamental questions, concluding that systemic problems required systemic solutions.

First among the topics that Native intellectual activists began prioritizing was the issue of Indigenous identity. In other words, what role should it play in Native students' education, and who should be in charge of establishing and maintaining that role? The nationwide discourse woven by years of research had shown BIA and public schools to be largely incapable of handling these questions in satisfactory ways for Native students and their communities. Thus, even while some BIA officials like Hildegard Thompson began calling for students to let education "strengthen [their] pride in being an American, an Indian, and an individual of worth," Native activists and their allies were largely unconvinced that such rhetoric portended any fundamental transformation in how the BIA operated.[48]

Murray and Rosalie Wax, both of whom had contributed to the Workshop on American Indian Affairs, criticized the bureau for expecting its new educational programs to suddenly win over Native communities after decades of failure and resentment.[49] They noted that officials had seemed too willing to blame Native communities for being "apathetic" to the BIA programs. "Our own observations," they wrote, "are that 'apathy' is a convenient label to apply to people who don't happen to agree with the program that a government official or other reformer happens to be *pushing*. Frankly, when we went to Pine Ridge, we did expect to see apathetic people. Instead we saw people [with a] lust for life."[50]

Robert Dumont encountered a similar positive energy in his summer program for Oglala Sioux school children in 1964. The program had no attendance requirements, but by embracing community rhythms for day-to-day life and celebrations, "the program moved rapidly and quickly became a *regular part of the community*," drawing in students who showed up by seven o'clock in the morning each day, before program leaders had even set up for the day.[51] These moments revealed for Dumont and other activists the potential for positive change that might emerge from a true connection between a Native community and its schools. Nowhere did Dumont mention a "frightening separation" between students and their educational center, as did the Emory University researchers in South Dakota schools just over a year before.[52] In a brief summer program of heightened community participation,

Dumont already saw promise but looked for permanence: "How can we unify the school and the community?"[53]

In answering this question, Native people in the mid to late 1960s began proactively turning back the momentum of a previous era's terminationist policies through their own efforts to take control of their education systems. Fortunately, the federal government's proactive stance toward addressing poverty in the 1960s opened the door for ambitious Native leaders to adapt government platforms and arenas for their own purposes. They seized temporary opportunities for community-driven projects funded by the Johnson administration's "Great Society," hoping to demonstrate the type of initiative that merited more permanent community control. As they did so, Native-driven schools arose as tangible sites of Native American self-determination—years before that term became a common phrase in domestic American politics.[54] These new and transforming institutions, while often local in their immediate impact, also further contributed as sites of research, writing, and publication, adding power to the Native-driven national discourse on education and leadership training.

As they built up and broadcast a national conversation on the problems of American schooling for Native students, Native intellectual activists in the early 1960s quickly and convincingly constructed an image of a broken system in need of fundamental changes. The evidence they accumulated and disseminated powerfully supported their arguments for reworking the entire relationship between Native students and American schools, and for placing greater control over that process in the hands of Native people themselves.

Creating New Sites of Native Control in American Education

As editor of the *Journal of American Indian Education* in 1965, Dr. Bruce Meador furthered the perspectives of Native leaders like Robert Dumont, whose research had underscored the potential cultural breaks for Native students in assimilationist American schools. Meador relied on his own research experience with students in bilingual and bicultural settings, and flatly rejected a false choice between "the white man's world" and "the Indian world."[55] He sought to refocus the entire discussion of Native American schooling on a student-centered goal, achieving students' complete potential as members of the overall community. "I would suggest," wrote Meador, "that the more fundamental question is whether or not we should educate the Indian [student] to become a self-actualized person. Should he be taught to appreciate his native language, the language of his father and mother? The customs of his parents? I believe the answer is clearly yes. It seems reasonable to assume that the child who does not view his heritage with confidence has special difficulty in becoming what he is potentially."[56] Meador did not specifically mention higher education in his call for "self-actualization" for Native American students. Still, the principle applied to students of all ages experiencing any type of education. Native activist Sun Bear (Ojibwe) expressed his own similar feeling through *Many Smokes*, a national magazine: "the American Indian stands at the threshold of a new time in history."[57] Young Native people, he asserted, were in the midst of a "Renaissance" and a "rebirth of [their] culture," beginning to take an active interest in learning from their histories and controlling their futures.[58] In the late 1960s and into the 1970s, Native intellectual activists increasingly saw this type of "self-actualization" as possible not simply on an individual basis but in a broader, more collective sense, through greater control of their education. Once that vision became tangible, they turned to higher education in particular as a crucial force for building sustainable routes of access to the highest levels of training, and for maintaining political, economic, and social leadership in their communities.

The late-1960s educational discourse reflected this strong momentum for self-determination in the context of schooling. Jack Forbes continued to act as a prolific advocate in this direction, working toward his own proposal of an American Indian University but also showing support for other projects that promised to bring about "higher learning [that was] *both Indian-controlled and Indian-centered*."[59] His university proposal in many ways mirrored Henry Roe Cloud's vision at the American Indian Institute in the early twentieth century. Forbes's tireless spirit and his willingness to reach out to others also helped him act as a bridge between multiple generations of leaders who worked in a growing body of intellectual activism, sustaining the central goals of Cloud's vision and sharing in its modern reconstitution.

By 1965 Forbes was corresponding directly with Sol Tax, D'Arcy McNickle, and several of the founders of the NIYC regarding organizational strategies and potential sources of funding for Native-driven projects in higher education.[60] The NIYC soon began conducting research in collaboration with the Far West Laboratory for Educational Research and Development, where Forbes worked as a director.[61] During this time Forbes also developed connections with Navajo educational leaders, who eagerly pursued their own opportunities at community control in schooling.[62] The fabric of correspondence that Forbes helped weave clearly illustrates the strength of the movement toward Native-driven education by the late 1960s. It was a shared conversation that balanced the individual contributions of a wide range of capable activists with a willingness to collaborate across organizational and tribal boundaries.

Central to the optimism these activists felt was the prospect of a shift toward government backing, put into motion by President Lyndon Johnson's Office of Economic Opportunity (OEO) in the mid-1960s. As part of Johnson's larger effort to aid poverty-stricken areas across the country, federally funded community action programs allowed many Native communities to develop proposals and run programs designed to boost economic development in a wide variety of ways. Reservation communities throughout the country immediately utilized the opportunities under the OEO to fund programs in education—from expanded preschool to remedial training for high school dropouts to adult basic education and job skills training.[63] A crucial example of this initiative is the quick formation by Navajo councilmen and educators of Demonstration in Navajo Education (DINE), a nonprofit corporation designed to receive and administer funds for OEO educational programs.[64] Though the OEO was far from universally praised among Native reformers, the programs it funded provided a crucial breathing space for efforts at Native control to take root and demonstrate their own merit.[65]

Perhaps the most transformative of these demonstrations began in 1966, when the OEO funded an entirely tribally controlled, bilingual school for young children on the Navajo reservation— the Rough Rock Demonstration School.[66] In her account of the school's history, Teresa McCarty underscores the importance of this experimental program, noting that the Native administration and community control represented at Rough Rock marked "a course of action that forever changed . . . Indigenous schooling in the United States."[67] Although "this little school [sat] in an isolated community, sixteen miles from the nearest pavement, where the average education for the adults [was] one year," the principles that guided it resonated throughout the country.[68] And although Rough Rock served young children, its Native administration and creative curriculum served as examples translatable to any level. Even in its early days, Rough Rock's supporters proudly pointed out that the "school belongs *entirely* to the Navaho people, through the local school board and the Board of Directors. [The] BIA and OEO have turned over all funds to DINE, Inc. with 'no strings attached.' The local Board of Education operates the school and sets all broad policy."[69] After only six months of operation, the tangible demonstration of these principles of Native control had already attracted attention from thousands of visitors from across the country, interested in all types of schooling.[70] Over fifty Native American tribes were represented among the visitors—the clearest sign available that the discourse surrounding the push for Native-driven education had continued to strengthen on a national scale.

The introduction of tribal control at Rough Rock was an important administrative change, but it signified far more than that. The "demonstration" aspect—the "cultural identification" expressed through the school's faculty, staff, and curriculum—is what drew such encouraging attention.[71] Observers noted the uniquely Navajo

Indian-Controlled and Indian-Centered

curriculum, which "[made] Navaho culture a significant and integral part of the school program [whereas] in many [other] schools, students [were] directly or indirectly pressured into giving up their Navaho cultural heritage."[72] Rather than focus solely on standards of individual achievement, the school was "organized around principles of kinship, family, and communalism" in way that allowed for and encouraged Navajo cultural knowledge to be passed between adults and children.[73]

At Rough Rock, suddenly the means to protect and endorse expressions of tribal identity had materialized within the school setting. No longer did there exist a sharp divide between the administrators and the community. This type of educational program had been expressed as a hypothetical and hopeful philosophy—an intellectual proposal for a perceived problem. Now, the administrators, faculty, students, and community members at Rough Rock acted out a tangible process of self-determination in Native American education.

As Robert Roessel—"Bob" to his colleagues—pointed out in a speech soon after Rough Rock's opening, the people within the community did not fail to notice the gravity of this moment. "On the Navaho Reservation . . . there are Bureau of Indian Affairs schools, which in Navaho is called a 'Washington Beolta' (Washington school). Public schools, which are attended by 95 percent of the Navahos, are called 'Belagona Beolta' (the white man's school). Up until eight months ago these and the mission schools were the only kinds which Indians attended."[74] But Rough Rock created the need for an inventive new term in Navajo Nation. There was "now a new type of school which I think has real significance: 'Dineh Beolta' (The People's school, the Navaho school)."[75]

While he applauded the community for largely embracing Rough Rock's experimental methods, Bob Roessel and his wife, Ruth (Navajo), also deserved credit for the leadership they provided. Bob had earned his doctorate in education at Arizona State University, helped found that university's influential Center for Indian Education, and also served on the Presidential Task Force on Indian Affairs.[76] His persistent desire to immerse himself in

Navajo cultural knowledge and practice over many years had also earned him the respect and admiration of many community leaders, some of whom came to consider him "one of the people."[77] Ruth's father was a Navajo medicine man, and as a teacher she worked from a place of deep Navajo knowledge in her efforts to implement education as a holistic experience, involving constant interaction between an individual and his or her surrounding culture.[78] The Roessels' achievements drew national and pantribal attention but never prevented them from exuding enthusiasm for local activism, as they helped build community engagement and support not only for Rough Rock but for subsequent Navajo education projects as well.

Before long, Native people throughout the country began seeing Rough Rock as a positive example of a fundamental change in the relationship between their students and the education system. Moreover, Navajos and several other tribes began targeting higher education as a crucial arena for introducing new sites of Native control. In 1968 the OEO approved a proposal to for the creation of Navajo Community College, and the tribe's approval of an all-Navajo Board of Regents represented an affirmation of Native authority at the first tribally controlled, reservation-based college in the country.[79]

By 1972 half a dozen tribal colleges and universities had been founded throughout the country. The American Indian Higher Education Consortium (AIHEC) formed the following year as a support base and information-sharing group for these new and economically vulnerable institutions. Topics often included practical efforts for developing curricula, reaching out to rising students within the community, and negotiating with government bodies.

As reservation-based sites of higher education and publication, the first wave of TCUs brought an important new layer to the national discourse on Native schooling that had grown throughout the 1960s. Many common themes still connected various tribes, reservations, and institutions across the country, but the schools were also dedicated to the goals of individual tribes and thus added a deeper connection to local communities. Navajo

Indian-Controlled and Indian-Centered

Community College, for example, produced texts that focused heavily on Navajo-specific issues such as tribal history and the tribe's contemporary relationships with state and U.S. government bodies.[80] Through the *Sinte Gleska College News*, faculty members at that South Dakota college discussed ongoing efforts to secure funding and develop curricula, encouraged students to enroll in Lakota-centered cultural programs, and published editorials on the benefits of education in challenging racial stereotypes.[81]

For all the early tribal colleges, progress toward full control came in stages, and collaboration with outside institutions was often necessary. Bismarck Junior College, Mary College, the Universities of South Dakota, Colorado, and Minnesota, and other institutions offered initial extension programs on reservations in North and South Dakota.[82] Navajos, too, worked closely with Arizona State University, Northern Arizona University, and other area schools throughout the planning of Navajo Community College.[83]

These tribes, however, indicated firmly their intentions to exercise their own initiatives. Explicit references to autonomous, Native control echoed through the various goals and mission statements expressed by these colleges, as they attempted to create "real alternative[s]" rather than simply importing an outside form of education to their communities.[84] In Navajo Nation, the term "by Navajos, for Navajos" became a common refrain in the dialogue produced by Navajo Community College president Ned Hatathli and his colleagues.[85] And at every school, mission statements stressed some variation of a similar sentiment concerning cultural identification: "tribal studies are an integral part of all courses offered," for instance.[86] Still, the willing collaboration between tribal educators and outside institutions underscores the central vision of these early TCUS—that tribal identity was encouraged not as a static concept but as a crucial step in a dynamic mission to build and maintain a body of adaptable Native intellectual and professional leaders.

Like Henry Roe Cloud decades before, Native intellectual activists on the national and local levels in this era viewed BIA and public schooling as failing to serve Native students in meaningful ways—in both cultural identification and professional training. Like Cloud's American Indian Institute, TCUs now sought to support young Native leadership by approaching both of these seemingly disparate educational realms in tandem. Their community-centered missions, however, also allowed them to more tightly focus on tribal notions of leadership in ways that Cloud's eclectic scope could accomplish only in a general sense.[87] For Sinte Gleska College, this focus meant offering courses such as "Lakota music and dance, Sioux history and culture, [and] Lakota thought and philosophy."[88] For Navajos, it meant providing courses in Navajo studies to develop a firm rootedness in the language, the clan system, and the original Holy People.[89] From that baseline of tribal identity, TCUs' founders argued, students could have the strength to go on and engage the mainstream American systems of education and economics, better prepared to succeed because of an authoritative sense of self and group identity.[90]

For the leaders of these early schools, succeeding meant much more than being able to freely teach Native history and culture. As outlined above, their communities experienced high dropout rates, difficult economic prospects, and social ills related to poverty and alienation. Tribal leaders thus saw TCUs as pivotal tools in attacking those economic and social ills. Navajos, for example, sought to train medical professionals to improve health care on the reservation through the work of their own people. They sought to do the same in education by training their own teachers, and in natural resource management by training engineers and lawyers as a strategy for reducing their reliance on outsiders for assistance.[91] In these ambitions of an early tribal college can be seen the building blocks of self-determination.

The tribal college model's focus on the immediate community, however, did not require the rejection of a broader, national vision of Native intellectual leadership as envisioned by someone like Henry Roe Cloud in the second decade of the twentieth century or Jack Forbes in the 1960s. While TCUs' mission statements expressed particular tribal goals, these early documents also borrowed from one another and revealed a shared purpose.

Sinte Gleska College, for example, sought to "facilitate individual development and tribal autonomy" by instituting career training alongside "educational resources uniquely appropriate to the Lakota people," who were "rooted to the Reservation and culture [while] concerned about the future" of that community as well.[92] Part of the same mission, however, was a broader hope that Sinte Gleska and TCUs in general would serve as "a model for Indian-controlled education."[93] At Turtle Mountain and Standing Rock Community Colleges, mission statements similarly promoted unique tribal perspectives and community-centered economic goals alongside a broader sense of "Indian control" and "the cultural and social heritage of the Indian people."[94] In this way, the espoused missions of the early tribal colleges and universities displayed a vision of an adaptable form of Native intellectual leadership that tethered the concerns of Native American people in a local and national context.

Ultimately, the willingness of TCUs to collaborate in forming AIHEC, to share organizational and pedagogical ideas, and to collectively strive for greater protective legislation showed the belief that Native intellectual leadership on a national scale could be developed through distinct, community-oriented sites. Tribal colleges and universities could work toward the same broad vision as Cloud's American Indian Institute or an American Indian University envisioned by Forbes, while also addressing particular tribal goals and community needs. And even as reservation communities embraced tribal colleges, Cloud's and Forbes's visions of off-reservation centers of Native-driven higher education would endure as well.

Tribal Colleges and Universities as Demonstrations of Self-Determination

The linkage between education that supported Native or tribal identity and the capability to succeed in diverse and adaptable ways was the culmination of an argument that took years to outline, articulate, and demonstrate. The rapid expansion of a discourse on Native American education from 1961 onward encouraged

Native people and their allies in education to share their ideas and experiences.

Their first step was assessing the state of education for Native students in America. The broad problems in the relationship between Native students, their communities, and their schools were not necessarily new. In many ways, these problems stretched back generations, to a time when Euro-American schooling for Native people served as a tool for cultural assimilation. The legacies of this particular aspect of settler colonialism should not be underestimated. Native responses to these obstacles were not new, either. But the ability and willingness of Native intellectual activists to research and discuss these problems—and to share in a growing discourse with interested people across the country—was rapidly growing by the summer of 1961 and beyond. Growth in the number and reach of Native publications and organizations created a conversation that highlighted Native American students' struggles with problems in schooling that deeply harmed the overall well-being of their communities. Widespread perceptions of cultural separations between teachers, administrators, students, and parents led to low achievement levels and high dropout rates.

Individual educators and government agents with the Bureau of Indian Affairs sought to address these issues by urging students to take pride in their history and heritage. But the BIA could not simply overturn its legacy in the eyes of many Native leaders, and tribal control over the administration and curricular vision of schooling became the most promising path toward truly meaningful change. This change, they asserted, would bolster a student's sense of self by privileging culturally relevant expressions of identity as the foundational source of authority for a student's growth in any field. In the effort to overturn a legacy of forced assimilation, this philosophy became a useful tool for Native people to craft and promote their own paths to leadership.

Increasingly, Native leaders and their allies tapped into a growing movement for Native American self-determination—the ability of a tribe to collaborate with outside governments for assistance but to retain essential authority over its own programs. Native-driven institutions of education became key hubs for expressing in tangible ways the goals of self-determination. Tribal colleges and universities were especially important because of their prominence within their communities and their dedication to immediately addressing tribal issues such as access to professional leadership and to further higher education. These institutions also became important rhetorical platforms in their own right, contributing to the ongoing discourse on Native American education by producing their own texts.

This movement grew not simply as an effort to preserve a static notion of culture and history for its own sake. Rather, like Henry Roe Cloud, the new generation of Native intellectual activists behind this movement understood the encouragement and protection of tribal identities as an essential step in building adaptable leadership and, in turn, ameliorating the social, economic, and educational problems of modern Indigenous communities. The simple but profound argument for Native-driven education was summed up in the mission statements of the early TCUs, as they repeatedly endorsed a balanced concept of Native leadership that was culturally rooted in tribal knowledge and values while capable of applying academic tools to "concrete problems."[95]

This argument took years to develop, and the final expression of it through Native-driven schools could not provide a definitive sense of its absolute vindication. Indeed, poverty and unemployment have persisted beyond the initial era of TCUs and into the twenty-first century.[96] But by the final years of the 1970s, several TCUs had already become recognized candidates for full accreditation from the North Central Association of Secondary Schools and Colleges (NCA).[97] The NCA's award of full accreditation to Navajo Community College in 1976 came as a form of vindication for all TCUs, which shared the common goal of improving the lives of their community members. The NCA praised Navajo Community College for its "outreach and continuing education programs which provide much-needed community services" to Navajos.[98]

Endorsement from and collaboration with the broader American education system became an important sign of permanence and validation for the early TCUs, but enthusiasm among the student body showed even before accreditation. At Sinte Gleska, Oglala Lakota, and Turtle Mountain Community Colleges, enrollment increased or remained steady throughout the first several years after founding.[99] At Navajo Community College, enrollment increased while retention approached 90 percent—a symbolic reversal of the near-90 percent dropout rate that Bob Roessel had estimated for Navajos at off-reservation colleges.[100]

As the initial wave of TCUs worked toward strengthening their programs and securing accreditation, the 1978 Tribally Controlled Community Colleges Assistance Act provided a permanent source of funding for existing schools and for a second wave of new institutions that spread the movement onward.[101]

As mentioned above, many reservations across America continued to struggle with persistent poverty and high unemployment, and those with TCUs did not necessarily escape these problems. Over the years, however, the long-term dedication of the tribes responsible for supporting these institutions has periodically been rewarded by encouraging feedback. A survey of 1980s graduates of Turtle Mountain Community College showed an unemployment rate of just 13 percent, compared with 55 percent on the reservation as a whole.[102] Several other TCUs reported employment rates for graduates in a similar range.[103] Researchers also uncovered limited but encouraging results as students transitioned from TCUs to other segments of American higher education. In one case study from the early 1990s, Native students who attended Salish Kootenai College before transferring to the University of Montana fared markedly better in grade point average and rate of graduation than those who went straight from high school to the university.[104]

Researchers, educators, business leaders, and students themselves continue to find encouraging signs in the work of tribal colleges and universities in the twenty-first century.[105] Moreover, recurring signs of validation such as the Higher Learning Commission's approval of Diné College's transition to a four-year institu-

Indian-Controlled and Indian-Centered

tion with multiple bachelor's degree programs continue to bolster the original vision of these schools.

While these anecdotal results do not show TCUs as a panacea for all reservation communities, that goal was never the heart of the argument for these schools. Rather, Native intellectual activists over the course of many decades argued simply but crucially for the worthiness of their own worldview, their own intellectual development, and their own paths to leadership. The most important element of the argument was also the most fundamental, summed up in a simple but powerful phrase or two: "by and for Indians," as Henry Roe Cloud had printed on the front page of his school newspaper, or "Indian-controlled and Indian-centered," as Jack Forbes put it. In the trying early days of the tribal college era, this old but still relevant sentiment was yet again being redeployed, this time in the language of self-determination: "As a young Navajo has expressed it, 'How can we change without destroying ourselves?' While self-determination does not answer this question, it allows Native Americans the freedom to wrestle with it."[106]

FOUR

An Exercise in Tribal Sovereignty

The Early Years of the Tribal-College Era

On a summer Saturday in 1968, at Fort Defiance, Arizona, Navajo Nation commemorated the centennial of the "Treaty of Peace between the U.S. Government and the Navajo Tribe."[1] The June 1 Treaty Day Festival included a parade with dozens of entrants, "Indian dance groups . . . marching bands and a drill team," and "two little old ladies, wizened but spry and in good humor, [who] carried away first prize in the Old-Timers category."[2] What made these "little old ladies" such an important part of the Treaty Day celebration? They were twin sisters, over one hundred years old, whose lives directly coincided with a key era in Navajo history. Born in the time of the "Long Walk to exile at Fort Sumner," New Mexico, in 1864, their lives traced the "century of progress" following the Treaty of 1868.[3] Behind them lay an ambivalent century—a modern era of peace but also one of hardship brought by a legacy of settler colonial conquest and the restrictions of reservation life for Native people in the United States. Ahead lay still more uncertainty. As tribal chairman Raymond Nakai noted, progress had been "quite good," but Navajos "were still lagging behind their neighbors economically."[4] Still, hope resonated in his voice as he pledged that the tribe would work tirelessly to move from a century of progress toward the "next century—the century of achievement."[5]

Raymond Nakai was motivated by the prospect of increased tribal control in the 1960s, and from the beginning of his tenure as chairman he had been instrumental as an outspoken proponent of placing schools at the center of that vision for greater self-determination. As he urged Navajos to enter a new and more prosperous era, events already in motion seemed to represent an affirmative answer to his call. Less than two months after the Treaty Day celebration, the tribal council approved an all-Navajo board of regents for the newly formed Navajo Community College (NCC), the first tribally controlled college on reservation land in the United States.[6] Classes would not commence for another six months, and yet the early dedication to Navajo control signaled the school's stance as community-driven and community-focused from its inception. Soon, NCC would become a centerpiece for the types of celebrations illustrated above. At other reservations across the country as well, tribal colleges and universities (TCUs) would rise as the newest hubs of a Native-driven activist effort toward fundamental change in the relationship between Indigenous students and American higher education.

Establishing Footholds in the American Higher Education Landscape

Given the increasing weight of reservation-based institutions in this new development, the focus will shift slightly in this chapter. The central theme of the story remains the same. From Henry Roe Cloud onward, the activists in this history were focused on "getting out a Native and national leadership" through the construction of myriad creative hubs of Native intellectual activism for greater control of and access to higher education and training.[7] Now, however, individual tribes and communities come into greater focus. Focusing narrowly on this era—roughly 1968 to 1978—reveals in great detail the moment when reservation communities first seized the opportunity to reinvigorate in tangible ways a Native intellectual activism that had been building for years. Through this perspective, the topics that mattered most to the founders of these schools become more visible. As financial and academic viability hung in the balance for these fledgling institutions, what principles did their founders consider most important, and what fundamental missions did they pursue most aggressively?

In crafting their responses to these questions, those supporting tribal colleges and universities linked the language and phi-

An Exercise in Tribal Sovereignty

losophy of Native American self-determination to their efforts in higher education. Comanche scholar LaDonna Harris and others have written of self-determination as a movement that focuses on bringing about "effective sovereignty [and] self-sufficiency" for Native communities, often by "partnering with their neighbors, the nation, and the world for mutual advancement."[8] This contemporary understanding of self-determination matches well the practical efforts of tribal colleges and universities, which from the beginning sought to endorse tribal identity and protect Native sovereignty while also collaborating with mainstream American institutions for educational support and financial security.[9] Indeed, TCUs can be considered one of the longest-lasting tangible demonstrations of this approach to Native American self-determination.[10]

The federal government under Lyndon Johnson's administration in some ways helped give this concept traction through the new Office of Economic Opportunity (OEO), which assisted community-led projects such as Rough Rock Demonstration School at the elementary level and NCC in higher education.[11] Johnson's domestic effort to build a "Great Society" sought to aid the country's poor, and opened these and other new avenues for Native people to bring resources into their communities and empower their own leaders. At the onset of the 1970s, Richard Nixon would also express the federal government's support of Native American self-determination.[12]

And yet, just as in the preceding decades, the fight for greater Native empowerment in the 1960s and 1970s would often require a deft sense of when and how to adapt to and collaborate with mainstream power structures in America. In their efforts to build and institutionalize paths to leadership through higher education, TCUs' founders and advocates employed Native intellectual strategies and discourses with deep roots. While the particular events of the self-determination era and the various federal programs of the 1960s and 1970s may have presented truly new opportunities, key principles remained compatible with a long line of Native activism. Strategic adaptation of powerful structures and resource channels would be as necessary as ever, while at the same time, the centering of Indigenous culture and bodies of knowledge would remain vital for these new institutions' missions. Just as Henry Roe Cloud had done at the American Indian Institute and Haskell Institute decades before, TCUs in the 1960s and 1970s sought to engage and collaborate with the dominant models of American education, while placing creative control over those models in the hands of individuals and communities supporting Native identities.

Even as this movement took on new forms in the tribal college era, it remained at once local and national. The practical and philosophical construction of each TCU was a unique development but also held clear ties to the growth process at other schools. While each tribal college began with its own ideas for academic achievement and community outreach—making the idea of a "typical" TCU somewhat unrealistic—these institutions did share much in common, often intentionally so. Collaboration and information sharing among these schools and their related publishing platforms remained a key part of the tribal college movement.

The earliest groups to take on the challenge of running tribal colleges were the Navajo, the Turtle Mountain Band of Chippewa Indians in northern North Dakota, and three different Siouan communities in the Dakotas—Pine Ridge, Rosebud, and Standing Rock. All five of the schools—Navajo Community College,[13] Turtle Mountain Community College, Oglala Lakota College, Sinte Gleska College,[14] and Standing Rock Community College[15]—were founded within a span of five years, and were key members in the formation of the American Indian Higher Education Consortium (AIHEC) in the early 1970s.[16] As in previous generations of Native activism and organization, the founders of these five schools were often small clusters of energetic and singularly driven individuals who could patch together alliances of reservation leaders as well as young Native scholars. They combined their diverse bodies of knowledge and shared a tenacious drive toward a common goal for greater access and control of higher education for their people.

In a relatively short period, they laid the groundwork to not

An Exercise in Tribal Sovereignty

only bring alive a new type of institution but to ensure long-term stability as well. They collaborated with older American colleges and universities, secured necessary funding from government and private-sector sources, and continuously worked toward greater protection in terms of accreditation and legislation that would benefit new TCUs in the future. At the same time, they collaborated in establishing academic and cultural missions with tribal communities and Native students at large in mind. Eventually, these efforts were rewarded with a sense of validation and permanence, as TCUs became cornerstones of their communities and created an institutionalized connection between Native students and American higher education. As a sign of the success of those early efforts, all five of these institutions remain active today.

Within this group, Navajo Community College will serve as the primary example in this chapter, because of its leading role as the earliest of these schools and because of the relatively high population of its home community and its student body. While the bulk of the source material concerns NCC, the institutions shared connections and commonalities that highlight the overall intellectual collaboration of the early tribal college era.

As mentioned above, one of the elements that separated the tribal college era from previous developments in Native-driven education was an increase in governmental and institutional support. Early in the twentieth century, the Clouds had struggled constantly to support the American Indian Institute with inconsistent funds from private donors and charitable organizations. Even at the government-run Haskell Institute, Cloud was forced to confront massive restrictions in funding, enrollment, and curricular freedom in the midst of the Great Depression. In the postwar period, the looming prospect of American Indian termination policies forced Native activists to argue for the very existence of their unique communities and identities. With the tribal college era of the 1960s and 1970s, some powerful actors in American politics and education finally began to support the idea of Native American self-determination, and TCUs in particular. This chapter is largely framed by that support—beginning with the tribal projects funded by the Office of Economic Opportunity in the 1960s, and concluding with the passage of the Tribally Controlled Community College Assistance Act of 1978 (TCCCA Act), which helped lay out a permanent scaffolding of federal support for existing and prospective TCUs.[17] Despite the importance of these federal policies, this infrastructure of support was secured only because of the determined advocacy of Native activists.

Bringing the ideas of self-determination into practice through tribal colleges and universities took years of persistent work on both national and local levels. Well before the Office of Economic Opportunity agreed to fund Native American education projects—indeed, well before the OEO existed—Native activists were laying the intellectual foundations for those projects. Some national organizations—such as American Indian Development, the Workshop on American Indian Affairs, and eventually the National Indian Youth Council—dedicated themselves to these projects. At the same time, however, reservation leaders also began imagining programs that could address community-specific educational needs.

In the early postwar period, Navajos began envisioning large-scale educational improvements as a key factor in confronting poverty on the reservation—not by assimilating but by striving for a space within the system of federal funding in which a uniquely Navajo identity could flourish.[18] In a 1953 speech to his tribal council, Navajo tribal chairman Sam Ahkeah sought to make this sentiment more tangible by highlighting particular goals. He called for new programs in higher education as a potential tool for placing Navajos in vital positions as lawyers and conservationists working on the tribe's behalf.[19] In the late 1950s, increasing royalties from the tribe's natural resources gave tangible backing to these educational ambitions. Rather than disperse these profits in lump sums to tribal members, the Navajo tribal council looked to effect a more prolonged positive impact, establishing scholarship funds to encourage greater participation in higher education.[20]

Even a call for increasing educational programs was never a simple, one-sided issue. Some Navajos pointed to the ever-changing demands of the American economy and questioned the possibility of a truly Native identity surviving in modern American society.[21] But there were always strong voices—even among students themselves—arguing that a Native identity was not simply possible but essential for survival.[22] Higher education came to represent for many the path toward increasing tribal strength politically and legally, taking full control of natural resources, and safeguarding community livelihood by addressing the shortage of Navajo professionals like teachers, doctors, and nurses.

In the first years of the 1960s, Dillon Platero, chairman of the education committee of the Navajo Tribe, gave further direction to this energy for continued educational advancement among his tribe. He began corresponding with government bodies, charitable foundations, and interested activists in Native education such as Jack Forbes about the possibility of supporting a new center for higher education on Navajo land.[23] In his writings, Platero asserted his desire that wherever an institution might be founded, Native control should prevail.[24] As early as 1960, he expressed his concern that "programs that were not sanctioned by the Navajo people [had] been rather unsuccessful. When we see the enthusiasm [to go on to high school or college] among the students themselves," he wrote, "then we would like to provide some type of education for them beyond their [current] program."[25]

Taken together, the rhetorical stances of Ahkeah and Platero displayed the balanced vision of Native education that stretched back to Henry Roe Cloud's American Indian Institute. They revealed in one sense a straightforward drive to secure higher levels of education and professional leadership for Native people. They also showed, however, the strategic vision of appropriating the dominant American models and transforming them into a unique system that was designed, maintained, and experienced by Native people in a way that validated Native identities.

One of the first routes toward a concrete expression of this vision arose with the Office of Economic Opportunity, formed in 1964. The OEO became an important tool for handling much of the Johnson administration's war on poverty in the United

States, reviewing proposals and distributing funds for community-led programs.[26] Reservation communities throughout the country eagerly harnessed newly available OEO funds for education and other community projects. Included in this group of reservations were all four of the communities that would join the Navajo in founding the first wave of TCUs—the Turtle Mountain, Pine Ridge, Rosebud, and Standing Rock reservations in North and South Dakota.[27] For their own part, Navajos secured a separate office—the Office of Navajo Economic Opportunity—to facilitate those OEO projects across their large reservation.[28] As a sign of the OEO's willingness to pursue Native control, the Navajo office featured an executive board on which a majority of members were Navajo representatives and not outside officials.[29]

Bob Roessel, long-time activist and educator among the Navajo, saw an opportunity with OEO programs to put tribes' own plans into action. He argued that a key reason many Native people embraced this new platform was the basic fact that it bypassed the Bureau of Indian Affairs (BIA).[30] The BIA in the 1960s still carried a deep-seated reputation among Native people as a "paternalistic" agency whose primary contact with reservation communities involved "dictat[ing] to Indian groups what they could or could not have or do."[31] In contrast, Roessel saw the OEO as taking up an "encouraging posture," rather than a dogmatic one.[32] With this change, Native activists like Navajo chairman Raymond Nakai immediately sought to secure a space in which their own creative energy could finally be recognized as the driving force in addressing community projects. By 1965, leaders at the Turtle Mountain, Pine Ridge, Rosebud, and Standing Rock reservations had also laid the early groundwork for tribally controlled higher education by instituting a broad range of educational activities through the OEO. Many of these initiatives were explicitly directed toward vocational training and adult basic education, but "the interest shown in [these] activities [was] very apparent" from the beginning, which would prove crucial for expanding the size and scope of tribal control over educational efforts in the ensuing years.[33]

Navajos first highlighted the essential implications of Native-driven schooling projects not in the form of a college but in early education, at the Rough Rock Demonstration School in 1966. The early success of this school—and its explicit dedication to bilingual learning and expressions of tribal culture under the guidance of Navajo educator Ruth Roessel—represented an important demonstration of the promise of self-determination in education, and only strengthened the resolve of community-focused activists who wanted to apply a similar model to higher education.[34]

For Navajo Nation, the higher education model began to take shape in 1968, when the OEO agreed to fund a community college project.[35] Dr. Sanford Kravitz, as a leader of the OEO's efforts to fund worthy Community Action Programs, had been an early proponent of Rough Rock Demonstration School and other Native-driven education projects. In the ensuing effort to found Navajo Community College, he became "instrumental in obtaining initial OEO funding."[36] Navajo leaders would make up the board of regents and design the curriculum and overall academic mission, but would also seek the committed support of outside donors, educators, and the government.

The patchwork of contributions to NCC's founding was exhibited in several distinct ways. For one, the Navajo tribe worked closely with officials at Northern Arizona University and Arizona State University in 1966 and 1967 to determine the potential need for and feasibility of a reservation-based community college.[37] This early planning process was a necessary step in securing the founding grants from the OEO. Even as the OEO endorsed the plan and became the primary financial backer, Navajos in NCC's early years continued to explore a broad range of options for support. They garnered approximately 20 percent of the school's budget from private grants and donations, while the tribe itself contributed another 20 percent.[38] Almost immediately, tribal leaders also sought to raise $10 million for the construction of a permanent, central campus on the reservation, one that might truly represent a Navajo-centered creation.[39] Until that campus could be completed, the tribe came to an agreement to utilize classroom space at a new BIA high school campus in Many Farms,

Arizona.[40] These early efforts to cooperate with the OEO, the BIA, and outside educational and charitable institutions were necessary steps in bringing NCC into a favorable but finely balanced relationship with the established systems of American higher education and politics. Much like the American Indian Institute some fifty years before, Native leaders at Navajo Community College worked to retain control over the school's mission and administration, while also ensuring that students' accomplishments were supported with proper resources, as well as respected by outside institutions and employers.[41]

Despite the assistance of the Office of Economic Opportunity, the founders of Navajo Community College understood the need for a long-term funding solution. In the summer of 1969, Bob Roessel stepped down as NCC president and moved to the position of executive vice president, with Ned Hatathli entering as the first Navajo president of the college.[42] Hatathli projected strength in both his physical presence and his rhetoric, unabashedly pursuing a greater sense of Navajo influence over every aspect of the school's development. Soon, a college council was formed within the tribal government, further solidifying a sense of Native control in the school's administration. Still, Hatathli understood the necessity of continued collaboration. With the school's administrative structure taking shape, he and Roessel continued a push for protective legislation and greater funding to ensure NCC's growth. This need for expansive support became especially apparent as the tribe strove for construction of a new campus site near Tsaile, Arizona.[43]

One of the significant barriers to greater stability for early tribal colleges was a general lack of state funding. While state laws in Arizona or the Dakotas might include benign language regarding cooperation with tribes, such statements rarely led to concrete funding opportunities, as states argued that Native American education was a federal matter.[44] As early as April 1968, the *Navajo Times* pointed out this difficulty, lamenting the rigidity of the state government's position.[45] "There appears to be no way," one Navajo journalist wrote, "that Arizona tax money could be used to subsidize the Navajo college, unless drastic amendments to the

An Exercise in Tribal Sovereignty

educational laws are passed."[46] The *Navajo Times* writers were right in perceiving the entrenched nature of this roadblock; four years later, the situation had not changed. "It must be remembered," read a 1972 NCC report to the tribal council, "that the State of Arizona, which provides full support for state-operated junior colleges, contributes absolutely nothing to Navajo Community College."[47] The lack of state funding thus stood out as a reminder that not all structures or discourses guiding mainstream American society could be cracked open by Indigenous activist efforts.[48]

Fortunately, NCC found an ally on the federal level in Congressman Wayne Aspinall, a Democrat from Colorado who chaired the Committee on Interior and Insular Affairs.[49] Aspinall had gained respect for Navajo educational leaders like Dr. Guy Gorman and the Roessels over the course of several meetings, in part because of their dogged drive toward their vision but also because of their willingness to engage the congressman in a personal, caring manner.[50] Aspinall sought to return the favor by attending the dedication ceremony for the opening of construction at the Tsaile campus site in the spring of 1971. Aspinall described the ceremony in striking terms, relating that he had "felt the power of God" during the Navajo prayers.[51] From then on, he was fully committed to pursuing further supportive legislation. Perhaps his most lasting collaborative effort with school administrators was his influence in the passage of the Navajo Community College Act (NCC Act) in December of 1971. Under this new legislation, NCC could receive up to $5.5 million in construction funds for the new campus.[52] Even more important, the act provided for "an annual sum for operation and maintenance of the college" at the same per-capita rate that was used to fund other federally supported Native American schools.[53] This legislation's significance lay not simply in the money it provided but in its apparent endorsement of a new era of self-determination undertaken at NCC. It showed that a Native-driven project could garner the same level of support as an established BIA institution.

Despite the victory that the Navajo Community College Act represented in principle, there were immediate concerns about its practical implementation. In the spring of 1972, the *Navajo Community College Newsletter* conveyed the school administration's disappointment in what it perceived as a lack of commitment from the BIA to apply the act to its full extent.[54] Indeed, the bureau had requested less than the maximum funding allowed under the NCC Act's terms for the 1973 budget, and had in turn been awarded less than that request. As a result, school officials scrambled to raise approximately $900,000 for 1973, rather than the $500,000 they had expected to contribute.[55] The NCC Act did represent a positive commitment from the federal government, and its funds provided necessary resources in the growth of the tribal college movement. Still, this incident and others like it served as a reminder to Native intellectual activists that even in an era when the federal government espoused its endorsement of self-determination, forces within the system could always be shifted against them in threatening and unexpected ways.

At the Turtle Mountain, Pine Ridge, Rosebud, and Standing Rock reservations, Navajo Community College provided a positive illustration of tribally controlled higher education but could only rarely serve as a perfectly replicable model. Pine Ridge's Oglala Lakota College, for example, serves as a useful illustration of the trajectory faced by these four communities. Oglala Lakota arose like NCC from a years-long tribal effort to institutionalize higher education and build on the momentum of OEO projects.[56] But unlike the OEO educational projects at Navajo, those at Pine Ridge did not immediately transition into start-up grants for a community college. Pursuing multiple alternate routes, Pine Ridge's Lakota leadership in 1969 and 1970 secured temporary partnerships with the University of Colorado and Black Hills State College, which offered reservation-based courses to their own students as well as tribal members. In 1971 tribal leaders took the next step by officially founding Oglala Lakota College, cobbling together a meager school budget from a variety of sources. By the following year, the primary source of funding became the BIA, which, as indicated above, developed a reputation among the early TCUs for failing to fund these schools at the maximum allowable limits.[57]

An Exercise in Tribal Sovereignty

Even with the daunting challenges of securing start-up funds and the misgivings about the role of the BIA, the early TCUs remained resilient. One key tool that Turtle Mountain, Oglala Lakota, Sinte Gleska, and Standing Rock Community Colleges all eventually utilized was Title III of the Higher Education Act of 1965. One of Title III's expressed purposes was to "assist in the establishment of cooperative arrangements" between existing colleges and "developing institutions," so that those developing institutions might offer higher education to students otherwise "isolated from the main currents of academic life."[58] Both Oglala Lakota College at Pine Ridge and Sinte Gleska College at Rosebud formalized partnerships with Black Hills State College through the help of Title III grants, while Turtle Mountain partnered with North Dakota State University, and Standing Rock with Bismarck Junior College.[59]

These partnerships under Title III increased the influence of established American colleges and their faculties in the growth process of TCUs, while ostensibly providing a level of financial stability. In truth, however, early TCU administrators like Jim Shanley (Assiniboine) were wary of overreliance on such grants, concluding that "you didn't know if [the money] was going to be there from year to year."[60] Despite the difficulties of working under Title III and other partnerships, tribal officials often saw the agreements as a necessary and pragmatic form of protection—a worthwhile adaptation of the American educational framework that opened up breathing space for new TCUs to secure and legitimize their place in the higher education landscape. As Wayne Stein has written, a willingness to collaborate with and seek advice from established schools as well as from one another was a key characteristic in the success of the early tribal colleges, and almost every TCU had some form of a non-Native "sidekick" working to bridge the gap between the reservation and the mainstream power structures of American education and government.[61] Furthermore, this type of collaboration aligned with a well-established tradition among earlier Native intellectual activists. At the American Indian Institute in the late 1910s, when Henry Roe Cloud partnered with faculty and tutors from nearby Fairmount College, he appreciated the quality of instruction without viewing the relationship as a threat to his particular focus on Native leadership.[62] Decades later, D'Arcy McNickle and the other directors of the Workshop on American Indian Affairs similarly worked within the established system of American universities and colleges, all the while challenging students to utilize that education to better study the history and conditions of Indigenous communities and serve their Native people.[63] Tribal colleges and universities built on that tradition of pursuing a higher education that balanced outward collaboration with a focus on Native issues, and they instituted that effort within Native people's home communities.

To solidify productive relationships among the TCUs and bolster the effort to garner outside support, representatives from the developing schools formed the American Indian Higher Education Consortium in 1973. Although many individuals contributed to the strength of the TCU movement in these early years, Jim Shanley from Standing Rock Community College and Lionel Bordeaux (Lakota) of Sinte Gleska College are frequently mentioned as two of the most important figures in safeguarding unity among the schools and presenting a strong negotiating front to governmental and nongovernmental bodies when it came to financial support. Shanley, not yet thirty years old when entering the world of TCU and AIHEC administration, was nevertheless "a force to be reckoned with" when it came to his advocacy of the early schools.[64] Shanley and others at AIHEC in the early years necessarily worked on multiple fronts, not only sharing curricular and community missions and strategies between schools but also developing deals with private sector donors and literally drafting proposed legislation that would eventually institutionalize funding for the schools.[65] In these efforts to garner additional assistance, however, Shanley credits Lionel Bordeaux above all for setting a tone of unity among the schools, continually encouraging greater Native ownership over the direction of the institutions, and demanding respect from outside organizations. Even at a young age—becoming Sinte Gleska's president in his early thirties—Bordeaux had a way of drawing people in

An Exercise in Tribal Sovereignty

to listen carefully to what he had to say, exerting a sort of gravity in the room that proved impactful on his listeners. On multiple occasions over the years, with millions of dollars at stake from powerful outside organizations like the Kellogg Foundation and the Ford Foundation, Bordeaux stood his ground on the unity of the TCU movement, insisting that any grants be made available to all TCUs, not simply the favored ones that fit the organizations' "romantic ideas" of what a tribal college should be.[66]

Individuals like Jim Shanley, Lionel Bordeaux, Stanley Red Bird (Sicangu Lakota), Janine Pease (Crow), and others both on and off the reservations proved not only principled in such instances but effective. These TCU advocates' personal influence was also crucial to the advancement of legislation such as the Tribally Controlled Community College Assistance Act of 1978 (TCCCA Act). From the early 1970s onward, this kind of powerful presence and commitment was crucial to the growth of the TCU movement, when the early schools were only half-jokingly described as little more than "fifty dollars and a typewriter."[67]

As mentioned above, AIHEC proved vital in coordinating assistance on grant writing and sharing information on the details of useful legislation such as the Higher Education Act.[68] Beyond the initial concerns over funding, the group also facilitated cooperation in developing curricula, carrying out new research, and exploring routes to accreditation. From its inception, AIHEC thus served a dual purpose as a supportive hub for the member TCUs as well as a unified point of contact with outside organizations and the federal government. It rose as yet another example of how this particular vein of intellectual activism remained at once local and national, dedicated to greater Native leadership and control, and consciously open and adaptable when seeking the support of non-Native advocates.

Pursuing Native-Driven Curricular and Community Missions

The partnerships they formed with outside schools, foundations, and government organizations signaled early TCUs' willingness to balance an innovative push for tribal control with a pragmatic acknowledgement of the strengths and resources of the established American education system. As they articulated their own curricular and community missions, however, an emerging intellectual vision connected TCUs not just to their home communities and to one another but to a deeper thread of Native intellectual activism as well.

The core of that vision was a two-pronged effort explicitly laid out in the founding documents and mission statements of TCUs: to provide positive experiences in the study of Native history and culture while also enabling Native students to become more likely to succeed according to mainstream American systems of education and economics. Despite particular tribal lenses, this vision was woven into each TCU's mission with remarkable continuity, and held the central threads of a Native intellectual activism pursued by the likes of Henry Roe Cloud as early as the 1910s. At Turtle Mountain Community College, for example, the founding administration in the early 1970s sought "to create an environment where the cultural and social heritage of the Indian people can be brought to bear through the curriculum," and in turn to "establish an administration, faculty, and student body involved in exerting leadership within the [Turtle Mountain Chippewa] community."[69] Just as Cloud had at the American Indian Institute, the founders of the early TCUs envisioned Native and tribal history and culture as fundamental to modern Native American leadership, rather than as part of a static past. At Oglala Lakota College, the mission statement similarly expressed a desire to "assist in the development of Sioux culture" in an active, ongoing process, as an "attempt to solve the social, political, and economic problems plaguing the reservation."[70] Navajo Community College pursued the same dual purpose, tethering the immediate educational and vocational needs of its community members to the active study and development of Native cultures.[71] At NCC this dual purpose was also prefaced by a statement that spelled out in plain terms the fundamental importance of self-determination in education. "It is essential," the board of regents wrote in 1968, "that educational systems be directed and controlled by the society they are

An Exercise in Tribal Sovereignty

intended to serve," and within those systems, "each member of that society must be provided with an opportunity to acquire a positive self-image and a clear sense of identity."[72]

Oral histories on the founding of Navajo Community College illustrate just how important this concept was for the school's founders, who developed NCC with both non-Native and Navajo concepts of intellectual leadership in mind.[73] They understood that many traditional Navajo leaders within the community would be hesitant to recognize the leadership of a young generation that did not possess a deep knowledge of Navajo cultural beliefs and practices, regardless of higher education degrees and certificates.[74] But the authors of NCC's early mission statement did not seek to protect Navajo identity in a way that simply separated students from other cultural systems. Rather, they insisted, the empowerment that came from self-determination—from rooting students in a home community and a home identity—would be essential in navigating the demands of the broader modern world. "Members of different cultures," they wrote, "must [also] develop their abilities to operate effectively . . . in the complex of various cultures that make up the larger society of man."[75]

As with the founding documents of the other schools, NCC's objectives thus echoed an approach to Native leadership built on principles similar to those articulated by Henry Roe Cloud early in the twentieth century. In particular, Cloud had repeatedly argued that cultural pride and positive expressions of Native identity provided a foundation that *enhanced* rather than detracted from the overall goal of adaptable Native leadership.[76] The early tribal colleges of the 1960s and 1970s built on this idea and accentuated it, bringing a philosophy of Native and national leadership through higher education into more direct contact with reservation communities. As they provided degree programs for students who might transition to careers and institutions off their reservations, they also demonstrated a firm commitment to the social and economic goals of their home communities.

Navajo Community College illustrated this point through a variety of early programs. For example, Navajo Adult Basic Education formed as one of the most versatile of NCC's initiatives, with sections as diverse as "Job Development, Tribal Work Experience, Community Development," courses on the causes and effects of alcoholism, and an extension program with the University of Arizona.[77] By 1972 fourteen sites across Navajo Nation offered these programs, showing that the tribe's push for a permanent central campus would not prevent NCC from remaining active in reaching out to as many community members as possible. As part of that goal, the school participated in a "Career Opportunities Program" for "teacher aides [to] work with children in the classroom or dormitory."[78] Career Opportunities students at NCC gained classroom experience in the reservation's elementary schools in preparation for their careers as educators. Other TCUs adopted this method as well, and it aligned with the general goal of extending a philosophy of self-determination over a larger portion of the education system. As with the American Indian Institute, officials at Navajo Community College also hoped to study and improve agricultural and natural resource possibilities on the reservation. Navajo farmers and ranchers felt the impact of NCC through the Community Agriculture Program, which disseminated strategies in crop and soil management, irrigation, livestock raising, and marketing.[79] The Community Agriculture Program was supplemented by a farmers' cooperative that helped organize the leasing of basic equipment. Through these myriad services, NCC immediately signaled that tribal colleges would do more than simply import existing models of higher education to their communities—they would reshape those models in ways that made them more adaptable to the particular goals and needs of their people.

Adapting to the needs of community members carried over to the student body as well. Tribes were eager with their new schools to control curricular programs but also to reform the fundamental relationship between Native students and institutions of higher education. The founders of Navajo Community College understood well the problems Native students had commonly encountered in mainstream American higher education. With few peers and hardly any faculty, counselors, or advisers

An Exercise in Tribal Sovereignty

coming from a Native background, Navajo students in nonreservation schools had reported that they felt "pushed aside" by others, or that others too quickly interpreted their reserved personalities as "ignorance."[80]

To prevent this type of alienation at NCC, administrators thought deeply about remodeling the entire experience of attending college. For students pursuing an associate's degree, the "Inquiry Circle" became an innovative tool in that effort.[81] This open-ended counseling format allowed a student to bring up "any question, problem, difficulty, or conflict he would like to resolve. It may be a question about his relationship with other people, his values and beliefs, his view of the world . . . [or] his career."[82] Further seeking to correct the perceived blind spots evident at nonreservation institutions, NCC also provided counselors and student aides who would be allowed to come to students' homes and discuss issues unfamiliar to parents and family members who lacked college experience.[83] These extensive services aimed to retain Navajo students and prepare them and their families for possible transitions to off-reservation schooling and careers. But they also sought to overturn entrenched legacies of American schools, which had been characterized by a "frightening separation" between educators, students, and their families.[84]

Addressing that legacy of separation through proactive services allowed TCUs to extend the type of work envisioned not just by Cloud but by the directors of the Boulder Workshop in the 1950s and 1960s—utilizing the benefits of aligning with the American higher education system while encouraging students to remain rooted in their Native cultures and cognizant of the strengths of their own people's leaders. Unlike these previous efforts, however, TCUs now carried this work directly to reservations, and institutionalized it as a recognizable pathway for a greater number of students.

Perhaps nothing was more vital to this reshaping of the higher education model than a concerted effort by tribal colleges to place Native American studies at the center of the curriculum. By organizing curricula that grew around a central base of Native and tribal studies programs, the founders and educators of early TCUS embraced the understanding that cultural factors could never be divorced from the learning process, no matter the subject.[85] This understanding, furthermore, was portrayed in TCUS' curricula as an opportunity to impact the present and future rather than as a reason to retreat to the past. In other words, while TCUS sought to root students in cultural knowledge that stretched to immemorial pasts, they also emphasized particular events in tribes' histories with settler colonialism and modern contexts that in turn impacted the social, economic, and political circumstances of students. In this way, Native and tribal studies programs became a necessary tool in the pursuit of the intellectual vision outlined in their mission statements.

Navajo Community College provides perhaps the clearest illustration of this multilayered approach to Native studies. In its early years, NCC benefited from a strong philosophical agreement between its top administrators and its Navajo studies educators. The school's first president, Bob Roessel, wholeheartedly supported his wife Ruth as the director of Navajo studies, and when Ned Hatathli soon stepped in as the school's first Navajo president, that advocacy continued. Hatathli clearly expressed his desire that the Navajo studies program would act not as a "veneer" but as "the heart of Navajo Community College."[86] This sentiment was also echoed by tribal chairmen—first Raymond Nakai and later Peter MacDonald—who privileged the bodies of knowledge held by Navajo elders and hoped the Navajo studies program would become a source of individual and collective pride for students.[87]

With administrators and educators aligned, Navajo studies became a vehicle for a unique approach to higher education. As a sign of the level of commitment to the program, Navajo studies coursework was required rather than optional. The overall program included over thirty courses, with about half focusing on pantribal issues and the others addressing specifically Navajo topics, sometimes taught only in the Navajo language.[88] To support this extensive program, NCC streamlined the qualifications for Navajo studies instructors, recognizing that academic qualifications according to the norms of American academia were often less relevant than a deep knowledge of the material and an ability to teach that material.[89] Pursuing this route, the program was "staffed entirely by full-blood Navajos," by 1971.[90] In her role as director of the program, Ruth Roessel was not simply an administrator but an experienced educator with a firm grounding in Navajo culture. Her father was a Navajo medicine man, and an appreciation for that type of deep cultural knowledge helped shape the program.

Even for NCC administrators who had grown up with a firm sense of their tribal history, the process of constructing this curriculum became an important moment of reflection and recommitment to the teaching of that knowledge.[91] In the early years, Navajo Community College president Ned Hatathli encouraged administrators and educators to undertake a deep study of traditional Navajo forms of the education process, and to consider how those traditional teaching methods could inform a modern higher education effort.[92]

Students in the Navajo studies program often began by encountering some of the most basic teachings of a Navajo approach to life. For example, Wilson Aronilth Jr., who taught Navajo studies at NCC from its inception, emphasized the Navajo clan system as the foundation of all identity.[93] The clan system traced a direct and personal connection to the very origins of the Navajo people. Knowledge of this deep connection, Aronilth hoped, would engender confidence in a student's individual sense of identity and place in society, while also underscoring a shared past as a source of collective strength.[94] As with so many Native intellectual activists and educators of the era, Aronilth saw his teaching as much more than a lesson in history or cultural tradition. He interpreted his work as directly relevant to many of the problems facing reservation communities in modern America—generational divides, broken families, depression—which he saw as stemming from a crisis of identity.[95] Ruth Roessel related that for many students who had been relocated to urban areas throughout the country, returning to NCC and entering Navajo Studies in this way was an intensely emotional experience:

They wanted to come back and they wanted to learn about the culture, they wanted to learn about who they are. So it was real sad in my class, you know, some of them said, "I don't speak Navajo and I don't know anything about it," their tears coming down. It's just—it's just really, really touching, those things. So I told them . . . "This is what makes you a Navajo, you may not speak your language, but you can read about all these things, and that's what makes you a really strong person," I said . . . "You can learn more about yourself, and where the Navajo come from, and have a full knowledge, and you can gain it—and that makes you a Navajo." So that's what they did.[96]

For Aronilth and Roessel, reconstructing positive expressions of Native identity in modern America would never be done by abandoning one source of knowledge for another, or attempting to take on an entirely new identity. Instead, as Aronilth put it, he felt that students must first enter a "learning and re-learning process of what our forefathers taught us," understanding their cultural values but also "why [we] use these values."[97] From there, students could "understand cross cultural ideas through comparison, participation, and discussion of values," thus constructing a balanced body of knowledge and a balanced worldview.[98]

In many cases, discussions of contemporary implications were much more direct. In an early Navajo studies text that she helped author for the program, Ruth Roessel addressed myriad topics like tribal relations with governments, reservation economic development and land management, the relevance of Supreme Court cases for Native sovereignty, and examples of self-determination.[99] Roessel sought to ensure that the Navajo studies program and her text in particular were infused with a powerful Native voice, allowing her activist stance to shine through in her descriptions of the contemporary relationships between tribes and American governments.[100] Crucially, Ruth Roessel's own voice as an educator carried a weight among her community and her students. As her assistant Evelyn Anderson observed, "She's very knowledgeable in the tradition. . . . She not only dresses [but] she speaks and she eats and she sleeps . . . everything's [in the] tradition [and] that opens an eye" to her presence and draws the attention of students.[101] Under Roessel's direction, the program also required students to attend seminars on current affairs impacting Native people, and encouraged attendance at events such as the National Congress of American Indians conference.[102]

Roessel's willingness to combine the multiple layers of cultural, historical, and contemporary studies in her program aligned well with the school's mission statement and with the long line of intellectual activism to which she added. This effort was also mirrored at the other early TCUs. At Sinte Gleska College, an "Ethnic Studies Curriculum Development" project sought to bring Native worldviews into discussions on topics ranging from politics to science to poetry, while workshops were set up to reexamine the roots of common Siouan cultural practices.[103] The Sinte Gleska curriculum, like NCC's, also encouraged students to engage with contemporary Native issues and organizations such as the National Indian Education Association. Through these diverse applications, a core of Native studies at tribal colleges and universities carried out the schools' curricular and community missions in powerful and proactive ways, and reshaped the experience of higher education for Native students.

Early TCUs sought to expand their innovative influence outside the curricular realm as well. Publishing newsletters, books, and other materials quickly became a way to privilege tribal perspectives and to harness an established educational and rhetorical instrument for the particular goals of Native people. This method was not entirely new. Henry Roe Cloud had understood well the empowering aspect of publishing, devoting much of his time at the American Indian Institute and Haskell to creating forums on Native issues and disseminating his own writings.

No school in the tribal college era seized this opportunity more aggressively than Navajo Community College, where the press became not simply a necessary device for the daily needs of the institution itself but a powerful platform for voices all across Navajo Nation.[104] This work initially overlapped with the Navajo studies curriculum, with Ruth Roessel writing enthusiastically of the opportunity to teach from a perspective that relied primarily "upon those sources which originate from the Navajos themselves."[105] Over time, the NCC Press expanded to publish Navajo perspectives on some of the tribe's most important historical topics and modern developments. True to her word, Roessel was instrumental in privileging Native sources, editing or collecting Navajo accounts for at least five books during NCC's first five years.[106] One of these, *Navajo Stories of the Long Walk Period*, was considered "the first Navajo account of the traumatic events surrounding" the Navajo exile to Fort Sumner in the 1860s.[107] Another work collected Navajos' stories of the government-imposed livestock reduction program during the Great Depression.[108]

Through these projects, the NCC Press privileged Native voices in print in ways that had rarely been done before. It gave Navajos an additional platform in their effort to assert the strength of their own perspectives and bodies of knowledge. Like the college itself, the press acted as a demonstration of a tribe appropriating the established American tools of intellectual empowerment for Native-driven purposes. As it did so, it became another clear example of TCUs acting as hubs of Native American self-determination, and contributed directly to the enhancement of a long line of intellectual activism. It also helped to illustrate that tribal colleges and universities sought to accomplish much more than a simple importation of an existing higher education model. They pursued curricular and community missions that in some ways aligned with mainstream American educational models, but that also emphasized the enormous relevance of Indigenous culture, history, and identity to their students' everyday lives in modern America.

Seeking Permanence and Validation

The sense of balance that permeated the overall missions of early tribal colleges and universities was also built into the effort to establish a greater sense of permanence for the schools. Early TCUs' administrators and advocates understood that the most plausi-

An Exercise in Tribal Sovereignty

ble path to truly institutionalizing this new model of higher education required solidifying their relationships with mainstream American educational and political systems through accreditation and legislation. At the same time that they sought these outside forms of validation, however, they would need to ensure that their community members still recognized these institutions as Native American entities.

For Navajo Community College, the enthusiastic push for a newly constructed campus became one of the essential factors in establishing the school as a permanent pillar of the reservation community. From the moment of NCC's inception, the Navajo Tribal Council had begun a drive to acquire construction funds. Thanks to the generosity of board of regents member Yazzie Begay, land for a campus site became available near Tsaile, Arizona.[109] With the added financial assistance of the Navajo Community College Act of 1971, the ambitious campus project was spurred onward and became an early point of pride for NCC's advocates.[110] To understand the true significance of this construction project, it is useful to take a careful and deliberate look at how the new campus fit into Navajo Nation in both a physical and philosophical sense.

The chosen campus site in Tsaile sat in the heart of Navajo Nation, nestled among the rugged Chuska Mountains. The landscape of this area vividly brought to mind both the power and the beauty of nature. The rocky bluffs and mesas jutted out from the desert and asserted their immediate physical strength. At the same time, their subtle mixes of reds, browns, and oranges suggested a softness. The site was beautiful but also remote. At the outset of the campus project in 1971, there barely existed a functional road to service construction personnel, let alone the hundreds of would-be students, faculty, and staff expected to attend in the future.[111]

While this relative obscurity seemed to make the Tsaile site an unlikely fit for a community college, Begay and other Navajo advocates saw a benefit in rooting the school "in the heart of the reservation."[112] Not only would the new location keep NCC within a one-hour drive for over one-third of the Navajo population, but it would also represent in a very real sense a protected space, located near the center of the reservation and free from any negative connotations associated with existing BIA facilities.[113]

The notion of the new campus as a protected space for Navajo identity was a powerful metaphor, but it was also grounded in physical realities. As Navajo studies instructor Wilson Aronilth Jr. writes, the importance of the location of the new campus stemmed from its position within the traditional Navajo homeland, as marked out by the four sacred mountains that correspond to the cardinal directions.[114] Beginning in the east was *Sisnaajiní* (Blanca Peak, Colorado), adorned with a white shell. According to the Navajo tradition from which Aronilth taught, a lightning bolt fastened this mountain to Mother Earth. To the south lay *Tsoodzil* (Mt. Taylor, New Mexico), colored turquoise. A stone knife fastened it to the earth. In the west was *Dook'o'oosliid* (San Francisco Peaks, Arizona), colored yellow and dressed with abalone shell, and tied to the earth with a sunbeam. And to the north lay *Dibé Nitsaa* (Hesperus Mountain, Colorado), colored with black jet, and fastened to the earth with a rainbow beam. For Aronilth, each of these mountains also signified a particular type of emotion or mindset, meant to evoke positive thinking, good health, social unity, or general harmony. As literal landmarks, they helped map out the boundaries of the traditional homeland, while their ties to the origins of the Navajo people gave them a cultural grounding and made them a sort of "shield from evil, harm, and danger" that might threaten Navajo identity.[115] The new NCC campus, located within the bounds of these four sacred mountains, was meant to draw on and reflect the strength that they demonstrated.

Nowhere was the connection to the sacred markers of Navajo homeland and identity more apparent than in the design for the Culture Center, a campus building meant to evoke in Navajos the same reverence that the White House or Mount Vernon might for other Americans.[116] For the planning of this particular project, the board of regents entrusted a group of Navajo medicine men, who hoped to display for students and other visitors

An Exercise in Tribal Sovereignty

a connection between the contemporary tribe and the original Navajo Holy People. They designed sanctuary walls within the building to resemble "the mythological home of the Sun," who had built a special dwelling for Changing Woman.[117] The walls of the sanctuary would be made of the same materials as the four sacred mountains—white shell, turquoise, abalone shell, and jet.[118]

A similar thought process pervaded the "design and structure" of the "entire campus . . . [which] was made to represent the traditional Navajo" lifestyle.[119] For example, all buildings' main entrances faced east, calling to mind the traditional setup of a Navajo dwelling, the hogan.[120] Dorms sat on the west side of campus, as the west side represented the resting place in the home. The campus library held a vital position at the center of campus, reflecting a firm belief in the power of its knowledge as a source of great life and energy, as "the center of the Hogan is where the fire burns."[121] The attention to detail in each of these steps meant that the campus itself became a forceful, physical reminder of the connections between contemporary students and the origins of Navajo identity.

Even before construction began, a ceremony in April of 1971 ensured that as Navajo Community College grew to meet the demands of modern American higher education, it would also maintain connections to older traditions of tribal knowledge.[122] At the dedication ceremony, "a traditional cane [or *gish*] was used in planting the seed of NCC."[123] A medicine man planted "white and yellow corn . . . for the blessing of the college," and the seed was meant to "grow and develop into a beautiful spirit of Navajo education."[124] It was during these prayers that Congressman Wayne Aspinall "felt the power of God" and was filled with hope for NCC's future.[125] With the site properly blessed, construction began in the summer of 1971 and, with the encouragement of president Ned Hatathli, builders employed a construction workforce of which 95 percent were Navajos.[126] Truly, NCC's permanent home was developing through the work of its own people's hands, and was emerging as yet another example of how TCUS could refashion established models to fit their own needs and become Native-driven projects.

As reservation communities embraced the tribal college movement, TCUs' advocates understood the need to establish a similarly strong position within the larger systems of American education and politics. The clearest test in the early years concerned the ability of tribal college graduates to transfer their credits or certificates to off-reservation schools. At Navajo Community College, tribal officials and educators had worked with faculty at Northern Arizona University and Arizona State University in the planning process. Still, they were eager to see how NCC credits would transfer to other schools throughout the country. In 1972 administrators noted with satisfaction that "NCC students with the Associate of Arts degree have been accepted with full credit . . . at institutions in other parts of the country. No student has been denied credit, including that received in Navajo culture and language courses."[127] This example became an early sign of validation for the tribal college movement, especially as courses in Native cultural studies and language were accepted alongside general studies and vocational credits.

Despite the early acceptance of NCC credits and the positive academic partnerships that had aided Turtle Mountain, Oglala Lakota, Sinte Gleska, and Standing Rock community colleges, supporters of the early tribal colleges agreed that an effort toward full accreditation would better secure their standing. To achieve that goal, all five schools worked with the North Central Association of Secondary Schools and Colleges (NCA). The road to full accreditation generally required multiple visits from NCA staff to assess curricula, teaching, and administration, and could last seven years or more.[128] This lengthy process was often made more challenging for TCUs by the tenuous nature of their funding. Still, the collaborative network provided by the American Indian Higher Education Consortium enabled the schools to share advice on conducting the necessary self-studies and administrative preparations to meet NCA standards.[129]

In the meantime, TCUs continued to pursue their missions, gaining confidence from incremental signs of permanence and validation. In the fall of 1973, for example, Navajo Community College officially moved to its permanent site in Tsaile, a long-awaited step in the school's growth. Enrollment could expand at the new site, and "90 percent of the previous semester's students returned for the second semester" in the 1973–74 school year, an encouraging figure that showed an almost complete reversal of the troubling dropout rate for Navajos in other postsecondary schools.[130] The curriculum at NCC also began featuring a summer fine arts program that became a "flourishing" pantribal hub.[131] A *Navajo Times* article in the summer of 1976 discussed at length the impact of decorated faculty and eclectic influences on the summer program. Ceramics courses brought in students from as far away as New Jersey, while a bilingual Navajo theatre ensemble performed original plays written by the instructors—"members of the Native American Theatre Ensemble of New York."[132] Well-known Acoma poet Simon Ortiz became another popular guest instructor as well. This summer program—and the positive response it received—was an important signal that the effort toward outside collaboration and validation could occur alongside an ongoing demonstration of Native leadership through administration, instruction, and positive expressions of Indigenous identity.

Just three weeks later, as if in agreement with the praise of the *Navajo Times*, the NCA awarded full accreditation to Navajo Community College, making it the first fully accredited tribal college on reservation land.[133] As perhaps the most significant endorsement, the NCA review committee noted the "clarity of philosophy and objectives" at NCC, along with the "unity of the Board of Regents, faculty, and staff, [who were] supportive of that philosophy."[134] The NCA's approval of Navajo Community College's guiding principles represented in essence an endorsement of the potential future for Native American self-determination in education. Just as important, that sense of validation extended to the entire tribal college movement. By 1978 Turtle Mountain, Oglala Lakota, Sinte Gleska, and Standing Rock were all well on their way to the same goal, having reached the stage of recognized candidates for accreditation.[135]

At the same time, the persistent lobbying of AIHEC's members finally began gaining momentum among elected officials in

Washington DC. As long-time tribal college administrator and supporter Wayne Stein has written of this effort, the early years of AIHEC's existence were often a struggle to find common ground between the energetic optimism of its members and the skepticism or plain indifference of representatives in Congress.[136] Over time, however, AIHEC's members won key allies, thanks in large part to their determination to seek out any elected official from states in which TCUs had been founded. In particular, James Abourezk, a Democratic senator from South Dakota, proved an interested advocate. Abourezk served as the first chairman of the Senate Select Committee on Indian Affairs, beginning in 1977, giving him a vital influence in supporting future legislation.[137]

In October of 1978, AIHEC's effort to win legislative support for their cause finally reached a key milestone, with the passage of the Tribally Controlled Community College Assistance Act.[138] The act provided a sense of fiscal stability for TCUs by making grants available through the Department of Health, Education, and Welfare—and by *requiring* the dispersal of a minimum number of grants to existing TCUs within the first year of its passage.[139] The legislation encouraged the department to seek the advice of tribal governments and Native American organizations, and explicitly sought to support schools that "demonstrate[d] adherence to stated goals, a philosophy, or a plan of operation which [was] directed to meet the needs of" Native people in particular.[140] Administrators at TCUs immediately applauded this development. Sinte Gleska's president Lionel Bordeaux, for example, wrote in his school's newsletter that he viewed "the funding of this bill [as] necessary to [the school's] survival."[141]

Even as the TCCCA Act became a reality and represented a greater collaborative step toward strengthening the early tribal colleges, the founders of these schools realized that TCUs could quickly become sites of vehement philosophical and political disagreement, even among supporters. At Navajo Community College, the death of President Ned Hatathli in 1972 contributed to a prolonged shake-up in leadership that Bob Roessel would later lament as a significant hurdle in the school's development.[142] After

An Exercise in Tribal Sovereignty

that time, Roessel argued, NCC became the focus of political dis-
agreements among Navajo Tribal Council members regarding
the best course for the school's future and its role in engaging
the larger American systems of education and economics. Roessel was disappointed by the NCC administration's changes to the
initial vision of the curriculum during the 1970s. He criticized
the administration for too readily deemphasizing Navajo studies and breaking the program up "into little pieces," rather than
keeping it as a central pillar.[143]

This particular issue at NCC reflected a much larger philosophical divide between those who wanted TCUs and other Native
educational hubs to conform to the needs of the American economy and those who—like the Roessels—saw Indigenous studies as a crucial and uniquely appealing aspect of TCUs that must
remain the foundation.[144] Jack Forbes, too, came to see a danger
in early TCUs clinging too closely to the established models of the
American junior college. He argued that such a strategy would
not appeal to the most ambitious and qualified Native students
and faculty, and would in turn detract from the effort to develop
Native leadership that could impact American intellectual circles
on a high level.[145] As usual, Forbes was perceptive in his observations; the debate over this balance was something all early tribal
colleges grappled with from their inceptions, and it will likely
continue to some degree for as long as TCUs exist.

As a result of the philosophical battles in leadership and curricular direction, Navajo Community College suffered dozens of
resignations among its faculty and staff during the mid and late
1970s, and encountered difficulty even in accurately tracking and
reporting enrollment for funding purposes.[146] Bob Roessel, like
many other advocates, worried that these struggles could dam-
age the school's reputation and cause hesitation within Congress
regarding the prospect of further supportive legislation. To this
day, the legacy of these pressures and struggles is a concern for
TCU supporters, and these issues remain a pressure point for politicians who argue against increased funding.[147]

In the midst of these challenges, however, supporters of the early tribal colleges also found cause for optimism. As full accreditation stood within reach in the late 1970s, the prospect of new supportive legislation signaled the chance for more Native communities to initiate their own efforts to increase access to and control of higher education. Looking backward from today's perspective, it is easy to conclude that the optimism of that moment has since been mixed with frustration, as dozens of subsequent schools have risen but often have been met by the same hurdles of funding and the same battles over curricular and vocational directions. The flashes of optimism that appeared in the 1960s and 1970s, however, are an important part of this history and deserve to be highlighted because they reveal the resilience of Native intellectual activists in the face of persistent challenges. Throughout the time that the TCCCA Act wove its way through Congress, promising greater financial security and another form of validation for the early TCUs, the schools remained dedicated to their particular missions and to what the founders of NCC called "an exercise in tribal sovereignty."[148]

In the winter of early 1978, Sinte Gleska College held a graduation ceremony for ten recipients of associate's degrees and dozens of students receiving their GEDs, or general equivalency diplomas.[149] In conjunction with graduation, the tribe held the annual *wacipi*—a special type of powwow. Trade and art shows featured handmade crafts. Banquets, musical performances, and dance contests for all ages lasted for three days. The entire community celebrated Lakota culture through the festivities' connection to tribal history. But the *wacipi* also encouraged a living, practiced identity—an indication of what it meant to be a part of the Lakota people in that year and in that moment. The fact that such an important expression of identity occurred in conjunction with graduation showed how central the young school had already become to the community. In another of South Dakota's tribal colleges—Oglala Lakota College—students encountered a curriculum that focused on the "whole person in balance," or *Wolakota*.[150] Across the country at Navajo Community College, students learned to value a connection with their original Holy People through the

An Exercise in Tribal Sovereignty

clan system, and they emphasized "living in a way of beauty," or in harmony with the world around them.[151] These unique concepts emphasized particular histories and philosophies, but all shared a connection to a long thread of Native intellectual activism that stretched back decades and incorporated individual activists, national organizations, and tribal leaders.

In the 1960s and 1970s this form of activism benefited from a shift toward greater support on the part of key allies in American government and education. On a basic level, this support allowed students in Native communities to gain greater access to higher education and ensuing circles of American professional and intellectual leadership than they had before. Some received GEDs or adult basic education while others completed associate's degrees, certificates, and other credits that would transfer to four-year universities off the reservation. But these schools did more than simply formalize a relationship between Native students and the established American educational, political, and economic landscape. They transformed that relationship into something new, and rather than merely import a model of higher education, they reshaped it into something that encouraged an ongoing demonstration of Native leadership, and that fit the particular needs of the tribal communities they served. In so doing, they became pillars of those communities and hubs of Native American self-determination.

With this dedication to Native administration and tribal focus, TCUs rooted students' education in cultural knowledge and practice that stretched back to time immemorial, while also emphasizing specific factors of tribes' histories with settler colonialism and contemporary politics that impacted students in immediate ways. In this process, tribal colleges built from and redeployed the essential principles of a long line of writers, educators, and students before them. They sought to demonstrate the relevance of Native identities in the modern world, and to institutionalize a path in higher education that prepared students to adapt to the realities of that world and to contribute to Native leadership in their own right.

FIVE

Embracing Pan-Indianism

*Off-Reservation Institutions and Their Place
in the Tribal-College Era*

E ven as the tribal college movement took root in reservation communities, Native leaders elsewhere maintained their long-developing efforts to cultivate national leadership on an intertribal basis. In a tumultuous era of social and political protest emerging in the late 1960s and early 1970s, intertribal activism became more visible than ever. Groups like the American Indian Movement (AIM) aggressively demanded greater accountability from government bodies regarding the recognition of Native people's individual and tribal rights. In turn, the administrations of Lyndon Johnson and Richard Nixon began to formalize the U.S. government's repudiation of American Indian termination policy and the endorsement of self-determination.[1]

Two institutions in particular captured what the tribal college movement could look like in this context, both within the structure of the Bureau of Indian Affairs (BIA) and purposefully divorced from it. In the latter effort, Jack Forbes's persistent activism for an American Indian University finally came to life in the form of Deganawidah-Quetzalcoatl University (D-Q University, or DQU), a small, pan-Indigenous school near Davis, California.[2] Within the BIA, Haskell Institute in Lawrence, Kansas, was transformed into a postsecondary school with a broader academic mission under the name Haskell Indian Junior College.

Together, the stories of these two institutions in the early years of the tribal college era help shine light on difficult questions regarding the fundamental nature of Native intellectual activism and self-determination in twentieth-century America. Some activists asked, How could true Indigenous intellectualism flourish in a

BIA school? How could Native American self-determination exist within the rules and structures established by the United States government? Others asked, How could any impactful reform come about *without* the assistance of non-Native people and the approval of powerful political forces? Why should Native activists *not* utilize the tools of the colonizer in their decolonization efforts? These fundamental questions regarding how and where Native activism should operate were intimately linked to questions about the nature of Native identity. In Forbes's work, especially, this tension occasionally rose to the surface as he appeared to struggle over the basic question, What should an American Indian University look like? Or even more simply, he seemed to ask in his writings, What did Native *identity* look like? Clearly, this question did not have one answer. But both D-Q University and Haskell Indian Junior College gave students the opportunity to explore it. Only one of these schools survives today, but both were linked to the era's Native intellectual activism, and both illustrated crucial elements of how the tribal college movement resonated beyond reservation communities, gaining strength in pantribal settings as well.

In principle, Jack Forbes remained a staunch opponent of government funding and oversight of D-Q University throughout its development in the 1970s.[3] This stance aligned with his philosophy of Native American self-determination but also revealed a possible gap between philosophy and pragmatism, presenting significant barriers to the effort to keep the fledgling school open. Initially ambitious for the prospects of an American Indian University that would draw students from all over the Americas, Forbes by the end of the 1970s expressed deep frustration in his writings. He articulated acutely the bitterness of a Native activist struggling for radical change in the face of powerful structural limits in American politics and education.

While Forbes attempted to cultivate a new generation of Native intellectual leaders outside the influence of colonial systems, a concurrent development was taking place at Haskell Institute. In the late 1960s and early 1970s, Haskell transformed from a vocational boarding school to a junior college model. Forbes and some other Native activists, perceiving the BIA's influence over Haskell as its central characteristic, refused to see the school as a true hub of Indigenous activism and intellectualism.[4] Many administrators and educators, however, saw Haskell's transition as an opportunity to push government structures and institutions farther into an acceptance of the swelling push for self-determination. For their own part, many of Haskell's students by the 1970s understood themselves as part of a broad movement toward a Native intellectual leadership that unequivocally embraced Indigenous expressions of identity.[5]

These schools were linked to the tribal college movement through common goals and administrative connections such as the American Indian Higher Education Consortium. Despite their fundamental administrative differences, DQU and Haskell shared an effort to perform the work of tribal colleges and universities (TCUs) in an off-reservation, intertribal setting. In this respect, they were in turn linked to the activism of Henry Roe Cloud in the early twentieth century. Cloud had envisioned Native intellectual leadership broadly, encompassing many forms of tribal and Indigenous identity and many different skill sets. His career in education had highlighted the struggle between creative Native leadership and the restrictions associated with federal administration and assistance. The stories of D-Q University and Haskell in the 1960s and 1970s would reveal new developments as well as enduring continuities in that tense relationship.

DQU and a Pantribal Vision of Native Intellectual Activism

By the time D-Q University first opened its doors to students in 1971, it had existed in Jack Forbes's mind for more than a decade.[6] Beginning in the late 1950s and continuing through the 1960s, Forbes consistently pursued the development of Native American self-determination and intellectual activism, and he considered an intertribal American Indian University a potential centerpiece of that effort. He first sent his university proposal to members of the Kennedy administration, Congressional representatives, and fellow educators and Native activists in 1961, but he continued to revise and disseminate his ideas throughout the ensuing decade.[7] Forbes never mentioned Henry Roe Cloud by name when discussing his proposal in the 1960s, but he was certainly familiar with Cloud's work, and his ideas and ambitions for the university project in many ways aligned with Cloud's vision at the American Indian Institute early in the twentieth century.

Unlike Cloud, however, Forbes, in his advocacy for the American Indian University project, drew clear rhetorical lines between settler colonial culture and that of Indigenous people. Christianity served as a key example. While Cloud had understood Christianity as one of several positive influences on his own life and—in combination with Native approaches to learning—as a vehicle for encouraging useful qualities in students' lives, Forbes emphasized Christianity's role as a fundamental tool of colonization against Native cultures.[8] In defense of an American Indian University, Forbes understandably prioritized the merits of Indigenous intellectualism and innovation but at times resorted to broad strokes in his language, such as his suggestion that Native activists needed to "reject white values."[9] Such statements reflected Forbes's intense commitment to working toward Native-driven intellectual activism but did not acknowledge the nuances involved in the type of work undertaken by the Clouds and other activists of the previous generations. After all, Henry Roe Cloud had not only emphasized the importance of Native history and contemporary Native issues but had maintained his own Native language and a commitment to reservation communities in a manner that Forbes would champion as a key starting point for grassroots activism in his own time.[10] A close examination of Forbes's work, in fact, reveals that it did share much in common with this deeper vein of intellectual activism promoted by Cloud and his allies. As they navigated layers of personal and collective culture and identity, the Clouds, McNickle, and other like-minded Native leaders hoped to bring about similar overall goals. They held higher education as a centerpiece for developing Native intellectual activism in modern America. In the process, they utilized and grappled with the

Embracing Pan-Indianism

mainstream American structures of education and politics, and were forced into compromises and contradictions much more complex than a dichotomy between "Native American values" and "white values."

The starting point of Native empowerment for both Henry Roe Cloud and Jack Forbes was a broad understanding of Indigenous identity—one that, for both men, reached beyond some of the commonly accepted boundaries of nation-state and tribe. Cloud frequently expressed the merits of his American Indian Institute in terms of benefits for Native people of the United States, but he strove for an eclectic student body and hoped to bring in students from throughout the Americas.[11] In 1922 he expressed a broad notion of common indigeneity when he wrote to his mentor and adoptive mother Mary W. Roe that he hoped their work would inspire "untold possibilities of good [for] the whole Indian race in the Western Hemisphere."[12] Less than six months later, his American Indian Institute accepted a Honduran student, and he wrote optimistically that the Institute considered "the Central American and South American Indians" within its potential scope.[13] Though the language barrier between this student and the faculty eventually served as a deterrent for additional efforts of the same kind, Cloud's actions revealed his optimism for an intellectual movement that prioritized common Indigenous experience and identity over tribal divisions.

In the 1960s Jack Forbes articulated a similar argument.[14] His original university proposal of 1961 focused primarily on issues facing tribes in the United States, but by 1965 his revised proposal included a section dedicated to "Inter-American Indian Affairs."[15] Forbes estimated that "30 million or more Native Americans outside of the United States are in need of programs similar to" those he envisioned for tribal members in the United States.[16] He incorporated his training as an anthropologist and historian into a framework that emphasized a common Indigenous experience with colonialism. In the late 1960s Forbes's language clearly displayed this inclusive understanding, as he frequently described recognized tribes in the United States as well as Chicanos as "tribal groups" or "Native Americans," connected by historical experiences as well as cultural and ancestral ties.[17] He argued that self-determination in the face of the colonial experience was best pursued by a united intellectual leadership that was intertribal and international.

Springing from this broad understanding of Native identity, Forbes's proposals for an American Indian University came to display ever more the ambitious spirit that Cloud had poured into the American Indian Institute decades before. Cloud had consistently written of the need for expansion of funding and enrollment for the Institute to make "the greatest strides" for "Indians of every tribe" and to become a true national center for Native leadership.[18] In the 1960s Forbes's plans for a university project echoed the same hopes for a nationwide—if not international—impact. With each year, as he honed and revised his vision, his ambition grew. In 1965 his proposal still carried the original focus on professional education in teaching, medical fields, and business, but it also brought in additional material on the need for programs in remedial work, agricultural development, law and tribal government, and even education for "social workers and government personnel" who worked within Native communities.[19] In this way, Forbes's expanding proposal sought to reach nearly every aspect of Native higher education, from college preparatory work to advanced research to interactions with government officials. This concerted effort to address contemporary Native issues also mirrored the work of the founders at Navajo Community College and the other TCUs. Forbes explicitly wrote that his university would "do much more than merely 'preserve' tribes" in its effort to produce "a marked improvement in tribal patterns of self-development and self-realization."[20]

Moreover, Forbes's inclusive view of Native identity also meant that his proposed project would attempt to stretch beyond national borders, acting as a "unique research center in tribal [and] inter-tribal . . . relations the world over. A comparative program," he concluded, "might well be of international significance."[21] In his 1965 proposal's final paragraph, Forbes summed up what he viewed as the potential impact of his work: "It could be *the* major effort in the 'war on poverty' in so far as tribal groups are concerned."[22]

Despite his bold language, Jack Forbes understood that to make a tangible impact, he must eventually strike a balance between his own ideals and the existing realities in American politics and education. Forbes's inclusion of the Johnson administration's phrase "war on poverty" hinted at that reality. By 1968 his revised university proposal captured the meeting point between boundless ambition and practical restraints.[23] This updated version maintained Forbes's broad academic vision but also referenced the particular developments of the late 1960s, such as the future of Navajo Community College and the potential trend at Haskell Institute toward a college model.[24] Perhaps sensing the possibility of his own project gaining traction, Forbes for the first time dedicated lengthy sections to the problems of funding his project and securing resources and faculty.

Just as Henry Roe Cloud had done in his original vision for the American Indian Institute, Jack Forbes expressed ambivalence about federal funding and oversight, warning that "bureaucratic administration would nullify the goals of a Native university."[25] He pointed to the large Bureau of Indian Affairs budget for education—as well as federal efforts to fund Howard University as an institution primarily for African American students—as evidence that the problem with funding lay not in whether the money existed. Indeed, he argued, the federal government could make "a simple decision" to "democratize its Indian programs" and fund an expansive, Native-driven project such as his from within the BIA's existing resources.[26] The key issue, Forbes concluded, was that the federal government would simply not commit serious BIA funds to a project that it could not administer directly. This fundamental understanding of the need for complete administrative control in the hands of Native people was a central pillar of Forbes's vision of self-determination and intellectual activism, and would remain a key difference between his project and the BIA's effort to refashion Haskell Institute in the same era.

From the late 1960s onward, Forbes took a number of concrete strides in rapid succession that brought his project into reality. In 1967 and 1968 he helped organize and formalize the California Indian Education Association (CIEA). This organization arose from a conference of approximately 150 Native educators and activists in the state who committed themselves to getting Native "parents, educators, and grassroots people organized in a pressure group" to push for immediate changes in schooling for Native American students.[27] The CIEA strove to approach the education system broadly, rather than to pin blame for poor student outcomes on any one issue. The group pushed Native parents to become more active in parent-teacher associations and in routine meetings with educators, hoping to raise awareness of negative stereotypes and systemic biases that impacted public schools from early childhood to postsecondary years.[28] One of the CIEA's most visible efforts involved pressuring colleges and universities to establish programs in Native American studies (NAS)—an initiative that would see fifteen separate California schools establish NAS programs between 1968 and 1978.[29] Though these new programs were often forced to stretch their budgets paper thin, they were an encouraging sign of the potential influence of the CIEA, which sought to link intellectual leaders like Forbes to ordinary Native parents and students at the grassroots level.

As a central part of the effort to institute NAS programs, Forbes took up a faculty position at the University of California–Davis in 1969.[30] He immediately began working with David Risling Jr. (Hoopa Valley) to organize the Tecumseh Center of Native American Studies, and in 1970 they were joined by Sarah Hutchinson (Cherokee).[31] At this time Forbes was still in his midthirties, and he quickly came to see Hutchinson and especially Risling as two of his closest colleagues and advisers.[32] He admired Risling's intellectualism but also his pure determination, calling him "a bulldog-like fighter for a brighter future for Native people."[33] Over time, Forbes considered Risling not only a friend but an "elder brother."[34]

Once together at the University of California (UC) Davis, Forbes, Risling, and Hutchinson began to imagine the Tecumseh Center as a sort of base of operations for pursuing Forbes's university project. The CIEA had already helped organize a feasibility study with funding from the Donner Foundation, which had also provided initial funds for Navajo Community College.[35] Originally dedicated to cancer research in the 1930s, the Donner Foundation became a key source of funding for many Native-driven projects, supporting initiatives in arts, culture, and especially education by the 1960s.[36] Following their feasibility study, Forbes and Risling began supporting the argument that surplus government land could be repurposed for the potential university.[37] By the summer of 1969, they had identified a former Army communications complex as a potential site.[38] The complex had "various large buildings suitable as dormitories, offices, [and] class rooms," and sat just a few miles outside Davis.[39] With a site identified, it became more and more imaginable that Tecumseh Center faculty, together with members of the CIEA, could act as volunteer organizers and teachers in the effort to get a university up and running. Students could plausibly utilize some of UC Davis's resources when necessary, or even take courses at both institutions.[40]

The strategy of pursuing the surplus Army land introduced one possibility that Forbes had originally feared—dependence on the federal government—but it also represented an opportunity to act out decolonization in concrete ways. In other words, while permission to use the land would come from the federal government, the ensuing development of the university project would be administered by Native leaders and dedicated to cultivating Native intellectual activism among its students. It was a strategy that fit perfectly into the context of the time and place, given the ongoing occupation of Alcatraz Island in nearby San Francisco Bay by Native activists calling themselves the "Indians of All Tribes."[41] The Alcatraz occupiers hoped to "re-claim" the island as a symbolic reversal of settler colonialism, and as a way to draw attention to a history of abuses that all Native Americans shared in their relationship with the U.S. government.[42] Forbes, Risling, and Hutchinson appreciated and drew on that same activist spirit but focused their attention more sharply on a less visible but more pragmatic plot of land. The targeting of a physical site close to Davis helped push the project into the final stages of formal organization.

By 1970 Forbes had worked with Luis Flores, head of Chicano studies at UC Davis, to solidify plans for a university administrative structure that would balance Native American and Chicano studies.[43] This increased incorporation of Chicano studies into the plan by 1970 paralleled the rapid growth of a broader Chicano activism in California at the time, as Chicanos in the 1960s had observed stubbornly inadequate schools for their children due to de facto segregation and academically conservative administrators, even at the university level.[44] The feeling of marginalization in educational institutions despite the espoused goal of equal opportunity could create shared ground between Chicanos and Native American tribes. In finally giving a name to the project—Deganawidah-Quetzalcoatl University—Forbes reached deep into precolonial intellectual history and sought to capture a shared Indigenous perspective.[45] "Deganawidah," wrote Forbes, was a "reformer and statesman," who "originated the concept of the League of Nations" among the Iroquois in the 1300s, while Quetzalcoatl "guid[ed] the Toltecs in their development of a superb civilization" before the arrival of the Spaniards.[46]

Soon, additional faculty from throughout the state pledged to support DQU's development—even if it meant volunteering their time—and the academic framework became clearer.[47] The model that emerged included four main areas of study: American Indian studies, Chicano studies, medical training, and a vocational program.[48] In the fall of 1970, D-Q University was officially incorporated as a nonprofit organization, and the DQU board began the process of applying to the Department of Health, Education, and Welfare (HEW) to take over the government surplus land site near Davis.[49]

At that moment, Forbes's decade-long goal to establish a platform for Native people "to acquire," "to transform," and "to create their own educational institutions" stood within reach.[50] His ambition and optimism remained a driving force as DQU's founders looked forward to translating their ideal model into a concrete reality. It is important to understand these years of persistent work leading up to that moment in the fall of 1970. It is important to understand the commitment by these educators and activists to a particular intellectual vision, and their dedication to goals of both inclusive collaboration and self-determination—which, for Forbes as well as for the founders of other tribal colleges and universities, were not necessarily at odds.[51] It is especially important to understand D-Q University in this moment of optimism because, in the years that followed, the institution's development would become heavily impacted by constricting forces in the established systems of American education and politics. From 1971 onward, DQU's story would become less about the intellectual vision of Jack Forbes and his colleagues than it was about the immense challenges and compromises facing activists attempting to reshape the relationship between Native students and American higher education.

The Concrete Struggles of Implementing the DQU Vision

The implementation of the D-Q University intellectual vision brought both excitement and immediate challenges. In the fall of 1970, DQU officials waited anxiously but confidently for the Department of Health, Education, and Welfare to approve their formal request to acquire the surplus land near Davis. They had already toured the complex multiple times, and were informed that theirs was the only application for the site.[52] In a few short weeks from September to November 1970, however, the DQU founders were blindsided by a series of mysterious reversals within HEW. First, they saw reports of a competing application submitted by UC Davis—a development that directly contradicted the information they had received not only from their contact in HEW but from the University of California Board of Regents. On October 30, HEW informed DQU that it was denying their application and awarding the site to UC Davis instead. As Forbes and his colleagues became increasingly aware of the illegitimate nature of this reversal—given that the UC Davis application was incomplete and unsanctioned by the board of regents—they quickly organized a two-pronged protest.[53] As faculty members with their careers now potentially compromised by this confrontation, Forbes and the other DQU administrators sought to appeal the decision through the established rules guiding HEW and the state's university system. At the same time, though, they helped organize and direct the energy of Native and Chicano student protestors at UC Davis and other nearby colleges, encouraging a peaceful occupation of the site beginning in November of 1970.[54] This two-pronged strategy proved effective, as the combined visibility of the "occupation, court action, and public education . . . succeeded eventually in forcing the [UC system] to repudiate its own defective application," effectively awarding the site to DQU.[55]

The combined strategy of the public protest by students and the legal challenge by faculty and staff became an immediate point of pride for Forbes. After all, despite his rhetoric against "white values," he clearly understood the necessity of occasionally operating "within the system" to bring about change.[56] He considered the linking of Native intellectual leaders and grassroots organizers and protestors a crucial part of the effort toward self-determination and a crucial part of DQU's mission.[57] It seemed fitting, then, that the very founding of the school would be a demonstration in the type of activism it would promote.

Still, the acquisition of the campus site was not without its foreboding signs for the embryotic D-Q University. Like the Alcatraz occupation, the protest at DQU was joined by many who had no real interest in the specific principles and goals of the original protestors.[58] Indeed, some of the most vocal and latest-arriving occupiers to the site had taken part in the Alcatraz protest and seemed more motivated by the public display of occupation than the long-term academic vision of DQU. While the original student occupiers dedicated themselves to the cause of legally establishing an innovative university, many newcomers "argued for simple seizure . . . according to a doctrine of 'Indian rights' which refused to recognize the legitimacy of negotiating with the white govern-

Embracing Pan-Indianism

ment."[59] This branch of occupiers gained influence as many of the original student protestors were forced to return to their studies at UC Davis and elsewhere, lest they fall behind in their academic standing and lose valuable scholarships. These conflicts between factions of occupiers were eventually resolved, although at some points DQU officials had to enlist the support of law enforcement to remove the most unwelcome and hostile protestors.

The overlap between the academic goals of students and faculty and the activist goals of nonstudents was to some degree intentionally courted. Forbes hoped to utilize DQU as a Native hub that connected intellectual training with grassroots action. But this relationship would prove an occasional flashpoint of tension throughout the school's early development, especially in an institution with an experimental mission and a lack of stable resources.

Just as troubling, the rather clandestine attempt to block DQU's application confirmed suspicions that officials within HEW and other segments of the federal bureaucracy—not to mention the UC system—might present active opposition to the entire development of the project. From that moment, hopes for robust support from the government were dampened, and any basic level of trust was damaged. Thus, while members of the D-Q University movement proclaimed "Deed Day" on April 2, 1971—the day when they finally achieved formal control of their campus site—the moment was rightfully a balance of celebration and trepidation.[60]

Throughout DQU's early history, Forbes sought to harness the positive elements of the collaborative energy that arose during the campus site occupation. Rather than denigrate, he wanted to feed on the emerging racial and ethnic activism represented by groups like the American Indian Movement. Despite the problems during the campus occupation effort, he understood a certain degree of tension and struggle as a necessary part of the development of DQU, especially considering the school's dedication to principles of self-determination through direct action.[61]

One of the earliest and most exciting of these efforts to reach Native communities was the Native American Language Education (NALE) project. NALE was actually a series of individual community programs that DQU helped organize and run with funding from the Office of Education.⁶² At the Zuni reservation in New Mexico from 1973 to 1975, DQU staff contributed to a curriculum development project that produced teaching materials in the Zuni language, meaning students could encounter a standardized American curriculum while aligning it to their native language in their home community. While DQU's contact with the program ended in the 1970s, the initial contributions of the NALE program were important for the establishment of a Zuni-controlled school district in 1980. Similar DQU extension programs impacted communities throughout California, with the school acting as a protective umbrella for Native-driven education projects that would have otherwise struggled for adequate staff and funding. In this way, DQU truly served as a hub of Indigenous intellectual activism, because leaders at the school could carve out resources from the mainstream channels of American government and education and could funnel that aid to otherwise marginalized grassroots projects.

Unfortunately, the effort to pursue Native and Chicano community development would also bring on serious complications for the fledgling university. In 1972 DQU received a grant of over $3 million from the Department of Labor to teach and assist migrant Mexican farmworkers in California over a two-year period. Part of the project's scope included the purchase of heavy farm equipment, and some DQU board members suggested rejecting the grant on the grounds that the project did not align in significant ways with the mission of a university. With such a large windfall at stake, however, the grant presented too many intriguing possibilities for the majority of board members to turn it down. Over time, the project became a sprawling and disjointed collection of activities. Multiple interest groups from outside the original DQU administration attempted to influence the project and, in so doing, impacted the direction and public perception of the school. The real damage to the university's reputation came almost two years after the project had closed. New directors in the San Francisco regional office of the Department of Labor suddenly accused DQU of mismanaging funds that had been used to purchase tractors for one of the project's extension sites. This accusation led to years of investigations into DQU's administration, which produced little evidence of mismanagement but represented in the eyes of the school's founders an opening for relentless harassment from the federal government.[63]

The university's commitment to linking intellectual training with real-world activism also drew the attention of leaders with a national focus. Most notable of these was Dennis Banks (Ojibwe), who joined the DQU faculty in 1975.[64] Banks had become perhaps the most visible Native activist of the era, thanks in large part to his role in the American Indian Movement. By 1975 AIM had already captured the attention of the public as well as the federal government for its connections to the Alcatraz occupation, the occupation of the Bureau of Indian Affairs offices in 1972, and the Wounded Knee takeover at the Pine Ridge reservation in 1973.[65] The Wounded Knee incident had resulted in criminal charges against Banks and other Native activists, but California governor Edmund "Jerry" Brown refused to extradite Banks to South Dakota.[66] In an era of intense government suspicion of minority activist groups, Banks's notoriety drew attention from the FBI, which in turn brought additional unwanted scrutiny to DQU as an institution. Many DQU personnel heartily supported Banks, but they became convinced by the late 1970s that the federal government was unfairly targeting the institution because of these connections, and because of the school's overall activist stance.[67]

While accusations of mismanagement and the ensuing negative press harmed D-Q University's reputation, the stubborn reality of low funding remained perhaps the most important obstacle to the school's overall development. Even as DQU received government grants, it lacked a permanent and secure base of general funding that could be used at the discretion of the university's directors.[68] Instead, DQU's various efforts depended on individual grants for finite projects, and faculty often taught courses on a volunteer basis.[69] These conditions contributed to uncertainty, which in turn prevented enrollment from growing at the ambitious rate that Jack Forbes had originally envisioned.[70] Hartmut Lutz, an instructor at DQU in the late 1970s, estimated the university's enrollment at approximately two hundred students per year—by no means an insignificant number but nowhere near Forbes's original vision of three thousand.[71] Given the reality of low funding and enrollment, DQU's accreditation was limited to the junior college level, which restricted the founders' ambitions for graduate and professional programs.[72] Despite this blow, Forbes and David Risling continued to draw up and discuss plans into at least 1974 in the hopes that one day DQU would develop a PhD track.[73] While the graduate program never materialized, the plans displayed the founders' commitment to their intellectual vision despite the enormous obstacles they faced.

At the end of the 1970s, Forbes was still unable to enact plans for four-year and graduate programs, but he nevertheless sought to reignite support for DQU's original intellectual vision.[74] In a piece titled "The Development of a Native Intelligentsia," he deftly articulated the mission that he believed DQU could still accomplish with adequate support. He wanted to "empower and strengthen the traditionalist intelligentsia" of Native communities, while training "younger people in such a way that they would be able to return to their communities and lead the intellectual and creative struggle for liberation."[75] In many ways, this goal echoed the mission statements at other TCUs throughout the country. Turtle Mountain Community College, for example, sought "to create an environment where the cultural and social heritage of the Indian people can be brought to bear through the curriculum," and in turn to "establish an administration, faculty, and student body involved in exerting leadership within the community."[76] Furthermore, DQU had joined the other TCUs in the American Indian Higher Education Consortium from its early days, and had sought funding under the Tribally Controlled Community College Assistance Act of 1978 (TCCCA Act).[77]

Forbes, however, did not emphasize his connections to contemporary TCUs or the long line of Native intellectual activism on which they built. He wrote his "Native Intelligentsia" piece

Embracing Pan-Indianism

in a time of dire financial straits at DQU—a time of frustration with the dearth of support and the abundance of harassment that he felt his school had suffered over the previous decade. The toll of his emotional investment appeared to impact the tone of his writing as he implored wearily, "Isn't it clear that we need to support an Indian-controlled university?"[78] While much of his frustration in this effort was directed at the federal bureaucracy, he implicated a swath of Native activists as well, painting the situation facing Native people as a clear choice between remaining "a servant of colonialism" or becoming "an avowed nationalist."[79]

In lashing out at the federal government and the Native people that he saw as unwilling to embrace his full commitment to self-determination, Forbes may have overlooked the nuanced work of not only the other TCUs but of past leaders such as Henry Roe Cloud, whose struggle outside the established channels of government funding and support at the American Indian Institute had shown so many similarities to his own work at DQU. Indeed, the American Indian Institute had been even freer of government funding and restrictions than Forbes's own effort had. Forbes also seemingly neglected the later efforts of people such as Elizabeth Bender Cloud and D'Arcy McNickle, who worked within the BIA when they viewed it as an empowering platform for Native people but rejected the bureau when they perceived it as a tool of termination. Forbes, prolific intellectual that he was, was perhaps so emotionally invested in his own effort to acquire support that he could not admit how it, too, constantly negotiated and inhabited the world of the colonizer and the world of the resister at the same time. In this mindset, it is understandable that he sought to portray his endeavor as particularly innovative, worthwhile, and indeed *necessary*—even if that meant overlooking the impact that others had made before him.

Hartmut Lutz, a visiting instructor at UC Davis and D-Q University in the late 1970s, became a valuable observer to this stage of Forbes's career. Lutz fully supported Forbes's philosophical stance on self-determination but more readily admitted the numerous compromises to that stance that became unavoidable at DQU. Lutz compiled a brief history of DQU during his time there, which provides a crucial perspective because of his position as both insider and outsider. He actively participated in and supported the school's mission but could also more easily step back and take a detached view of the role that the institution played in the grand scheme of Native activism in the 1970s.[80]

With this perspective, we can see that while D-Q University's early development never reached the lofty levels that Jack Forbes had projected, it nevertheless operated as an important site in the growing nationwide effort for Native American self-determination. It pursued many of the same goals as the other tribal colleges and universities but did so by "embracing Pan-Indianism" more explicitly than the reservation-based schools did, and by boosting grassroots education projects in numerous Native communities.[81] Additionally, DQU served as a lively hub of Indigenous cultural study and expression in much the same way that reservation-based TCUs did for particular tribes. When Dennis Banks was unable to return to the Dakotas for the Sun Dance in 1976, for instance, he helped construct the ceremonial grounds and organize the dance on the DQU campus instead.[82] And in 1978—a milestone year with the passing of the TCCCA Act—DQU remained dedicated to contemporary Native activism by helping to organize the Longest Walk. The walk saw Native protestors march across the continent from Alcatraz and DQU in the west to Washington DC in the east, "symbolically rever[sing] the process of destruction" during Euro-American settler colonialism.[83] In these and many other instances, D-Q University operated as a key center for the demonstration of a Native intellectual activism that was both philosophical and concrete, rooted in tradition and modern in its action.

The Reorientation of Haskell Institute

Jack Forbes and his colleagues may not have seen the full development they had hoped for at D-Q University, but they nevertheless sought to advance core principles that aligned with a long thread of Native intellectual activism stretching back to the early part of the twentieth century. DQU became an important complement to the reservation-based tribal college movement, representing as it did another Native hub in the ongoing development of a discourse on self-determination and Native leadership in higher education. That discourse found support in off-reservation settings, not only taking root at DQU but impacting the direction of the federal government's stance as well. The Bureau of Indian Affairs' transition toward a postsecondary academic model at Haskell Institute in the late 1960s and early 1970s can be seen as an illustration of that impact.

Like many BIA policy initiatives, the transition at Haskell was far from seamless and was in large part born out of the frustrations of a preceding strategy. Indeed, the bureau's plans for Haskell in the early 1960s showed quite a different approach. In those years, the BIA attempted to shape Haskell Institute not as a junior college with a broad academic mission but as a center of primarily vocational training for high school graduates. From 1960 to 1965, as Jack Forbes marshaled his argument for an intertribal university to train "experts on Indian history . . . anthropology, sociology, psychology, religion, and language," the BIA instead reorganized Haskell with an increasingly sharp focus on trade programs that included auto mechanics, plumbing, painting, and baking.[84]

While this reorganization phased out high school courses and allowed Haskell to operate as a postsecondary institution by 1965, the bare vocational focus was a stark contrast to the rhetoric of Forbes and other Native intellectual activists, and was palpable in Haskell's published materials. For instance, surveys on the progress of alumni focused almost exclusively on the occupations of former students, while even the school's mission statement and promotional bulletins in the mid-1960s praised "the assimilative value of the Haskell program" and the benefits of "off-reservation employment."[85] These materials—especially the updates on alumni career paths—were meant to show current and prospective students a vivid and personal image of the value of a Haskell education, and to provide encouraging displays of pride from graduates. But they were just as revealing in what they lacked. In page after page of alumni summaries, there never materialized an argument for Haskell as a supporter of broadly adaptable and particularly Native intellectual leadership.[86] In comparison with the deep discourse produced by Native educational reformers, Haskell's early 1960s publications appeared out of step—not only with contemporary activists like Forbes but with the efforts of the school's own former superintendent Henry Roe Cloud in the early 1930s.[87]

The sharp focus on vocational training and the broad endorsement of Haskell's "assimilative value" did little to counter arguments from Native activists like Jack Forbes and the early leaders of the National Indian Youth Council that the BIA was stubbornly paternalistic and narrow-minded.[88] Still, the BIA was never as monolithic as its critics might have argued. After all, individuals such as Henry and Elizabeth Cloud and D'Arcy McNickle had shown that at times, the power of the BIA could be harnessed and redirected in ways that aligned with the goals of Native activists.

In the late 1960s, BIA leadership under Commissioner Robert L. Bennett (Oneida) began to assist that redirection in the realm of education. Appointed by Lyndon Johnson in 1966, Bennett was just the second Native American selected as commissioner of Indian Affairs.[89] Though a long-time BIA employee, Bennett as commissioner immediately sought to reform and improve the bureau's relationship with Native communities, seeing the BIA's best role as that of a supporter for Native-led initiatives. He hoped to open up communication between Congress, the BIA, and individual reservations, and one of his particular areas of focus became Native representation in American higher education and law.[90] Though his brief tenure as commissioner ended with the incoming Nixon administration in 1969, Bennett remained dedicated to assisting Native intellectual activist efforts. He acted as founding director of the University of New Mexico Native American Law Center, assisted the Donner Foundation as a consultant, and encouraged the development of Haskell Institute as a junior college.

Though Bennett's departure necessarily impacted the tone of the bureau's leadership, the push toward a college model at Haskell continued—largely due to the efforts of a man named Wallace

Galluzzi. At first glance, Galluzzi seemed an unlikely force for shifting the BIA's mission at Haskell Institute to more closely resemble the goals of the tribal college movement. He was a non-Native man born and raised in an Italian-American family in western Pennsylvania.[91] When he joined Haskell's administration in the summer of 1963, he had spent his entire career—nearly fifteen years—in the bureau. His time in the BIA up to his arrival in Lawrence had largely overlapped with one of frustration for Native activists who saw the bureau as aligning too readily with goals of American Indian termination and rapid assimilation.[92] Finally, his first years at Haskell came in the midst of the school's overall push toward strengthening specific trade programs at the expense of nonvocational courses.

A closer look at his work, however, reveals that Galluzzi dedicated his career to expanding Native educational opportunities. After earning his education degree from Slippery Rock Teachers College in Pennsylvania, he had his first bureau experiences as a counselor and educator at the Standing Rock and Turtle Mountain reservations, and he eventually became responsible for overseeing higher education programs throughout the Dakotas.[93] Though he departed for Lawrence before the initiation of government funding that aided the early TCUs at Turtle Mountain, Pine Ridge, Rosebud, and Standing Rock, he took pride in expanding educational programs for students at those reservations, and was undoubtedly aware of the community-driven initiatives leading into the tribal college era.[94] And while his first years at Haskell came at a time of prioritizing vocational paths rather than a comprehensive academic mission, he showed that he was unwilling to continue pursuing that strategy if it proved ineffectual.

Galluzzi became principal of Haskell Institute in the summer of 1963, and during the first several years of his tenure the school completed its formal reorganization as a center of postsecondary vocational training. During that time, however, he monitored closely the shifting nature of Haskell's mission and the ways in which that shift impacted its student body.[95]

As principal, Galluzzi occupied the administrative position most intimately connected to the process of accepting and evaluating new students each school year. By the spring of 1968 he had seen enough of a shift among the student body to express serious concerns with the potentially negative impacts of Haskell's transition. "During the past five years," he wrote, "we have seen the caliber of student in regard to academic ability decrease rapidly each year."[96] He lamented the large number of college dropouts entering Haskell as a secondary option, and noted that Haskell did not appear to significantly ameliorate the dropout problem in its own right. Galluzzi's immediate plan called for restructuring the application process with more tangible prerequisites for prospective students, combined with greater collaboration between Haskell administrators, BIA officials in Washington, and contacts in reservation communities. Within months, these efforts would expand, as Galluzzi was promoted to superintendent of Haskell. From that point, he took on an instrumental role in reshaping the institute to not only address the issues he had tracked as principal but also to align with the more ambitious academic goals of the tribal college movement.[97]

As superintendent, Galluzzi immediately initiated an institutional self-study in the spring of 1969, which led to an evaluation later that year by outside educators to assess Haskell's strengths as well as areas requiring improvement and expansion.[98] The ensuing plan for transforming Haskell into a junior college developed rapidly and involved efforts to maintain vocational strength while significantly broadening the school's scope in terms of academic and community leadership. In Galluzzi's own words, he wanted to "elevate" Haskell's existing trade programs to turn out "professionals" rather than "journeymen," while also institutionalizing a more "comprehensive" academic offering.[99] Thus, while Haskell's administration expanded its auto mechanics and medical occupations programs, it also laid out the framework for associates of arts and associates of applied sciences degrees, with newly added divisions including humanities, social sciences, music, and art, as well as a distinct division for Native American studies.[100] With the expanded academic mission, the school became Haskell American Indian Junior College in the fall of 1970, and Galluzzi's position eventually shifted from superintendent to president.[101]

Galluzzi's effort to shape Haskell into a more ambitious academic institution built on his years-long work to expand Native opportunities in higher education, but it also overlapped with a symbolic shift in the federal government's stance on American Indian policy. In 1968 President Lyndon Johnson delivered to Congress a special message called "The Forgotten American," in which he criticized the policy of American Indian termination. Instead, Johnson endorsed a shift toward "maximum choice for the American Indian," in the form of programs that supported a philosophy of self-determination.[102] Though much of Republican Richard Nixon's political agenda differed from that of his Democratic predecessor, he took a similar stance on the topic of self-determination. In the summer of 1970, just before Haskell would officially begin its new life as a junior college, President Nixon echoed Johnson's "Forgotten American" speech and put his own voice behind the movement toward self-determination.[103] Members of Congress also supported this rhetorical push for a new era in American Indian policy, and that support only buttressed Haskell's new initiative.[104]

As at the other early tribal colleges and universities, the accreditation process at Haskell forced the administration to demonstrate a detailed understanding of how it could successfully enact its new academic programs. The process was an opportunity for the school's leaders to clearly articulate their ambitious vision in a way that mirrored the process at other TCUs. By 1971 that vision was taking form in Haskell's stated goals and objectives, which discarded the previous emphasis on the school's "assimilative value" and instead preached "knowledge and skills concerning Indian culture" and Native "communities and families."[105]

Galluzzi's emphasis in forming the broad new mission at Haskell only became clearer over time. As part of his overseeing the accreditation effort, Galluzzi in 1973 wrote a piece on Haskell's future that, while only two pages in length, read like a manifesto for increased Native access to and control of higher education, with Haskell as a centerpiece.[106] In the opening sentence, he clearly expressed his desire that Haskell should serve not the goals of assimilation as conceived by American government officials but the goals of Native people—"the reservation Indian; the urban Indian . . . the identity-seeking Indian; the contemporary Indian; the traditional Indian . . . the non-English speaking Indian; the English speaking Indian."[107]

In the concise but powerful paragraphs that followed, Galluzzi outlined as tangibly as possible his plans to push Haskell to "identify more closely with Indian communities" through more than mere rhetoric.[108] He recognized the ever-changing needs of not only Native students but Native communities and tribal governments in the modern world, and pledged to address those needs through a comprehensive program aimed at broad intellectual leadership. In that vein, Galluzzi proposed that Haskell initiate educational extension programs to tribal governments and their enterprises. As a concrete example of this attempt at outreach, Haskell began offering courses for college credit at nearly two dozen reservations.[109] In vocational pursuits, Galluzzi repeated his assertion that the school should work to move beyond "journeyman" trades and strive for "management and executive" levels of training.[110] On the academic program, he noted the importance of core courses in education, social work, and law but argued that "Haskell also has the responsibility for becoming . . . an authority in Indian culture. Its expertise should encompass the development of Indian leadership [and] tribal structures in the area of government, justice, and management."[111]

By framing the projections for Haskell's future as a "responsibility," Galluzzi provided an important acknowledgment of the federal government's position as one of *obligation*. In other words, Haskell was obligated to pursue the many and varied educational needs of Native students in modern America, and in Galluzzi's mind this pursuit was possible only through true collaboration with Native American people themselves. A true acceptance and endorsement of this position was a key component in working toward a philosophy of self-determination. Galluzzi made his position even clearer in his suggestion that Haskell's future should include, essentially, diminishing his own role as a non-Native administrator, and "changing the control of the college from the

Bureau of Indian Affairs to an Indian government body such as the Haskell Board of Regents."[112]

In the institutional study that followed this brief statement, Galluzzi's voice remained a strong presence. In language that called to mind Henry Roe Cloud, D'Arcy McNickle, and the founders of the reservation-based TCUS, Haskell's mission was characterized as the pursuit of a "comprehensive learning process" that could "adapt to meet the needs of the Indian community."[113] As he oversaw the transition at Haskell, Galluzzi thus pushed the school sharply away from a narrow-minded assimilative mission. Instead, he positioned the new Haskell Indian Junior College to carry out a broad mission of academics and service that aligned with the tribal college movement as well as an even deeper vein of Native intellectual activism in higher education.

The ambitious goals laid out by Galluzzi and his staff in the early 1970s quickly found a general sense of support among the Haskell faculty and students.[114] In practice, however, the transition was difficult for many who disagreed on exactly how it should take place. Among faculty and staff, an effective transition required collaboration between those who had spent years pursuing the old vocational model and those who had recently joined and were thus dedicated to the new junior college mission.

Even among students, stark differences of philosophy regarding Native American education and activism became apparent. In the early 1970s, surveys of Haskell graduates showed that many were deeply concerned about the transition. Multiple recent graduates worried that students in the new program were gaining an undue sense of power and entitlement, while one alumnus expressed "displeasure with the 'red power' infiltrating Haskell."[115] These responses indicated that even in an institution like Haskell—with all the bureaucratic support upholding it—the process of changing the landscape in Native American higher education rarely found universal acceptance.

More important than the school-specific issues they addressed, however, these responses showed that Haskell was in many ways dealing with issues relevant at any tribal college. Indeed, if "the red power" were truly gaining a foothold among Haskellites, it represented yet another example of how Haskell's transition toward a junior college model helped bring it into the same discourse on Native activism that impacted the other TCUs and institutions across the country. And though this vision for an intertribal educational and cultural center was largely shaped by a non-Native official at a BIA institution, the fundamental objectives in fact aligned quite closely with another, more explicitly activist intertribal effort—that of Jack Forbes at D-Q University.[116] Perhaps Haskell's students shared more in common with the students at DQU than would have been apparent at first glance.

As Henry Roe Cloud had envisioned in his brief and frustrating tenure in the 1930s, Haskell in the 1970s began pursuing an educational model that represented more than a government-run vocational training center for Native Americans. Though still a bureau-controlled entity, Haskell was laying the groundwork for a broader educational mission that would allow students the freedom to pursue a wide variety of intellectual and professional goals while expressing in myriad ways what it meant to be a Native student in modern America.

For their part, Haskell's students seemed to embrace this vision and make it their own. Throughout the 1970s, Haskell remained as diverse as ever, consistently pulling in students from more than eighty tribes and more than thirty states.[117] Student publications like the annual yearbook placed a firm emphasis on Native identity in its many sources and forms—"always adaptive, always resourceful . . . able to meet the challenges of a new time."[118] "The Haskell graduate," one article asserted, "is well-prepared to assume, intellectually and emotionally, a responsible and rewarding role in a traditional or modern society."[119] More than simply choosing one path or another, however, the writer portrayed contemporary Native students as able to learn and live "in one world [layered by] many cultures."[120]

Outside observers agreed that this assessment of Haskell's role as an important contributor to the modern landscape of Native education was more than flowery rhetoric. During the final stages of the accreditation process in the late 1970s, evaluators from the North Central Association of Secondary Schools and Colleges (NCA) praised Haskell faculty and staff for their preparation and ability to promote positive academic development among students. The NCA also singled out the Native American studies program as a vital piece of the overall institutional mission, noting that it had "the potential to help the college increase its national reputation for uniqueness and excellence."[121]

As the process of accreditation drew to a close in 1978 and 1979, students demonstrated their commitment to Native intellectual development at Haskell much as they did in other TCUs. For example, just as Sinte Gleska College in South Dakota had celebrated its graduates with the Lakota *wacipi* in early 1978, students in Lawrence closed the spring semester of that same year by taking part in the annual Haskell Pow Wow.[122] Haskell paired celebrations with a conference titled "The Right to Be Indian," a two-day meeting that balanced cultural demonstrations with a day-long discussion on the government policies impacting Native American self-determination.[123] The meeting brought in experts in law and education, including Sam Deloria (Dakota), director of the University of New Mexico Native American Law Center; and Ruth Roessel, a founder of the Rough Rock Demonstration School and of Navajo studies at Navajo Community College.[124] This intertribal event and others like it—addressing vital issues of education and politics that faced Native people on a national scale—represented much of what leaders from Cloud to Forbes had pursued for decades. The conference also provided another concrete example of how Haskell participated as a legitimate Native hub in the development of intellectual activism and the expanding tribal college movement.

The Multiple Realities of the Tribal College Movement

A new reality began setting in at Haskell in the 1970s. The school's students had always taken pride in their training, but now they also pursued broader academic missions in higher education. The new scope helped students envision themselves as leaders exhibiting Native identities in a collective as well as an individual sense, which made the school a key contributor to the tribal college movement and in turn to a long line of Native intellectual activism. In many ways, it was a transformation like the one Henry Roe Cloud had sought to bring about at Haskell four decades earlier. Even contemporary antagonists of the BIA like Jack Forbes would almost certainly have admitted that Haskell's students in the 1970s were gaining real opportunities "to think, to pioneer, to plan, to propose, to explore, [and] to create new visions" as "members of the Native intelligentsia."[125]

Despite this reality, the framework laid out by an unyielding proponent of decolonization like Forbes—a framework that labeled the bureau an instrument of colonialism—was also grounded in its own reality. The problem for Forbes did not concern the experience of a single student or even an entire cohort at Haskell but rather the basic structure behind the school. It lay in the fact that, as had so often happened before, a change in emphasis within the BIA or the federal government at higher levels could reshape or even shut down the entire project. After all, the transition at Haskell that brought the school into the tribal college movement had taken place just a few years after an entirely different initiative that focused on assimilative vocational training.

Forbes was not the only voice warning of the possible damages of this fundamental dependence on the bureau structure. At the Right to Be Indian Conference on Haskell's campus in 1978, for example, Sam Deloria spoke of a perception among Native people that federal programs and funding seemed to run dry as soon as Native communities were no longer perceived as "poor, sick, and dumb."[126] Deloria thus gave voice to the feeling that while the government ostensibly acknowledged its responsibility to Native Americans, in reality it failed to reward innovation among Native people or to sustain true collaboration with the most successful Native initiatives. Haskell had benefited from the active leadership of a capable and committed individual in Wallace Galluzzi, but there was no guarantee that his vision would prevail when his time had ended. Even Galluzzi himself had sought

Embracing Pan-Indianism

to address this issue, suggesting as early as 1973 that Haskell be placed beyond the direct control of the bureau and in particular seek a deeper and more diverse range of funding possibilities.[127] Two years later, Haskell's funding continued to come entirely from the BIA, as efforts to garner additional grants under the Higher Education Act of 1965 and the Vocational Education Act of 1963 were denied.[128] The school's status as a federal institution guaranteed it the BIA funding but also prohibited it from obtaining monies from a host of alternative sources.[129] In the 1979 accreditation evaluation by the NCA, the lack of deep and secure financial support remained a concern that was identified not only by Haskell administrators and supporters but by the outside evaluators as well.[130] Unfortunately, while some legislation in recent years has ostensibly opened up opportunities for Haskell to access more Department of Education funding, the basic reality of this structure has remained essentially unchanged to the present day.[131]

This was the frustrating reality that Forbes saw when he viewed the Bureau of Indian Affairs as an antagonist in his pursuit of decolonization and self-determination. Though he could not have predicted in the late 1970s what the next several decades would hold for DQU and Haskell, his skepticism regarding bureau control in efforts at Native self-determination was perceptive.

Still, it is important to acknowledge the optimism of the moment and the intertwined goals that made that optimism possible. After all, many Haskellites saw themselves—in their coursework as well as in events like the Right to Be Indian Conference—as an important part of the development of leadership impacting not just their particular school but all of Indian country. And for all their differences in background and affiliation, leaders at DQU and Haskell in the 1970s ironically shared much in how they perceived and pursued comprehensive higher education for Native people. In both cases, they acknowledged the benefit of bringing together individuals who expressed myriad forms of Native identity, and saw a need to link Native intellectual leadership on a national scale to local reservation leadership. At institutions that at times appeared drastically different, students and faculty constructed programs that accomplished these similar goals. Because of this activism, these individuals and the institutions they influenced represented important complements to the reservation-based tribal college movement, and have been key contributors to a decades-long thread of Native intellectual activism.

Conclusion

Ideas Have a Way of Living

H istorian Daniel Cobb has described Native activist efforts in postwar America as a layered composition, "a series of over- lapping parts that were at once distinct and interrelated."[1] Cobb's description also fits well the longer history outlined in these pages—the effort for greater Native access to and control of higher education and, in turn, for greater intellectual leader- ship and empowerment in modern American systems of politics and economics. Like the many twisting wires that form a steel cable, Native leaders and their non-Native advocates from Henry Roe Cloud onward added their own particular voices and tangi- ble contributions to this growing project, but their efforts were often intertwined. While displaying the unique contributions of Cloud and other key individuals, this history also shows how each in some way remained connected to a core activist effort that involved entire communities of people.

Over the course of his two decades directing the American Indian Institute and Haskell Institute, Henry Roe Cloud con- structed and sought to embody a complete vision of Native intel- lectual activism. He worked from a basic understanding that Native leadership must be at once culturally rooted and adaptable to modern challenges. In this way, he moved beyond the simplis- tic efforts at assimilation that dominated American Indian policy throughout much of his lifetime.[2] His educational and adminis- trative efforts instead explicitly placed value on adaptation, work- ing to both preserve and actively rely on Indigenous histories, languages, cultural practices, and identities.[3] For his own part, Cloud maintained his Native language and connections to his reservation community while achieving the highest levels of training in the mainstream American education system. He sought to establish a similar path for his students, expanding Native access to and preparedness for higher education. At the same time, he demonstrated how Native control could transform that educational effort to more directly address the specific challenges facing Indigenous people.

In Cloud's absences from the American Indian Institute, his wife Elizabeth Bender Cloud often stepped in and acted as the head administrator for extended periods.[4] After Henry's death in 1950, her capability as a Native intellectual leader revealed itself even more clearly. She spoke against federal termination policy and straightforward assimilation, attempting instead to redirect the energies of interested white Americans toward the persistence of Indigenous identities through programs that placed funds and creative control in the hands of Native community leaders.[5] In particular, she continued to push for a greater public dedication to increasing Native access to higher education and professional training.[6] In these ways, Elizabeth carried forward much of the educational vision that she and Henry had built early in the twentieth century. She also embodied that vision's emphasis on adaptability, strategically forming her rhetoric to face the new challenges of the postwar era, and even advancing an early argument for Native American self-determination in spite of the apparent pressures of termination.[7]

Elizabeth Bender Cloud's work also overlapped directly with that of D'Arcy McNickle, through the organization and implementation of American Indian Development (AID) in the early 1950s. McNickle had already become an influential figure in the Bureau of Indian Affairs (BIA), and AID's mission to develop community-led programs among Native people was in some ways a result of his frustration with the bureau during the Congressional push toward termination.[8] McNickle showed his willingness to work within the power structure of the BIA when possible but to abandon it when it ceased to serve his mission as a Native activist. Like the Clouds, McNickle had long understood Native leadership as most effective and impactful in modern America when it incorporated diverse sources of knowledge and power—tribal and pan-Indian, Native and non-Native.[9] By the late 1950s and early 1960s, McNickle began to infuse this fundamental understanding of Indigenous leadership into an effort to reshape the relationship between Native students and the American system of higher education. Through the Workshop on American Indian Affairs in Boulder, McNickle joined others like Cherokee scholar Bob Thomas in challenging young Native students to utilize their college educations in ways that directly impacted their reservation communities and Native people nationally.[10]

The Boulder Workshop in turn fueled the foundation of the National Indian Youth Council (NIYC), which in the early 1960s dedicated itself to expanding a discourse on the need for change in systems of schooling for Native American students.[11] Throughout the 1960s, as this discourse grew, it involved researchers, teachers, students, and tribal leaders in ways that highlighted particular community issues as well as systemic problems in American Indian education. Over time, the conversation increasingly focused on the argument for Native control in schooling as a necessary measure in addressing some of the factors that prevented Native students from reaching and excelling in higher education.

One of the pivotal voices in this 1960s discourse came from Jack Forbes. Forbes personified the hub of a growing discourse that became at once local and national. He corresponded directly with the directors of the Boulder Workshop, the founders of the NIYC, and the leaders in tribally controlled education projects like the Rough Rock Demonstration School and Navajo Community College.[12] He also put immense effort into forming the discipline of Native American studies within mainstream colleges while still developing his own proposal for an intertribal university. In that project, he hoped to link Native intellectual activism with community-led grassroots projects. Forbes did eventually achieve his goal of founding a unique center of Indigenous higher education, but his project also appeared in conjunction with a larger tribal college movement that impacted students both on and off reservations. Forbes, like the others, made his own distinct impact, but he did it in ways that complemented and added layers to the decades-long work of a diverse body of Native activists.

These stories did not take shape in a vacuum. Throughout the telling of this history, one of my central goals has been to display Native activists in their own words, and to reveal how vibrant their discourse was. In so doing, I have privileged a particular chorus of leading voices, but it is important to recognize that these individuals were also supported and joined by countless others who worked in tribal councils, reservation schools, and off-reservation organizations.[13] Furthermore, in addition to the web of discourse they created throughout Indian country, these Native voices were also intimately bound to the broader realm of changing forces in America. At each stage, the leaders examined here were forced to grapple with powerful trends in the dominant discourses shaping modern American cultural and political life.

Henry Roe Cloud presents a clear example. He emerged from a boarding school system that quite explicitly sought to erase forms of Native identity on an intimate level, only to preserve his Native language and pursue an effort to cultivate Native intellectual leadership on both community-wide and national scales. His American Indian Institute arose as a center of this leadership, supporting demonstrations of Native identity in a time when ideas of "100 percent Americanism" gained strength in the public discourse. At Haskell Institute, he brought a similar vision but was constricted by policy changes in the face of the Great Depression.

Other Native leaders interacted with the trajectory of American history in similar ways. Elizabeth Bender Cloud and D'Arcy McNickle attempted to utilize the promise of the New Deal in John Collier's BIA but eventually faced a powerful Congressional push for American Indian termination that in many ways reflected a larger shift toward cultural assimilation after World War II. In the 1960s and 1970s, ideas of multiculturalism, self-actualization, and self-determination gained renewed strength, allowing McNickle, Jack Forbes, Ruth Roessel, and others to take advantage of opportunities for Native leadership, especially in higher education. In every phase, these leaders sought to bend and shape the esteemed elements of American cultural and political life to serve their cause of greater Native access to and control of higher education and leadership training.

Viewing the intimate connections between this Native history and the larger trajectory of American history helps us better understand the actions and reactions of Native people in particular eras. Doing so in a long-term framework can also provide a more nuanced understanding of some understudied aspects of Native activism. Specifically, this story helps reveal not only how Native intellectual activism survived the strongest pushes toward American Indian termination but also how certain core themes of that activism were carried through with remarkable continuity. This story helps deemphasize the idea of a "pendulum" of federal policy alternating between support for and attacks on Native Americans' tribal identities and trust status. Instead, this work focuses on the Native individuals and their advocates who maintained networks of personal and philosophical connections while continually adapting their activist efforts to the unique challenges and opportunities of each era.

From the 1970s onward, there has been an explosion of tribal colleges and universities throughout the country, and they have displayed a remarkable degree of continuity with the goals and philosophies of the early movement toward tribal control in education.[14] One example of this continuity is revealed in the mission statements and curricular goals in publications by TCUs over the past several decades. At Bay Mills Community College in Michigan, for instance, the mission has been "to integrate traditional Native American values with . . . general education as a way of preparing students to assume responsible roles in their respective communities."[15] More evidence of this sentiment comes from Sisseton Wahpeton Community College in South Dakota, chartered in 1979 and accredited in 1990. The college's "guiding philosophy" has included the goal that students "participate with competence in both the Indian and the non-Indian worlds, and to appreciate the merits of both."[16]

Today, scholars of Native American higher education continue to emphasize the importance of these themes. For example, Gregory Cajete (Santa Clara Pueblo), Stephen Sachs, and Phyllis Gagnier (Algonquin) have argued that the most pressing issue in Native American education remains the need to create a "contemporized, community-based education process that is founded on traditional tribal values, orientations, and principles but that simultaneously utilizes the most appropriate concepts and technologies of modern education."[17] These statements—from several distinct voices in distinct contexts—all align with the original guiding vision of the tribal college movement. That vision begins with the basic philosophy of self-determination in schooling and seeks to aid Native communities by balancing the protection of Native culture and identity with educational and professional training adaptable to the realities of modern America.

In addition to their continued dedication to these principles, tribal colleges and universities have also demonstrated a significant and tangible impact on the cultural and socioeconomic health of their communities. While the presentation of hard data in this vein has been sporadic and incomplete, it has been encouraging. The limited research displays both qualitatively and quantitatively the benefits TCUs have made and continue to create for Native people.

One of the most important qualitative results of TCUs is that they "have turned the balance of power" in favor of Native administrators, educators, and their communities.[18] With greater control in tribal colleges and universities, Native leaders can "create educational curricula that simultaneously allow them to build their community infrastructures and to promote participation in the larger . . . society of the United States."[19] Depending on factors such as natural resources, geopolitical position vis-à-vis American industries, and a host of other variables, TCUs can use tribal control to bridge the gaps for their students in specific, directed ways. For example, Little Big Horn College in Montana recently collaborated with the Australian-American Energy Company to offer programs in which students earn certificates or associate degrees while simultaneously gaining skilled training toward energy industry jobs paying six-figure salaries.[20] Many TCUs also partner with nonreservation colleges and universities, combining to develop shared programs that can ameliorate tuition and fee barriers while collaborating on cultural interests like Indigenous studies and Native language preservation projects.[21] One recent exemplar of these partnerships is the Navajo Oral History Project, a collaboration between Diné College and Winona State University that created dozens of filmed and transcribed interviews of Navajo elders' oral histories.[22] These projects indicate possibilities for true collaboration with non-Native entities rather than a dependence solely on the basic labor demands of outside economic forces. These efforts also align with the adaptable goals of self-determination as defined by Comanche writer and activist LaDonna Harris, who emphasizes "living well in [Native] communities while partnering with neighbors, the nation, and the world for mutual advancement."[23]

Large-scale quantitative data has also recently supported the work that TCUs perform. A 2019 report compiled by Gallup and the American Indian College Fund (AICF) represents the largest survey of its kind on the relationship between TCUs, their alumni, their reservation communities, and the modern American educational and economic landscape at large. Compiling responses from nearly five hundred Native graduates and thousands of non-Native alumni nationwide, the report arrived at several overlapping conclusions that definitively support the missions of TCUs. First, they found that tribal college alumni are much more likely to report that their school prepared them for life outside college than did college graduates nationally or Native American graduates at other schools.[24] Relatedly, TCU alumni were more likely to report both engagement with and interest in their postgraduation jobs. And, just as in Native educational hubs from the American Indian Institute onward, Native American students coming out of TCUs are engaged in and pursue careers in a variety of fields, in direct contradiction to the generations-long trope that Indigenous students are best funneled into specific and limited types of labor.

The survey explored five areas of self-reported well-being: physical, community, financial, social, and career. The only category where TCU alumni did not equal or surpass all college graduates and Native college graduates nationally was in physical well-being.[25] By contrast, however, TCU alumni self-report substantially higher than their national peers in terms of community, social, and career well-being. These results are undoubtedly related to the above-mentioned feelings of engagement and interest in the work that these alumni do, but it is also encouraging to see that these results also stretch beyond the workplace to factors of "supportive relationships and love in your life" as well as "feeling safe and having pride in your community."[26] The most powerful and compelling explanations for these positive results can sometimes be summed up in the simplest language: "TCU graduates (59%) are almost twice as likely as American Indian graduates nationally (33%) to strongly agree that their professors/instructors *cared about them as a person*."[27]

Given this striking gap in how Native students feel treated and supported in different types of institutions, it seems obvious that TCUs should be strengthened to an extent that would allow them to expand their roles—that they are afforded opportunities to increase the breadth and depth of their academic offerings while maintaining the support structures that are both innovative and rooted in foundations of Indigenous and tribal culture.[28] And yet, while these recent results signal the positive impacts that tribal colleges and universities have made for Native people, critics can still point to the persistent struggles that many reservations experience with poverty, high unemployment, and low graduation rates, and they can note that even communities with TCUs do not quickly or easily escape these same problems. Certainly, more than fifty years after the birth of the tribal college era, mountains of work remain to be undertaken for these institutions. As the AICF acknowledges, Native students today continue to earn college degrees at rates well below other demographic groups.[29] But definitive research findings in fact only strengthen the argument for supporting what TCUs have done since their early days, what they currently do in maintaining their original missions, and what kind of expanded role they could play in the future.

Fundamental Questions for the Present and Future of Native-Driven Higher Education

The work done by Gallup and AICF is important for bringing greater clarity to and advancing a conversation around some fundamental questions. First, do tribal colleges achieve their goals of bolstering the well-being of Native communities, rooting higher learning in relevant cultural ideas and practices, and bridging the gap between reservation populations and the modern American landscape of higher education and professional development in meaningful ways? Unequivocally, as the data from two decades' worth of graduates shows, the answer is yes.

Second, are TCUs contributing to the development of a national intellectual and professional leadership that the Clouds, McNickle, Forbes, and others sought to cultivate over the past century? I have argued that in their philosophical underpinnings and in the seeds of positive results that they bring about, the answer is again yes. This question, though, is more difficult to answer confidently in the affirmative.

In a strict sense, any institution that advances higher learning and is both culturally rooted in Indigenous and tribal identities and adaptable to modern American structures of educational, economic, and political power is one that clearly advances the work of Henry Roe Cloud and the others. But it would also be correct to point out that Cloud, a Yale graduate himself, hoped to cultivate an elite level of intellectual and professional leadership at the American Indian Institute, and at Haskell in his brief time there. The financial difficulties of TCUs, along with the fact that many remain focused on two-year programs and vocational training, have meant that the tribal colleges in most cases remain community colleges in the true sense of the term rather than recognizable hubs of national leadership development. Indigenous students and faculty who seek to work in master's or PhD programs, law schools, or elite undergraduate programs generally find their way to mainstream American institutions. This reality is not a problem in and of itself. A problem occurs, however, when a TCU has the vision and the ambition to push for expanded degree offerings, extracurricular resources, outreach programs, and deeper and higher-profile faculty bodies but is prevented from doing so because of a fundamental and perpetual lack of basic funding. Even worse is when a school languishes in terms of its already existing facilities and programs, struggling just to survive.

Detractors of the tribal college movement seek to quickly brush aside this reality by picking out statistics that show what tribal colleges receive from the government in terms of per-degree or per-student dollars.[30] Tribal colleges deal with a legacy of barriers to the "traditional" academic track, meaning the time to completion is generally longer and the graduation rates tend to be lower than at a mainstream public or private university. As a result, the per-degree funding statistic can be intentionally selected to make a dubious argument that in comparison with more established schools, tribal colleges "spend lavishly," as former Montana state representative Tom Burnett put it.[31] Per-student funding statistics can also be misleading. From generations of settler colonialism and the ensuing relocations and restrictions, tribal reservations are often grossly disadvantaged economically, and their student bodies are in general less able to pay high tuition. Tribal colleges pull in some funds from their own tribal economic efforts, a patchwork of scholarships and grants, and meager tuition and fees revenues, but they rely for the bulk of their funding on the federal government.[32] Thus, while per-student dollars from the government might reach $9,200 at Diné College, for example, that number represents by necessity a much higher percentage of the operating budget than at a more established public university.[33] Because of these factors, a school's yearly operating budget—viewed in relation to its student body—provides a clearer overall snapshot of what is actually required to maintain creative and impactful institutions that can feed the ambition of students and faculty.

As an example, consider Wichita State University (WSU), a modest public university whose campus buildings and fraternity houses today literally border the very same plots of land where Henry Roe Cloud established the American Indian Institute over a century ago. When WSU went by the name of Fairmount College in the early 1900s, faculty there even collaborated with the AII. Wichita State currently works with an annual operating budget of approximately $398 million.[34] With a student population of around sixteen thousand, the university spends nearly $25,000 per student, per year, in overall costs.[35] At the nation's most prestigious public schools, the figure annually soars beyond this number by tens of thousands of dollars per student. Even on the Navajo reservation, with the longest-running TCU, Diné College can achieve an annual operating budget of roughly $20,000 to $22,000 per student, which still falls short of the resources of a mainstream public university like WSU.[36] The situation at other reservations can be much more bleak, especially as these institutions often seek revolutionary change in their communities regarding their relationship to institutions of higher education.

Part of the problem is that existing legislation is often not utilized to its fullest extent by the federal government, a frustrating continuity with the earliest days of the tribal college movement. As recently as 2011, the U.S. government issued only 66 percent of the allowable per-student funds to TCUs under the Tribally Controlled Community College Assistance Act and "no funding for the non-Indian students that compose about 20 percent of all TCU students."[37] Finally, "state and local governments have no obligation to allocate funding to tribally chartered institutions," again underscoring the fact that any tightening of the federal allocations is sorely felt by these schools.[38]

Even at off-reservation Haskell, an institution that garners a unique role within the Bureau of Indian Education (BIE) and could ostensibly act as *the* national hub of Indigenous intellectual development in higher education, the relationship with the federal government and its potentially vast resources is disheartening. Because of Haskell's unique place and mission, it ambitiously pledges to provide higher education tuition-free to Native enrollees. The United States government, in the form of the BIE, openly espouses its alignment with Haskell's mission, explicitly acknowledging "a trust and treaty responsibility to provide eligible Indian students with a quality education that reflects the unique cultural, geographic, and socio-economic circumstances of Indian Country."[39] Moreover, the BIE pledges to financially support "innovative services, and a commitment to academic excellence."[40] But the funds fall short of that rhetoric. Haskell, which by its nature does not raise revenue through tuition, receives just around $14,600 per student, and in fact saw a *decrease* in funding from 2019 to 2020. Haskell was forced to cut its storied football program in 2015. In 2017 track and field was cut. These moves were made strictly to save money by any means necessary, as the school seeks to keep pace with necessary improvements in facilities and technology. But they put a needless damper on the morale of students and employees, coming at a time when Haskell should have been celebrating its record numbers of college degrees awarded in 2016 and again in 2017.[41] The disconnect between the mission that Haskell undertakes, the supportive rhetoric of the BIE, and the bottom-line resources funneled to the school is striking. Unfortunately, it calls to mind the words of Sam Deloria, speaking at the Right to Be Indian Conference on the Haskell campus over forty years ago. Deloria suggested there was a feeling among Native people that federal programs and funding seemed to run dry just at the moment when Native communities were preparing to move past a perception of being "poor, sick, and dumb."[42]

If the BIE truly wishes to account for "the unique cultural, geographic, and socio-economic circumstances of Indian Country," they might begin by naming them more explicitly. They are the injustices that have historically been brought to Native communities by the machinery of settler colonialism. They are stolen lands, forced relocations, despoiled natural resources, and generations of identity-attacking educational institutions. When viewed in this honest language, perhaps the trust and treaty responsibility can take on greater gravity. The circumstances named here have left significant hurdles that obviously remain fundamental to discussions of resource allocations to cover instruction, counseling, health and wellness, extracurricular and community out-reach programs, the potential establishment and maintenance of university endowments, and so on. As the BIE acknowledges, it provides the primary funding for a school like Haskell in its effort to address the above circumstances and transcend them. If the fulfillment of this commitment is to be a priority, should Haskell be hamstrung by an operating budget that pales in comparison with public universities in its own state? Should TCUs on reser-vations be confined to thoughts of survival rather than working toward growth and innovation?

I hope this history can contribute not only to the historical scholarship on Native intellectualism and activism but also to con-temporary discussions of these ever-present questions in Ameri-ca's policy toward Native people. A key aspect of Native American history and Indigenous studies today is the effort to not only advance scholarship about Native people and their communi-ties but to serve those people and their communities. I hope my work will offer a useful—if modest—tool in that effort by reveal-ing the deep history of both continuity and innovation, from the work of Native intellectual activists like Henry Roe Cloud to the still-developing efforts in higher education and Native American self-determination more broadly. Part of the value of the sources employed in this history has been the ability to capture Native intellectual activists in those moments when the challenges became toughest. It must have been difficult, for instance, for Henry Roe Cloud to pen thank-you letters for five- and ten-dollar dona-tions when by the 1920s his American Indian Institute required $1,500 per month to operate.[43] Similarly, Jack Forbes's weariness and fatigue in the late 1970s seemed to leap from the page as he admonished, "Isn't it clear that we need to support an Indian-controlled university?"[44] These examples echo what Lucy Mad-dox has observed—that even the most eloquent and determined Native leaders have found it difficult to bend modern American discourses and political forces to their needs, and have suffered "difficulties and frustrations that, in hindsight, can seem unavoid-able and even predictable."[45]

The sources utilized in this history, though, have also captured Native intellectual activists in moments of unbridled optimism, and it is crucial to understand that the optimism was—and is—no less warranted than the frustration. I hope this history sheds light on that optimistic energy not simply for the sake of a feel-good story about the underdog. Rather, I hope it reveals how that energy in many distinct instances brought about real change for Native communities and individuals; how that energy can still serve many of its original goals even as it innovates; and how that energy, with greater investment and commitment from responsible parties, can still do much more to realize those goals in the future.

Sixty years ago, Ute student Joan Noble witnessed this energy and delivered an admonishment to her fellow founders of the National Indian Youth Council. As she observed the exciting activist spirit for leadership growing among her peers, she spoke of it with a quiet urgency, as if it were a small flame, and wrote simply, "Let us not let it die in our hands."[46]

FIG. 7. A mural at D-Q University displays pan-Indian themes, date unknown. Center for Southwest Research, University of New Mexico (Lee Marmon Pictorial Collection, PICT 2000-017, box 7, folder 9, item #6).

FIG. 8. A student of D-Q University works on a campus mural, date unknown. Photo courtesy of *Tribal College: Journal of American Indian Higher Education*.

NOTES

Introduction

1. Note on terms: I have tried to preserve the language and naming choices of my sources in their own time, so long as meaning remains clear. This will occasionally result in alternate spellings or the use of multiple names for one institution. For clarity and consistency, I use the names for the early TCUs and other institutions that are most relevant to and recognizable from the historical period and sources under study.

2. Ned Hatathli, "Navajo Studies at Navajo Community College," paper presented at EPDA Short Term Summer Institute, UCLA American Indian Culture Center, Many Farms, Arizona, 1971, https://files.eric.ed.gov/fulltext/ED082890.pdf.

3. Translation comes from Roessel Jr., "Right to Be Wrong," 2.

4. *Navajo Culture Center*; Aronilth, *Foundation of Navajo Culture*.

5. Adams, "Case Study," 26.

6. Higher Learning Commission, *Distinctive and Connected*; American Indian Higher Education Consortium, "About AIHEC," accessed May 1, 2016, aihec.org, http://www.aihec.org/who-we-are/index.htm. For examples of Native hubs, see Ramirez, *Native Hubs*; and Ramirez, *Standing Up*, 4–5, 18, 20.

7. Clark, "In Becoming"; House, "Historical Development."

8. Stein, *Tribally Controlled Colleges*.

9. Stein, *Tribally Controlled Colleges*, 1.

10. Brayboy, Fann, Castagno, and Solyom, *Postsecondary Education*.

11. Thelin, *History of American Higher Education*, 155–56.

12. Ramirez, *Standing Up*, 15. See also Bederman, *Manliness and Civilization*; Coulthard, *Red Skin, White Masks*; P. Deloria, *Playing Indian*; Fixico, *American Indian Mind*; and Raibmon, *Authentic Indians*. In terms of my specific historical topics, especially the reappropriation of American institutions and rhetorical platforms, I am also heavily influenced by Lomawaima, *They Called It Prairie Light*; Lomawaima and McCarty, *"To Remain an Indian"*; and Maddox, *Citizen Indians*.

13. Bhabha, *Location of Culture*; Ulick Peter Burke, Natalie Zemon Davis, and Patrick Joyce, "Cultural History," Making History, accessed March 1, 2017, http://www .history.ac.uk/makinghistory/themes/cultural_history.html.

14. Begay, Cornell, Jorgensen, and Kalt, "Development, Governance, Culture," 46.

15. Information on Henry Roe Cloud and the American Indian Institute is based on my own primary source research but also heavily reliant on the work of Renya Ramirez, anthropologist and granddaughter of Henry Roe Cloud. See especially Ramirez, *Standing Up*, for a comprehensive study of the Clouds.

16. Ramirez, *Standing Up*; Ramirez, "Ho-Chunk Warrior." See also Maddox, *Citizen Indians*.

17. For older examples of tribes appropriating Euro-American models of education, see Mihesuah, *Cultivating the Rosebuds*.

18. For an excellent brief outline of the impact of settler colonialism on the contexts and topics under study here, see Ramirez, *Standing Up*, 8–15.

19. Morgan, "Supplemental Report," 176–79. For broader assessments of the boarding school era see Adams, *Education for Extinction*; Lomawaima, *They Called It Prairie Light*; Child, *Boarding School Seasons*; Trafzer, Keller, and Sisquoc, *Boarding School Blues*; McDade, *Birth of the American Indian*.

20. For discussion of Native "cultural citizenship," see Ramirez, *Standing Up*.

21. Thelin, *History of American Higher Education*, 155–56.

22. See for example Haskell's newspaper, *Indian Leader*, May 24, 1935; Henry Roe Cloud to Dr. Will Carson Ryan Jr., August 7, 1934, box 135—Personal Correspondence, Haskell Series, NARA KC.

23. D'Arcy McNickle and Elizabeth Roe Cloud, "American Indian Development—A Project Sponsored by the National Congress of American Indians: First Annual Report," 1952, reel 54, Collier Papers, ASU, 3. See also Elizabeth Roe Cloud, "New Frontiers for the American Indian," 1952, box 68—Roe Cloud, Elizabeth, NCAI records, NMAI.

24. McNickle, "What Do the Old Men Say?"; McNickle, "Toward Understanding"; McNickle, "We Go On from Here"; McNickle, *They Came Here First*; McNickle and E. Cloud, "American Indian Development," Collier Papers.

25. McKenzie-Jones, "Evolving Voices of Dissent," 232.

26. Gerald T. Wilkinson to John Carlson, April 5, 1971, box 3, folder 35, records of NIYC. Wilkinson, as NIYC's executive director, relates that in the early years NIYC was "interested primarily in educational problems."

27. Jack D. Forbes, "A Proposal to Create an American Indian University," 1961, box 228—Native Higher Education and Colleges, Forbes Collection, UC Davis.

28. Rupert Costo to Dr. Jack D. Forbes, October 22, 1964, box 2—Jack Forbes: Correspondence, Forbes Collection, UC Davis.

29. Coulthard, *Red Skin, White Masks*; Warrior, "SAI and the End(s)," 222.

30. Jack D. Forbes, "American Tribal Higher Education," 1968, box 228—Native Higher Education and Colleges, Forbes Collection, UC Davis; Forbes, "Development of a Native American Intelligentsia," 75–88.

31. Cobb, *Native Activism*, 2.

32. Bederman, *Manliness and Civilization*, 10.

33. Bederman, *Manliness and Civilization*, 24.

34. Maddox, *Citizen Indians*.

35. Warrior, *Tribal Secrets*.

36. Ramirez, *Standing Up*.

37. In a broad sense, this line of thinking is also influenced by Fixico, for example *Indian Resilience and Rebuilding*.

38. See for example Crum, "Henry Roe Cloud"; Lomawaima, *They Called It Prairie Light*; McCarty, *Place to Be Navajo*; Pfister, *Yale Indian*; Ramirez, *Standing Up*; Stein, *Tribally Controlled Colleges*.

39. See for example V. Deloria and Wildcat, *Power and Place*; Jorgensen, *Rebuilding Native Nations*; Fletcher, *American Indian Education*; Harvard Project on American Indian Economic Development, *State of the Native Nations*.

40. "Henry Roe Cloud New Superintendent of Haskell Institute," *Indian Leader*, September 8, 1933, 6.

41. "Henry Roe Cloud New Superintendent," 6.

42. "Henry Roe Cloud New Superintendent," 6.

1. By and for Indians

1. Henry Roe Cloud to E. C. Sage, April 24, 1918, reel 2, records of AII. See also H. Cloud, "Education of the American Indian." For Cloud's commitment to expressions of Native identity among students, see the *Indian Outlook* (1923 onward) for the American Indian Institute, and the *Indian Leader* (1933–35) for Haskell Institute. In addition to Ramirez, *Standing Up*, works specifically focusing on Cloud include Crum, "Henry Roe Cloud"; Pfister, *Yale Indian*; and Tetzloff, "To Do Some Good."

2. Maddox, *Citizen Indians*; Allen and Piatote, "Society of American Indians."

3. Hertzberg, *Search for an American Indian Identity*, 204.

4. Collier quoted in "Haskell Needed for Future Work: Commissioner Collier Silences Rumors," *Indian Leader*, Fiftieth Anniversary Number, November 23, 1934.

5. Ramirez, *Standing Up*, 15. See also Bederman, *Manliness and Civilization*.

6. Martinez, *American Indian Intellectual Tradition*, 192.

7. For examples see H. Cloud, "Education of the American Indian"; "What Are the Aims of the American Indian Institute?" *Indian Outlook*, November 1, 1923, 4; and "Henry Roe Cloud New Superintendent of Haskell Institute," *Indian Leader*, September 8, 1933, 6.

8. Ramirez, *Standing Up*, 35, 107.

9. For examples see Henry Roe Cloud to W. S. Lank, October 26, 1923, reel 2, records of AII; "Ten Commandments of Success," *Indian Outlook*, November 1, 1923, 4; and Henry Roe Cloud, "Foreword," *Indian Leader*, September 7, 1934, 1, 6.

10. Ramirez, *Standing Up*, 4.

11. For U.S. examples see Adams, *Education for Extinction*; Child, *Boarding School Seasons*; DeJong, *Promises of the Past*; Hoxie, *Final Promise*; Lomawaima, *They Called It Prairie Light*; Lomawaima and McCarty, *"To Remain an Indian"*; and Trafzer, Keller, and Sisquoc, *Boarding School Blues*. For examples in other settler colonial nations see Jacobs, *White Mother*; Johnston, *Indian School Days*; and Miller, *Shingwauk's Vision*.

12. H. Cloud, "Education of the American Indian."

13. H. Cloud, "From Wigwam to Pulpit"; "Sunday Services," *Indian Leader*, February 9, 1934, 5. See also Ramirez, *Standing Up*.

14. H. Cloud, "From Wigwam to Pulpit," 338.

15. For a deeper discussion of the complicated relationship between the Roes and Henry Roe Cloud, as well as the use of "Cloud" versus "Roe Cloud," see Ramirez, *Standing Up*, for example 16–17, 112.

16. "Obituary: Walter C. Roe, of Oklahoma," *Missionary Review of the World* 36 (1913), 395.

17. Tetzloff, "To Do Some Good," 41.

18. Tetzloff, "To Do Some Good," 118.

19. Smithers, "Soul of Unity," 277.

20. For "Indigenous intellectual weapons," see Ramirez, "Ho-Chunk Warrior," 291. For "cultural citizenship," see Ramirez, *Standing Up*, 3, 215–16. See also Allen, "Introduction," 20.

21. Maddox, *Citizen Indians*, 16. See also Bederman, *Manliness and Civilization*.

22. H. Cloud, "Education of the American Indian."

23. Morgan, "Supplemental Report," 178.

24. Morgan, "Supplemental Report," 178.

25. For additional information on day-to-day experiences of boarding school students, as well as how the boarding school era fits into a larger story of American Indian assimilation campaigns, see Adams, *Education for Extinction*; Child, *Boarding School Seasons*; Hoxie, *Final Promise*; Lomawaima, *They Called It Prairie Light*; and Trafzer, Keller, and Sisquoc, *Boarding School Blues*.

26. Ramirez, *Standing Up*, 107.

27. H. Cloud, "Education of the American Indian," 208.

28. Morgan, "Supplemental Report," 177.

29. Warrior, "SAI and the End(s) of Intellectual History," 223–26.

30. H. Cloud, "Education of the American Indian," 206.

31. H. Cloud, "Education of the American Indian," 206.

32. Morgan, "Supplemental Report," 177; H. Cloud, "Education of the American Indian," 206.

33. H. Cloud, "Education of the American Indian," 207.

34. H. Cloud, "Education of the American Indian," 207.

35. H. Cloud, "Education of the American Indian," 207.

36. "Organization and Purpose," reel 2, records of AII.

37. Ramirez, *Standing Up*, 63–65; H. Cloud, "Education of the American Indian," 206.

38. Minutes of a meeting of the Indian Committee of the Home Missions Council, 1912, reel 2, records of AII.

39. "Proposed Constitution of the Roe Indian Institute," reel 2, records of AII.

40. See for example Ramirez, "Ho-Chunk Warrior."

41. H. Cloud, "Education of the American Indian," 205.

42. Thelin, *History of American Higher Education*, 145.

43. Thelin, *History of American Higher Education*, 145.

44. Henry Roe Cloud to E. C. Sage, April 24, 1918; Henry Roe Cloud to Mrs. J. F. Schermerhorn, March 7, 1923, reel 2, records of AII; "Organization and Purpose," AII.

45. Good and Teller, *History of American Education*, 237.

46. Henry Roe Cloud and H. W. Darling to Mrs. William T. Whitney, April 15, 1922, reel 2, records of AII.

47. Henry Roe Cloud to Mrs. A. E. Williams, March 7, 1931, reel 2, records of AII.

48. For further discussion of Cloud's "self-help" ideal, see also Ramirez, *Standing Up*.

49. "Organization and Purpose," AII; Henry Roe Cloud to Victor Gordon, August 9, 1917, reel 2, records of AII; "Estimate of Administrative and Maintenance Expense for the School Year, 1916–1917," reel 2, records of AII.

50. H. Cloud to Gordon, August 9, 1917.

51. H. Cloud to Gordon, August 9, 1917.

52. H. Cloud to Gordon, August 9, 1917.

53. "Organization and Purpose," AII.

54. "Organization and Purpose," AII.

55. Henry Roe Cloud, "The Need," *Indian Outlook*, February 10, 1924, 3; Henry Roe Cloud, "Peyote," *Indian Outlook*, March 1924, 2. For more on the context surrounding the use of peyote and debates among members of the Society of American Indians, see Maroukis, "Peyote Controversy."

56. Maroukis, "Peyote Controversy."

57. Maroukis, "Peyote Controversy," 177.

58. H. Cloud, "Need," 3; H. Cloud, "Peyote," 2.

59. Ramirez, *Standing Up*, 35.

60. Mrs. S. Thornton Hollinshead, "The American Indian, Life, Morals, Characteristics, Art and Traditions, Why We Should Conserve and Preserve Them," *Indian Outlook*, February 10, 1924, 6.

61. Henry Roe Cloud to Mrs. J. F. Schermerhorn, March 7, 1923, reel 2, records of AII. See also Ramirez, *Standing Up*.

62. "Indians Played Alto Flutes Long before Inventions by Whites," *Indian Outlook*, September–October 1924, 6; "Indians Give Corn to the Western Hemisphere," *Indian Outlook*, January 1925, 4; Rev. Richard H. Harper, "Some Indian Leaders, Past and Present," *Indian Outlook*, October–November 1925, 1, 3.

63. Smith, *Everything You Know*, 2–5, 166.

64. Smith, *Everything You Know*, 166.

65. Smith, *Everything You Know*, 166.

66. "Editor's Column," *Indian Outlook*, October–November 1925, 2–3.

67. "Editor's Column," 2. See also H. Cloud, "Foreword," 1, 6.

68. *Indian Outlook*, October–November 1925; *Indian Outlook*, December 1925; Mary A. Steer to Henry Roe Cloud, March 20, 1928, reel 1, records of AII.

69. Mary W. Roe, "The Daughters of the American Revolution in Indian Education," *Indian Outlook*, February 10, 1924, 4.

70. Henry Roe Cloud to Mary S. E. Baker, April 17, 1923, reel 2, records of AII.

71. Henry Roe Cloud to E. E. Olcott, January 10, 1923, reel 1, records of AII.

72. "Estimate of Administration and Maintenance Expense for the School Year, 1916–1917," reel 2, records of AII; E. E. Olcott to Henry Roe Cloud, July 29, 1924, reel 1, records of AII.

73. H. Cloud to Schermerhorn, March 7, 1923; H. Cloud to Mrs. J. F. Larkin, December 8, 1927, reel 2, records of AII; Office Secretary to Mrs. O. R. Dunlap, May 11, 1931, reel 2, records of AII.

74. Henry Roe Cloud to E. E. Olcott, October 24, 1927, reel 1, records of AII; Henry Roe Cloud to William Hill, October 24, 1927, reel 1, records of AII; Henry Roe Cloud to Mrs. Walter C. Roe, November 5, 1927, reel 1, records of AII.

75. Henry Roe Cloud to Mary Roe, November 5, 1927, reel 1, records of AII.

76. Henry Roe Cloud to Mrs. Walter C. Roe, March 25, 1927, reel 1, records of AII; Mrs. Henry Roe Cloud to Miss Edna R. Voss, March 8, 1932, reel 2, records of AII; Edna R. Voss to Mrs. Henry Roe Cloud, May 2, 1932, reel 2, records of AII; Henry P. Douglas to Mrs. Henry Roe Cloud, June 27, 1933, reel 2, records of AII.

77. Crum, "Henry Roe Cloud," 177. See also Ramirez, *Standing Up*.

78. Ramirez, *Standing Up*, 82.

79. Henry P. Douglas to Mrs. P. J. Skilton, March 25, 1932, reel 2, records of AII; Anna M. Scott to Mr. Henry P. Douglas, March 29, 1933, reel 2, records of AII; Henry P. Douglas to Mrs. F. H. Dickinson, September 10, 1936, reel 2, records of AII.

80. H. Cloud to Williams, March 7, 1931.

81. H. Cloud to Mrs. Walter C. Roe, March 25, 1927; Meriam, *Problem of Indian Administration* 59.

82. Meriam, *Problem of Indian Administration*, 58.

83. Szasz, *Education and the American Indian*, 16–17.

84. Meriam, *Problem of Indian Administration*, 64; Henry Roe Cloud to Mrs. Walter C. Roe, June 26, 1927, reel 1, records of AII.

85. Meriam, *Problem of Indian Administration*, 526.

86. Meriam, *Problem of Indian Administration*, 527.

87. Meriam, *Problem of Indian Administration*, 420.

88. Meriam, *Problem of Indian Administration*, 353.

89. Henry Roe Cloud to Mrs. David H. Doremus, January 3, 1928, reel 2, records of AII.

90. Tetzloff, "To Do Some Good," 126; Crum, "Henry Roe Cloud," 179.

91. Meriam, *Problem of Indian Administration*, 64, 345, 419.

92. Meriam, *Problem of Indian Administration*, 395. For more on Cloud's investigation of Haskell, see Tetzloff, "To Do Some Good," 140–41.

93. For examples see Ralph W. Allen to Henry Roe Cloud, August 16, 1933, box 135—Personal Correspondence, Haskell Series, NARA KC; and Henry Roe Cloud to

Dr. Rudolf Hertz, September 21, 1933, box 20—Henry Roe Cloud, Superintendent, Haskell Series, NARA KC.

94. John W. Tippeconnic to Henry Roe Cloud, August 20, 1933, box 135—Personal Correspondence, Haskell Series, NARA KC.

95. John Collier to Rev. Rev. Msgr. William Hughes, June 15, 1933, reel 18, Collier Papers, ASU.

96. Henry Roe Cloud to Gladys Skye, September 13, 1933, box 135—Personal Correspondence, Haskell Series, NARA KC.

97. John Collier to Eugene Lorton, July 21, 1933, reel 18, Collier Papers. For further discussion of this issue at other schools, see Lomawaima and McCarty, *"To Remain an Indian,"* 66–68.

98. Henry Roe Cloud to Ralph H. Case, September 13, 1933, box 135—Personal Correspondence, Haskell Series, NARA KC.

99. Henry Roe Cloud to Commissioner of Indian Affairs, September 1, 1933, box 135—Personal Correspondence, Haskell Series, NARA KC; Henry Roe Cloud to Commissioner of Indian Affairs, September 29, 1933, box 135—Personal Correspondence, Haskell Series, NARA KC; Henry Roe Cloud to W. J. Hutchins, November 20, 1933, box 135—Personal Correspondence, Haskell Series, NARA KC; Henry Roe Cloud to Robert D. Baldwin, November 23, 1933, box 135—Personal Correspondence, Haskell Series, NARA KC; Henry Roe Cloud to Commissioner of Indian Affairs, December 4, 1933, box 5—Conferences 1929–1935, Haskell Series, NARA KC.

100. Henry Roe Cloud to Commissioner of Indian Affairs, August 7, 1934, box 135—Personal Correspondence, Haskell Series, NARA KC.

101. H. Cloud to Commissioner, August 7, 1934.

102. Henry Roe Cloud to Dr. Will Carson Ryan Jr., August 7, 1934, box 135—Personal Correspondence, Haskell Series, NARA KC.

103. H. Cloud to Ryan, August 7, 1934 (emphasis mine).

104. H. Cloud to Ryan, August 7, 1934.

105. Collier quoted in "Haskell Needed for Future Work: Commissioner Collier Silences Rumors," *Indian Leader*, Fiftieth Anniversary Number, November 23, 1934, 17–18.

106. Collier quoted in "Haskell Needed for Future Work," 18.

107. Collier quoted in "Haskell Needed for Future Work," 18.

108. Henry Roe Cloud to John Collier, November 14, 1934, box 135—Personal Correspondence, Haskell Series, NARA KC.

109. "Henry Roe Cloud New Superintendent," 6.

110. Annette M. Lingelbach, "Indian Leadership: Reading Past History," *Indian Leader*, November 17, 1933, 9.

111. Annette M. Lingelbach, "Indian Leadership: Dancing from the Long Ago," *Indian Leader*, November 17, 1933, 6; Annette M. Lingelbach, "Indian Leadership: Indian Music," *Indian Leader*, December 22, 1933, 5–6; Annette M. Lingelbach, "Indian Leadership: Personal Contacts," *Indian Leader*, January 26, 1934, 5.

112. "Value of Mythology to a Race of People," *Indian Leader*, March 2, 1934, 1. See also "Indian Lore and Legends," *Indian Leader*, October 20, 1933, 1.

113. Lewis J. Korn, "An Indian Museum in Indian Hands," reprinted in *Indian Leader*, November 10, 1933, 3.

114. See also Warren, *Quest for Citizenship*, 167–69.

115. See for example "Opportunities for Indian Youth in Higher Educational Institutions," *Indian Leader*, March 30, 1934, 8; "News of Former Students," *Indian Leader*, May 25, 1934, 4; and "Commercial Graduates on the Job," *Indian Leader*, September 14, 1934, 4.

116. H. Cloud, "Foreword," 1.

117. "Notes of Interest," *Indian Leader*, April 20, 1934, 4; "A New Deal for the American Indian," *Indian Leader*, April 13, 1934, 1–3; "Letter to Highly Valued Superintendent," *Indian Leader*, May 3, 1935, 1.

118. Henry Roe Cloud, "Haskell and Her New Frontiers," *Indian Leader*, June 8, 1934, 14–17. For an example of dialogue on the legislation, see "The Indian Reorganization Act," *Indian Leader*, October 5, 1934, 1–5.

119. Henry Roe Cloud to Frank O. Jones, March 31, 1934, box 135—Personal Correspondence, Haskell Series, NARA KC; H. Cloud, "Haskell and Her New Frontiers," 14–17.

120. "Letter to Highly Valued Superintendent," 1.

121. For more on Cloud's work for educational provisions in the act, see Crum, "Henry Roe Cloud," 180–81.

122. Ramirez, *Standing Up*, 151–57.

123. For Cloud's discussion of a possible role as commissioner of Indian Affairs, see Henry Roe Cloud to A. M. Venne, May 14, 1934, box 135—Personal Correspondence, Haskell Series, NARA KC.

124. Ramirez, *Standing Up*, 151–65, 195.

125. See for example Ruth Roessel, *Navajo Studies*.

126. *Indian Leader*, May 24, 1935. The phrase "by Indians and for Indians" also appeared in early documents of the Society of American Indians, of which Cloud was a key member. See for example Allen, "Introduction," 3.

2. A New Spirit of Leadership

1. "Indian Reorganization Act of 1934," Public Law 73-383, *U.S. Statutes at Large* 48 (1934), 984–88.

2. Pfister, *Yale Indian*, 155–56; Ramirez, *Standing Up*, 143–46.

3. "Indian Reorganization Act of 1934."

4. For a more complete discussion of federal Indian termination policy in the postwar period, see Fixico, *Termination and Relocation*.

5. D'Arcy McNickle, "The Role of the National Congress of American Indians," 1959, quoted in Hoxie, *This Indian Country*, 335.

6. For an example of the acceptance of the pendulum metaphor and its contemporary prevalence, see *Encyclopedia of Politics in the American West*, ed. Steven L. Danver (Los Angeles: Sage Reference, 2013), s.v. "sovereignty, Native American," 615–17. For a more nuanced discussion of the topic and the alternatives to the pendulum metaphor, see Lomawaima and McCarty, *"To Remain an Indian."*

7. John Collier, "A Periodic Drive Renewed," *Indian Leader*, April 19, 1935, 1–2.

8. McNickle, "Four Years of Indian Reorganization," 11.

9. Tetzloff, "To Do Some Good," 168–70; Hoxie, *This Indian Country*, 310.

10. Hoxie, *This Indian Country*, 277–80.

11. Hoxie, *This Indian Country*, 285–86.

12. Fixico, *Termination and Relocation*, 64; Hoxie, *This Indian Country*, 321–22, 326, 328–29. Similarly, the Navajo Tribe did not vote to pass the Indian Reorganization Act but remained one of the tribes most interested in pursuing community control over their own programs, including in education. See for example Parman, *Navajos and the New Deal*.

13. Hoxie, *This Indian Country*, 310.

14. Almost immediately after starting his BIA position, McNickle began publishing a variety of articles on different facets of Native American policy. See for example McNickle, "Alaska—Getting Acquainted."

15. Parker, "D'Arcy McNickle: An Annotated Bibliography," 3.

16. Parker, *Singing an Indian Song*, 17–19, 27–29.

17. Parker, *Singing an Indian Song*, 27–29.

18. McNickle, "Straddle between Cultures." For a discussion of how McNickle's statements on Christianity affected his position as a federal employee, see Parker, *Singing an Indian Song*, 78–80.

19. Tetzloff, "To Do Some Good."

20. Henry Roe Cloud, "Foreword," *Indian Leader*, September 7, 1934, 1.

21. H. Cloud, "Foreword," 1.

22. See for example McNickle, *Surrounded*.

23. McNickle, "Straddle between Cultures," 30.

24. McNickle, "Four Years of Indian Reorganization"; McNickle, "What Do the Old Men Say?"; McNickle, "Toward Understanding"; McNickle, "We Go On from Here"; McNickle, *They Came Here First*.

25. McNickle, *They Came Here First*, 300. See also McNickle, "What Do the Old Men Say?"; Fixico, *Indian Resilience and Rebuilding*.

26. McNickle, "Four Years of Indian Reorganization," 8.

27. McNickle, "Four Years of Indian Reorganization," 8.

28. McNickle, "What Do the Old Men Say?"

29. McNickle, "Four Years of Indian Reorganization"; McNickle, *They Came Here First*, 280–83.

30. "A New Deal for the American Indian," *Indian Leader*, April 13, 1934, 1–3; "Notes of Interest," *Indian Leader*, April 20, 1934, 4; McNickle, "Four Years of Indian Reorganization." For McNickle's assessment of the allotment policy, see McNickle, *They Came Here First*, 271–80.

31. Henry Roe Cloud to James Arentson, August 3, 1934, box 12—Indian Education 1934–35, RG 75, Haskell Series, NARA KC.

32. Henry Roe Cloud to James Arentson, August 3, 1934.

33. McNickle, "Hill 57."

34. McNickle, *They Came Here First*, 293.

35. Fixico, *Termination and Relocation*, 91–94; Hoxie, *This Indian Country*, 319.

36. Cowger, *National Congress*, 30–31; Hoxie, *This Indian Country*, 317–18.

37. Cowger, *National Congress*, 30–31; Hoxie, *This Indian Country*, 317–19.

38. Parker, *Singing an Indian Song*, 108; National Congress of American Indians, "Charter Members at the Constitutional Convention, Cosmopolitan Hotel, Denver,

Colorado, November 15–18, 1944," accessed January 2, 2016, http://www.ncai.org/about
-ncai/mission-history/Founders_1944_Photo_Captions.pdf.

39. Hafen, "'Help Indians Help Themselves.'"

40. National Congress of American Indians, "The Founding Meeting of NCAI," accessed January 2, 2016, http://www.ncai.org/about-ncai/mission-history/the-founding -meeting-of-ncai.

41. McNickle effectively ended his work with the BIA with a leave of absence in 1952, although his resignation was not officially complete until 1954. See Parker, *Singing an Indian Song*, 132–36, 176.

42. "Statement of D'Arcy McNickle," ca. 1947, box 66—McNickle, D'Arcy 1943–54, NCAI records, NMAI. While this source does not contain an exact date, the context of the document reveals that it is McNickle's testimony for the President's Committee on Civil Rights, which met several times in 1947. See Juhnke, *President Truman's Committee*.

43. "Statement of D'Arcy McNickle," NCAI records, 426.

44. "Statement of D'Arcy McNickle," NCAI, 427.

45. "Statement of D'Arcy McNickle," NCAI, 427–28, 431–32.

46. "Statement of D'Arcy McNickle," NCAI, 427–28.

47. "Statement of D'Arcy McNickle," NCAI, 433–35.

48. Parker, *Singing an Indian Song*, 127–29, 132–36.

49. Parker, *Singing an Indian Song*, 129. For a more extensive study of Myer and his views of cultural assimilation, see also Drinnon, *Keeper of Concentration Camps*; and Fixico, *Termination and Relocation*.

50. House Concurrent Resolution 108, *U.S. Statutes at Large* 67 (1953): B132; Public Law 83-280, *U.S. Statutes at Large* 67 (1953): 587.

51. McNickle, "Four Years of Indian Reorganization;" McNickle, *They Came Here First*, 293–300.

52. D'Arcy McNickle and Elizabeth Roe Cloud, "American Indian Development—A Project Sponsored by the National Congress of American Indians: First Annual Report," 1952, reel 54, John Collier Papers, ASU. See also Elizabeth Roe Cloud, "New Frontiers for the American Indian," 1952, box 68—Roe Cloud, Elizabeth, NCAI records, NMAI. According to these sources, the first official projects of AID began in 1951. See also Parker, *Singing an Indian Song*, 138; and Cowger, *National Congress*, 123, for more on the early organization of AID.

53. E. Cloud, "New Frontiers for the American Indian," NCAI; McNickle and E. Cloud, "American Indian Development," Collier Papers.

54. McNickle and E. Cloud, "American Indian Development," Collier Papers, 3–4.

55. McNickle and E. Cloud, "American Indian Development," Collier Papers.

56. E. Cloud, "New Frontiers for the American Indian," NCAI.

57. Henry Roe Cloud to Mary W. Roe, March 25, 1927, reel 1, records of AII. See also Henry P. Douglas to Mrs. Henry Roe Cloud, June 27, 1933, reel 2, records of AII.

58. See for example the photo titled "Elizabeth Bender Roe Cloud," Elderviews website, November 18, 2012, https://elderviews.wordpress.com/2012/11/18/ahoogashinawega -brilliant-wings-the-roe-cloud-freeds/576920_3282061323370_1020267849_n/.

59. Tetzloff, "Elizabeth Bender Cloud."

60. Ramirez, *Standing Up*, 210.

61. E. Cloud, "New Frontiers for the American Indian," NCAI, 3.

62. Tetzloff, "Elizabeth Bender Cloud," 78.

63. McNickle and E. Cloud, "American Indian Development," Collier Papers, 7.

64. E. Cloud, "New Frontiers for the American Indian," NCAI, 1 (emphasis mine).

65. E. Cloud, "New Frontiers for the American Indian," NCAI, 3.

66. Elizabeth Roe Cloud, *Indian Affairs*, July 1952, box 68—Roe Cloud, Elizabeth, NCAI records, NMAI, 2.

67. E. Cloud, "New Frontiers for the American Indian," NCAI, 3.

68. E. Cloud, "Indian Affairs Newsletter," NCAI, 4.

69. McNickle and E. Cloud, "American Indian Development," Collier Papers, 7.

70. McNickle and E. Cloud, "American Indian Development," Collier Papers, 10.

71. E. Cloud, "New Frontiers for the American Indian," NCAI.

72. McNickle, "What Do the Old Men Say?" Quote is from McNickle, *They Came Here First*, 300.

73. Rosalie H. Wax, "A Brief History and Analysis of the Workshops on American Indian Affairs Conducted for American Indian College Students, 1956–1960, together with a Study of Current Attitudes and Activities of Those Students," 1961, box 144—American Indian Development, 1961–66, NCAI records, NMAI.

74. See for example "Seventh Annual Workshop on American Indian Affairs," *Indian Progress: Newsletter of the Workshop on American Indian Affairs, Boulder, Colorado*, March 30, 1962, box 3, folder 27, NIYC records.

75. Parker, *Singing an Indian Song*, 176.

76. Wax, "Brief History," NCAI, 16.

77. Wax, "Brief History," NCAI, 3–4.

78. AID, "Education for Leadership: The Indian People See the Future in Their Children," 1961, box 1, folder 12, NIYC records, 4.

79. Wax, "Brief History," NCAI, 1–2, 8–20.

80. Wax, "Brief History," NCAI, 8.

81. Wax, "Brief History," NCAI, 8–9.

82. AID, "Education for Leadership," NIYC records, 4.

83. AID, "Education for Leadership," NIYC records, 4.

84. V. Deloria, *Custer Died for Your Sins*, 84.

85. V. Deloria, *Custer Died for Your Sins*, 83–86.

86. V. Deloria, *Custer Died for Your Sins*, 86.

87. Deloria acknowledges Cloud's generation as the source of "creative thought in Indian Affairs," despite the experience of government boarding schooling.

88. See for example Henry Roe Cloud's discussion of the history of English settlement in Virginia, as cited in Ramirez, *Standing Up*, 168–69.

89. Lewis J. Korn, "An Indian Museum in Indian Hands," reprinted in the *Indian Leader*, November 10, 1933.

90. Martinez, *Life of the Indigenous Mind*, 184. See also Cobb, *Native Activism*, 25–29.

91. Bob Thomas to Clyde Warrior, n.d., box 3, folder 31, NIYC records.

92. For additional discussion of the workshop, see also McKenzie-Jones, "Evolving Voices of Dissent."

93. Cowger, *National Congress of American Indians*, 141.

94. "National Indian Youth Council Tentative Charter Membership," July 1961, box 1, folder 11, NIYC records. See also Shreve, *Red Power Rising*.

95. AID, "Education for Leadership," NIYC records, 4.

96. Henry Roe Cloud to Dr. Will Carson Ryan Jr., August 7, 1934, box 135—Personal Correspondence, Haskell Series, NARA KC.

97. Joan Noble to Herb Blatchford, July 30, 1961, box 1, folder 11, NIYC records.

98. "Jack D. Forbes," box 2—Jack Forbes: Correspondence, Forbes Collection, UC Davis.

99. McNickle and Cloud, "American Indian Development," Collier Papers, ASU.

100. "Jack D. Forbes," Forbes Collection. See also Sarah Cunnane, "Jack D. Forbes, 1934–2011," *Times Higher Education*, March 17, 2011, https://www.timeshighereducation.com/news/people/obituaries/jack-forbes-1934-2011/415484.article?storycode=415484, and Barbara Risling, "Lifetime Achievement: Jack D. Forbes," box 1—Jack Forbes: Chronology and Biography, Forbes Collection, UC Davis.

101. Jack Forbes, "5100 Miles by Rail," box 231—Jack Forbes: Early Writings, Forbes Collection, UC Davis.

102. Jack D. Forbes to Secretary of the Interior, June 28, 1957, box 2—Jack Forbes: Correspondence, Forbes Collection, UC Davis.

103. Forbes to Secretary of the Interior, June 28, 1957, 1.

104. Forbes to Secretary of the Interior, June 28, 1957, 1.

105. Forbes to Secretary of the Interior, June 28, 1957, 1.

106. See for example "American Indian University Brochures," box 2—Jack Forbes: Correspondence, Forbes Collection, UC Davis; Jack D. Forbes, "Suggestions for Improving Our Indian Program," 1960, box 2—Jack Forbes: Correspondence, Forbes Collection, UC Davis; and Lyndon B. Johnson to Dr. Jack D. Forbes, May 28, 1962, box 2—Jack Forbes: Correspondence, Forbes Collection, UC Davis.

107. Jack Forbes, "Professional Goals," 1956, box 2—Jack Forbes: Correspondence, Forbes Collection, UC Davis.

108. Risling, "Lifetime Achievement," Forbes Collection; Forbes, "Suggestions for Improving," Forbes Collection.

109. Forbes, "Suggestions for Improving," Forbes Collection, 1.

110. Forbes, "Suggestions for Improving," Forbes Collection, 2.

111. Forbes, "Suggestions for Improving," Forbes Collection, 2.

112. Forbes, "Suggestions for Improving," Forbes Collection, 2.

113. Forbes, "Suggestions for Improving," Forbes Collection, 2.

114. For examples from Henry Roe Cloud at Haskell, see Annette M. Lingelbach, "Indian Leadership: Reading Past History," *Indian Leader*, November 17, 1933, 9; and "Value of Mythology to a Race of People," *Indian Leader*, March 2, 1934, 1.

115. Jack D. Forbes to Drew Pearson, April 8, 1961, box 228—Native Higher Education and Colleges, Forbes Collection, UC Davis.

116. Forbes, "Suggestions for Improving," Forbes Collection.

117. Thelin, *History of American Higher Education*.

118. H. Cloud, "Education of the American Indian," 207. For more information on the perceptions of the directors of the Boulder Workshop, see Rosalie H. Wax, "Brief History," NCAI, 1–2, 8–20.

119. Forbes to D. Pearson, April 8, 1961.

120. Dr. Jack D. Forbes, "A Proposal to Create an American Indian University," 1961, in *Native American Higher Education: The Struggle for the Creation of* D-Q *University, 1960–1971*, by Jack D. Forbes, 1985, box 228—Native Higher Education and Colleges, Forbes Collection, UC Davis, 25.

121. Forbes, "Proposal to Create," Forbes Collection, 25, 27.

122. Forbes, "Proposal to Create," Forbes Collection, 25.

123. Forbes, "Proposal to Create," Forbes Collection, 25.

124. Forbes, "Proposal to Create," Forbes Collection, 29.

125. Forbes, "Proposal to Create," Forbes Collection, 28.

126. Forbes, "Proposal to Create," Forbes Collection, 28.

127. Forbes, "Suggestions for Improving," Forbes Collection.

128. Forbes to D. Pearson, April 8, 1961.

129. Forbes to D. Pearson, April 8, 1961.

130. Henry Roe Cloud to E. C. Sage, April 24, 1918, reel 2, records of AII.

131. Photocopies of Henry Roe Cloud's writing are found in box 72—Native Americans: General Topics and U.S. Tribes, Forbes Collection, UC Davis.

132. Henry Roe Cloud to Victor Gordon, August 9, 1917, reel 2, records of AII; "Organization and Purpose," reel 2, records of AII.

133. Forbes, "Proposal to Create," Forbes Collection, 27–28.

134. Forbes, "Proposal to Create," Forbes Collection, 33.

3. Indian-Controlled and Indian-Centered

1. Wesley, "Indian Education." From its inception, the *Journal of American Indian Education* was a diverse collection of original articles and reprints of research pieces by tribal officials and other Native leaders as well as non-Native educators and researchers.

2. See for example Thelin, *History of American Higher Education*, 303–10.

3. Ablon, "American Indian Chicago Conference"; Cobb, *Native Activism*.

4. "Declaration of Indian Purpose," 1961, box 1, folder 8, records of NIYC, 4–5.

5. Ned Hatathli, "Position Paper." Hatathli served as one of the early presidents of Navajo Community College.

6. Cobb, *Native Activism*, 52; McKenzie-Jones, "Evolving Voices of Dissent."

7. Cobb, *Native Activism*, 52.

8. Ablon, "American Indian Chicago Conference," 17.

9. "National Indian Youth Council Tentative Charter Membership," 1961, box 1, folder 11, records of NIYC; Minton, "Place of the Indian Youth," 29–32. See also Shreve, *Red Power Rising*, for example 14, 43, 47, 52, 54, 70, 187–91. For a sustained investigation of this type of activism in a long-term, local context, see Vicenti Carpio, *Indigenous Albuquerque*.

10. See for example Cobb, *Native Activism*.

11. For a cultural history of the first of the TCUS (Navajo Community College), its guiding principles, and its role in Native sovereignty, see Clark, "In Becoming."

12. Fixico, *Urban Indian Experience*, 124. See also Lomawaima, *They Called It Prairie Light*.

13. For example, see "Editor's Column," *Indian Outlook*, October–November 1925, 2–3.

14. Wilkins, *Hank Adams Reader.*

15. The most prolific collection of the varied perspectives on American Indian education is the *Journal of American Indian Education* itself, which has run from 1961 until the present. For earlier context see for example Clark, "In Becoming," 119–20, 124–25; and Iverson, *"For Our Navajo People."*

16. Aronilth, *Foundation of Navajo Culture,* ii–iii.

17. Iverson, *"For Our Navajo People,"* 108.

18. Wesley, "Indian Education," 4.

19. Wesley, "Indian Education," 5.

20. "Proposed Articles," 21.

21. "Proposed Articles," 21.

22. Jack D. Forbes, "Suggestions for Improving Our Indian Program," 1960, box 2—Jack Forbes: Correspondence, Forbes Collection, UC Davis; Thom, "For a Greater Indian America."

23. "Proposed Articles," 18.

24. Thom, "Statement of the National Indian Youth Council," 1.

25. Wilkins, *Hank Adams Reader,* 5–7.

26. Gerald T. Wilkinson to John Carlson, April 5, 1971, box 3, folder 35, records of NIYC. Wilkinson, as NIYC's executive director, relates that in the early years NIYC was "interested primarily in educational problems."

27. Shreve, *Red Power Rising,* 49–55, 108–14.

28. For example, see *Aborigine* 1, no. 1 (1962); and *ABC* 1, no. 1 (October 1963).

29. *National Indian Youth Council* (Gallup NM: National Indian Youth Council, 1961), box 3, folder 27, records of NIYC.

30. "National Indian Youth Council Named New Sponsor," 4; Shreve, *Red Power Rising,* 108–14.

31. *The Indian Progress: Newsletter of the Workshop on American Indian Affairs, Boulder, Colorado,* March 30, 1962, box 3, folder 27, records of NIYC.

32. See for example "Projects Planned," *ABC* 2, no. 4 (December 1964), 2.

33. See for example *ABC* 2, no. 4 (December 1964); and "Selections Committee Considers Applications for Aid," *ABC* 2, no. 5 (June 1965), 5.

34. "Oglala Sioux Educational Survey," 9.

35. "Oglala Sioux Educational Survey," 9.

36. Dumont, "Education and the Community," 3 (emphasis mine).

37. Lose, "Why We Need Our Education," 24.

38. Townsend, "Reading Achievement."

39. Townsend, "Reading Achievement," 10.

40. See for example Lomawaima, *They Called It Prairie Light*; Szasz, *Education and the American Indian,* 64–65; Child, *Boarding School Seasons*; and Reyhner and Eder, *American Indian Education,* 132, 163, 185–85, 202.

41. Nash, "Education Mission."

42. Wax and Wax, "Cultural Deprivation."

43. Kutsche, "Cherokee High School Dropouts," 27.

44. "Oglala Sioux Educational Survey," 9.

45. C. M. Charles, "Tutoring-Counseling Program."

46. Wesley, "Indian Education," 4.

47. "Navajo College Opens on Monday," *Navajo Times*, January 23, 1969.

48. Thompson, "You and Your Future," 4.

49. Wax and Wax, "Cultural Deprivation."

50. Wax and Wax, "Cultural Deprivation," 18 (emphasis mine).

51. Dumont, "Oglala Community School Program," 6 (emphasis mine).

52. "Oglala Sioux Educational Survey."

53. Dumont, "Education and the Community."

54. Wilkinson, *Blood Struggle*, 191–95.

55. Meador, "Pupil as a Person," 22.

56. Meador, "Pupil as a Person," 22.

57. Editorial, *Many Smokes* 1, no. 3 (1966).

58. Editorial, *Many Smokes* 1, no. 4 (1966).

59. Forbes, "American Indian University," 1.

60. Sol Tax to Dr. Jack D. Forbes, January 3, 1965, box 2—Jack Forbes: Correspondence, Forbes Collection, UC Davis; Melvin D. Thom to Dr. Jack Forbes, September 14, 1965, box 2—Jack Forbes: Correspondence, Forbes Collection, UC Davis.

61. For example, see "A Summary of the Indian Education Program," box 51—Native American Education Files, Forbes Collection, UC Davis; and Glen Nimnicht and Francis McKinley, "Recommendations to a Senate Investigating Committee on Education of Indians," 1968, box 51—Native American Education Files, Forbes Collection, UC Davis.

62. Jack D. Forbes to Robert Roessel, June 26, 1967, box 4—Jack Forbes: Correspondence, Forbes Collection, UC Davis.

63. Martin N. B. Holm to Commissioner of Indian Affairs Philleo Nash, May 13, 1965, box 4—Economic Opportunity Act Being Carried Out in the Aberdeen Area, RG 75, OEO-Indian Education, NARA DC.

64. Clark, "In Becoming," 153.

65. For example, see "Indian Glossary," ABC 2, no. 5 (June 1965), 7, where the NIYC lampoons the Office of Economic Opportunity, defining the OEO as "a state of confusion."

66. McCarty, *Place to Be Navajo*.

67. McCarty, *Place to Be Navajo*, xv.

68. Roessel Jr., "Right to Be Wrong," 2.

69. Reno, "Demonstration in Navaho Education," 2.

70. Roessel Jr., "Right to Be Wrong."

71. Reno, "Demonstration in Navaho Education," 3.

72. Reno, "Demonstration in Navaho Education."

73. McCarty, *Place to Be Navajo*, 86.

74. Roessel Jr., "Right to Be Wrong," 2.

75. Roessel Jr., "Right to Be Wrong," 2.

76. McCarty, *Place to Be Navajo*, 77–78.

77. Clark, "In Becoming," 186.

78. McCarty, *Place to Be Navajo*, 75–76.

79. Bill Nixon, "Navajos Plan College on Reservation," *Navajo Times*, April 25, 1968; "Council Approves Community College Board of Regents," *Navajo Times*, July 25, 1968. See also Clark, "In Becoming," for background on Navajo Community College founders' influences and philosophical goals for the college.

80. Ruth Roessel, *Navajo Studies*.

81. *Sinte Gleska College News*, November 1976; editorial, *Sinte Gleska College News*, January 1978, 1.

82. Stein, *Tribally Controlled Colleges*.

83. "Navajo Junior College Will Open at Many Farms in January, 1969," *Navajo Times*, May 16, 1968.

84. Gerald One Feather of the Lakota Higher Education Center, or Oglala Lakota College, quoted in Stein, *Tribally Controlled Colleges*, 41.

85. Ruth Roessel, *Navajo Studies*; Hatathli, "Position Paper."

86. Larry Belgarde, "Preliminary Self Study," 1974, quoted in Stein, *Tribally Controlled Colleges*, 88.

87. See for example Clark, "In Becoming," 88–89.

88. "Course Catalog," *Sinte Gleska College News*, January 1978.

89. Aronilth, *Foundation of Navajo Culture*, 71, 75–78, 119.

90. Clark, "In Becoming," 88–89, 227.

91. Hatathli, "Position Paper"; see also Roessel Jr., "Light in the Night," 26–29.

92. Sinte Gleska College catalog, 1984–86, quoted in Stein, *Tribally Controlled Colleges*, 70.

93. Sinte Gleska College catalog, 1984–86, quoted in Stein, *Tribally Controlled Colleges*, 70.

94. Belgarde, "Preliminary Self Study," quoted in Stein, *Tribally Controlled Colleges*, 88.

95. Belgarde, "Preliminary Self Study," quoted in Stein, *Tribally Controlled Colleges*, 88.

96. American Indian Higher Education Consortium and Institute for Higher Education Policy, "Tribal Colleges: An Introduction," February 1999, American Indian Higher Education Consortium, https://muspin.gsfc.nasa.gov/download/docs/papers/tribal_colleges_an_introduction.pdf.

97. Stein, *Tribally Controlled Colleges*, 52–55, 70–74, 87–90.

98. "NCC Granted Full Accreditation," *Navajo Times*, July 29, 1976.

99. Stein, *Tribally Controlled Colleges*, 54, 64, 85.

100. Enrollment figures from *Navajo Culture Center*; retention rate from House, "Historical Development," 76; dropout estimate from "Navajo College Opens," *Navajo Times*.

101. "Tribally Controlled Community College Assistance Act of 1978," Public Law 95-471, *U.S. Statutes at Large* 92 (1978), 1325–31.

102. Figures are from Paul Boyer, *Native American Colleges: Progress and Prospects* (Princeton NJ: Carnegie Foundation for the Advancement of Teaching, 1997), cited in American Indian Higher Education Consortium and Institute for Higher Education Policy, "Tribal Colleges," D-3.

103. Boyer, *Native American Colleges*, cited in American Indian Higher Education Consortium and Institute for Higher Education Policy, "Tribal Colleges," D-3.

104. Zaglauer, "Role of a Tribal College."

105. See for example Gallup and American Indian College Fund, *Alumni of Tribal Colleges*.

106. Adams, "Case Study," 26.

4. An Exercise in Tribal Sovereignty

1. "Treaty Day Celebration on Saturday," *Navajo Times*, May 30, 1968.

2. Front-page caption, *Navajo Times*, June 6, 1968.

3. "Fort Defiance," *Navajo Times*, June 6, 1968.

4. Nakai quoted in Roland C. Billie, "Treaty Day Gets in High Gear," *Navajo Times*, June 6, 1968, 1.

5. Nakai quoted in Billie, "Treaty Day," 1.

6. "Council Approves Community College Board of Regents," *Navajo Times*, July 25, 1968, 1.

7. Henry Roe Cloud to Dr. Will Carson Ryan Jr., August 7, 1934, box 135—Personal Correspondence, Haskell Series, NARA KC.

8. Harris, Sachs, and Morris, *Re-Creating the Circle*, vii.

9. Stein, *Tribally Controlled Colleges*, 14, 44–46, 88, 101. See also Paul Boyer, *Native American Colleges: Progress and Prospects* (Princeton NJ: Carnegie Foundation for the Advancement of Teaching, 1997); Boyer, *Capturing Education*. For frequent and sustained examinations of recent developments in TCUs, see *Tribal College: Journal of American Indian Higher Education*, which was begun in 1989.

10. Wilkinson, *Blood Struggle*, 191–95.

11. See for example Reno, "Demonstration in Navaho Education"; Lyndon B. Johnson, "Special Message to the Congress on the Problems of the American Indian: 'The Forgotten American,'" March 6, 1968, American Presidency Project, https://www.presidency .ucsb.edu/documents/special-message-the-congress-the-problems-the-american-indian -the-forgotten-american. See also Wilkinson, *Blood Struggle*, 191–95.

12. Richard Nixon, "Special Message to the Congress on Indian Affairs," July 8, 1970, American Presidency Project, https://www.presidency.ucsb.edu/documents/special -message-the-congress-indian-affairs.

13. Now Diné College.

14. Now Sinte Gleska University.

15. Now Sitting Bull College.

16. Stein, *Tribally Controlled Colleges*, 109. I have decided to use the school names that are most relevant to and recognizable from the historical period under study in this chapter, which covers roughly 1968–78.

17. "Tribally Controlled Community College Assistance Act of 1978," Public Law 95-471, *U.S. Statutes at Large* 92 (1978), 1325–31 (hereafter cited as "TCCCA Act of 1978"). See also "Message from the President," *Sinte Gleska College News*, November 1978, for a contemporary assessment of this act's importance; and Stein, *Tribally Controlled Colleges*, 115–18, for a brief discussion of the lobbying effort.

18. Clark, "In Becoming," 119–20, 123–25; Iverson, *"For Our Navajo People,"* 108.

19. Iverson, *"For Our Navajo People,"* 108.

20. Clark, "In Becoming," 123–25.

21. Clark, "In Becoming," 168.

22. Iverson, *"For Our Navajo People,"* 108–9.

23. Dillon Platero to Dr. Jack D. Forbes, June 14, 1961, box 2—Jack Forbes: Correspondence, Forbes Collection, UC Davis; Mary Gorman to Dr. Jack Forbes, July 31, 1961, box 2—Jack Forbes: Correspondence, Forbes Collection, UC Davis.

24. Platero to Forbes, June 14, 1961.

25. Dillon Platero, January 25, 1960, quoted in Iverson, *"For Our Navajo People,"* 110.

26. McCarty, *Place to Be Navajo*, 73.

27. Martin N. B. Holm to Commissioner of Indian Affairs Philleo Nash, May 13, 1965, box 4—Economic Opportunity Act Being Carried Out in the Aberdeen Area, RG 75, OEO-Indian Education, NARA DC.

28. Wilkins, *Navajo Political Experience*, 90.

29. *History and Semi-Annual Report.*

30. Roessel Jr., *Navajo Education, 1948–1978.*

31. Roessel Jr., *Navajo Education, 1948–1978*, 47.

32. Roessel Jr., *Navajo Education, 1948–1978*, 47.

33. Holm to Commissioner Nash, May 13, 1965.

34. McCarty, *Place to Be Navajo.*

35. Bill Nixon, "Navajos Plan College on Reservation," *Navajo Times*, April 25, 1968; "Council Approves," *Navajo Times.*

36. Oppelt, *Tribally Controlled Indian Colleges*, 34.

37. Ashe, *Survey Report*; "Navajo Junior College Will Open at Many Farms in January, 1969," *Navajo Times*, May 16, 1968; see also Oppelt, *Tribally Controlled Indian Colleges*, 34.

38. Roessel Jr., *Navajo Education, 1948–1978*, 70.

39. "Council Approves."

40. "Navajo Junior College Will Open."

41. Clark, "In Becoming," 182–83, 189–92.

42. "Ned Hatathli Named President of Navaho Community College," *Navajo Times* June 12, 1969; House, "Historical Development," 112.

43. "Navajo College Campus Dedicated," *Navajo Times* April 15, 1971; Oppelt, *Tribally Controlled Indian Colleges*, 35.

44. Stein, *Tribally Controlled Colleges*, 6.

45. Nixon, "Navajos Plan College."

46. Nixon, "Navajos Plan College."

47. *Report to the Navajo Tribal Council*, 49–50.

48. This issue remains a significant restriction on TCUs today. See for example Higher Learning Commission, *Distinctive and Connected.*

49. Roessel Jr., *Navajo Education, 1948–1978*, 60.

50. Clark, "In Becoming," 134–36.

51. Clark, "In Becoming," 136.

52. "Navajo Community College Act of 1971," Public Law 92-189, *U.S. Statutes at Large* 85 (1971), 646.

53. "Navajo Community College Act of 1971," 646.

54. "Fund Cut Severe Jolt to College," *Navajo Community College Newsletter* 4, no. 3 (March 1972).

55. "Fund Cut Severe Jolt."

56. Stein, *Tribally Controlled Colleges*, 41–42.

57. "Fund Cut Severe Jolt"; Stein, *Tribally Controlled Colleges*, 44.

58. "Higher Education Act of 1965," Public Law 89-329, *U.S. Statutes at Large* 79 (1965), 1229.

59. Stein, *Tribally Controlled Colleges*, 48–49, 65, 83, 97.

60. Shanley quoted in Bradley Shreve, "Takin' It to the Hill: A Conversation with Jim Shanley," *Tribal College Journal*, 28, no. 2 (Winter 2016), https://tribalcollegejournal .org/takin-hill-conversation-jim-shanley/.

61. Stein, *Tribally Controlled Colleges*, 78–81.

62. Henry Roe Cloud to Victor Gordon, August 9, 1917, reel 2, records of AII.

63. AID, "Education for Leadership: The Indian People See the Future in Their Children," 1961, box 1, folder 12, NIYC records; Rosalie H. Wax, "A Brief History and Analysis of the Workshops on American Indian Affairs Conducted for American Indian College Students, 1956–1960, together with a Study of Current Attitudes and Activities of Those Students," 1961, box 144—American Indian Development, 1961–66, NCAI records, NMAI.

64. Wayne Stein, personal communication, September 22, 2020; Shreve, "Takin' It to the Hill."

65. Shreve, "Takin' It to the Hill."

66. Wayne Stein, personal communication, September 22, 2020; Shreve, "Takin' It to the Hill."

67. Stanley Red Bird quoted in Beth Windsor, "Sinte Gleska College Celebrates Its Twentieth Anniversary: Beginning with Just One Broken Typewriter, the College Now Plans to Be a University," *Tribal College Journal* 3, no. 1 (Summer 1991), https:// tribalcollegejournal.org/sinte-gleska-college-celebrates-twentieth-anniversary-beginning -broken-typewriter-college-plans-university/.

68. Stein, *Tribally Controlled Colleges*, 78–81.

69. Larry Belgarde, "Turtle Mountain Community College Statement," 1974, quoted in Stein, *Tribally Controlled Colleges*, 88.

70. "Oglala Sioux Community College Survey," 1976, quoted in Stein, *Tribally Controlled Colleges*, 45–46.

71. Roessel Jr., *Navajo Education, 1948–1978*, 62.

72. "Philosophy and Objectives of Navajo Community College," quoted in Roessel Jr., *Navajo Education, 1948–1978*, 62.

73. Clark, "In Becoming," 88–89.

74. Clark, "In Becoming," 88–89.

75. "Philosophy and Objectives," quoted in Roessel Jr., *Navajo Education, 1948–1978*, 62.

76. Henry Roe Cloud, "Foreword," *Indian Leader*, September 7, 1934, 1; Annette M. Lingelbach, "Indian Leadership: Reading Past History," *Indian Leader*, November 17, 1933, 9.

77. *Report to the Navajo Tribal Council*, 28.

78. *Report to the Navajo Tribal Council*, 28.

79. *Navajo Culture Center*, 22–23.

80. "Young Navajos Discuss Problems," *Navajo Times*, June 6, 1968.

81. *Navajo Culture Center*, 18.

82. *Navajo Culture Center*, 18.

83. *Navajo Culture Center*, 18, 24–25.

84. "Oglala Sioux Educational Survey," 9.

85. See as an example Barden, *Self-Study*, 10.

86. Ned Hatathli, "Navajo Studies at Navajo Community College," 1–2, paper presented at EPDA Short Term Summer Institute, UCLA American Indian Culture Center, Many Farms, Arizona, 1971, https://files.eric.ed.gov/fulltext/ED082890.pdf.

87. Clark, "In Becoming," 162; *Navajo Culture Center*, 16.

88. Hatathli, "Navajo Studies," 1–2.

89. Hatathli, "Navajo Studies," 6.

90. Hatathli, "Navajo Studies," 1–2. For further examination of the importance of "blood," clan, and other categories and relationships for administrators at Navajo Community College, see Clark, "In Becoming." Multiple scholars have examined the problematic and potentially exclusionary elements of the concept of "blood" in tribal membership and recognition. For examples see Garroutte, *Real Indians*; Lowery, *Lumbee Indians*; Miller, "Seminoles and Africans"; and Edmo, Young, and Parker, *American Indian Identity*.

91. Clark, "In Becoming," 156–57.

92. Clark, "In Becoming," 156–57.

93. Aronilth, *Foundation of Navajo Culture*, 75–76.

94. Aronilth, *Foundation of Navajo Culture*, 119.

95. Aronilth, *Foundation of Navajo Culture*, 17–18.

96. Ruth Roessel in Maya Casilda and students of Diné College and Winona State University, *Ruth Roessel: Teaching Dine; The Living History of a Navajo Educator*, Navajo Oral History Project, 24 (2009), YouTube video, https://openriver.winona.edu/navajooralhistories/24/.

97. Aronilth, *Foundation of Navajo Culture*, 19, 22.

98. Aronilth, *Foundation of Navajo Culture*, 75.

99. Ruth Roessel, *Navajo Studies*.

100. Ruth Roessel, *Navajo Studies*, 48–55.

101. Evelyn Anderson quoted in Casilda and students, *Ruth Roessel*.

102. *Navajo Community College Newsletter* 1, no. 3 (October 1969).

103. "Indian Ethnic Heritage Studies Curriculum Development Project," *Sinte Gleska College News Letter*, November 1976.

104. *Report to the Navajo Tribal Council*, 11. See also *Navajo Community College Newsletter* 1, no. 1 (August 1969).

105. Ruth Roessel, *Navajo Studies*, 19.

106. Roessel Jr., *Navajo Education, 1948–1978*, 63–66. Examples of works include Ruth Roessel, *Papers on Navajo Life*, Ruth Roessel, *Navajo Studies*; Ruth Roessel, *Navajo Stories*; Ruth Roessel, *Role of Indian Studies*; and Ruth Roessel and Johnson, *Navajo Livestock Reduction*.

107. Roessel Jr., *Navajo Education, 1948–1978*, 63.

108. Ruth Roessel and Johnson, *Navajo Livestock Reduction*.

109. House, "Historical Development," 110.

110. "Navajo Community College Act of 1971."

111. *Report to the Navajo Tribal Council.*

112. House, "Historical Development," 110.

113. House, "Historical Development," 104.

114. Aronilth, *Foundation of Navajo Culture*, 12, 30–34.

115. Aronilth, *Foundation of Navajo Culture*, 30.

116. *Navajo Culture Center*, 39.

117. *Navajo Culture Center*, 40, 41.

118. *Navajo Culture Center.*

119. Aronilth, *Foundation of Navajo Culture*, 12.

120. Aronilth, *Foundation of Navajo Culture*, 12–14.

121. Aronilth, *Foundation of Navajo Culture*, 14.

122. "New NCC Campus at Tsaile Lake Dedicated," *Navajo Community College Newsletter* 3, no. 4 (April 1971).

123. Aronilth, *Foundation of Navajo Culture*, 10.

124. Aronilth, *Foundation of Navajo Culture*, 14.

125. Clark, "In Becoming," 136.

126. *Navajo Culture Center*, 28.

127. *Report to the Navajo Tribal Council*, 15.

128. "NCC Granted Full Accreditation," *Navajo Times*, July 29, 1976.

129. Stein, *Tribally Controlled Colleges.*

130. House, "Historical Development," 105; previous dropout estimate from "Navajo College Opens on Monday," *Navajo Times*, January 23, 1969.

131. "Fine Arts Flourishing at NCC," *Navajo Times*, July 1, 1976.

132. "Fine Arts Flourishing at NCC."

133. "NCC Granted Full Accreditation."

134. "NCC Granted Full Accreditation."

135. Stein, *Tribally Controlled Colleges*, 54, 72, 90, 106.

136. Stein, *Tribally Controlled Colleges*, 112–17.

137. Ryser, "American Indian Policy Review Commission," 38–39.

138. "TCCCA Act of 1978."

139. "TCCCA Act of 1978."

140. "TCCCA Act of 1978," 1326.

141. "Message from the President," *Sinte Gleska College News*, November 1978.

142. Roessel Jr., *Navajo Education, 1948–1978*, 81.

143. Roessel Jr., *Navajo Education, 1948–1978*, 76.

144. Roessel Jr., *Navajo Education, 1948–1978*. See also Clark, "In Becoming," 168, 182–83, 189–92.

145. Forbes, "Development of a Native American Intelligentsia," 80.

146. Roessel Jr., *Navajo Education, 1948–1978*, 71.

147. See for example Tom Burnett, "The Tragedy of Tribal Colleges," James G. Martin Center for Academic Renewal, June 9, 2013, https://www.jamesgmartin.center/2013/06/the-tragedy-of-tribal-colleges/#.U84JZ-NdXJD.

148. Mike Mitchell quoted in Clark, "In Becoming," 212.

149. "1978 Graduation and Annual Wacipi," *Sinte Gleska College News*, February 1978.

150. Reyhner and Eder, *American Indian Education*, 302.

151. Aronilth, *Foundation of Navajo Culture*, 78. See also Link, *Navajo*.

5. Embracing Pan-Indianism

1. Lyndon B. Johnson, "Special Message to the Congress on the Problems of the American Indian: 'The Forgotten American,'" March 6, 1968, American Presidency Project, https://www.presidency.ucsb.edu/documents/special-message-the-congress-the-problems-the-american-indian-the-forgotten-american; Richard Nixon, "Special Message to the Congress on Indian Affairs," July 8, 1970, American Presidency Project, https://www.presidency.ucsb.edu/documents/special-message-the-congress-indian-affairs.

2. Jack Forbes, "Brief Proposal for D-Q University," 1970, box 228—Native Higher Education and Colleges, Forbes Collection, UC Davis; Lutz, *D-Q University*; Frank-Cardenas, "Rise and Fall of D-Q University."

3. Forbes, "Development of a Native American Intelligentsia," 75–88.

4. Forbes, "Development of a Native American Intelligentsia," 75–88.

5. See for example "Story of Haskell," *Indian Leader*, Yearbook Issue, 1976, 162–65; and Fred Rednest, "Right to Be Indian Conference Held at Haskell," *Indian Leader*, May 19, 1978, 2.

6. Jack D. Forbes, "A Proposal to Create an American Indian University," 1961, box 228—Native Higher Education and Colleges, Forbes Collection, UC Davis.

7. For a list of recipients, see "American Indian University Brochures," box 2—Jack Forbes: Correspondence, Forbes Collection, UC Davis. For examples of the proposal and revisions, see Forbes, "Proposal to Create," Forbes Collection, and Jack D. Forbes, "American Tribal Higher Education: A Proposal," 1965, box 228—Native Higher Education and Colleges, Forbes Collection, UC Davis.

8. Henry Roe Cloud to W. S. Lank, October 26, 1923, reel 2, records of AII; see also "Ten Commandments of Success," *Indian Outlook*, November 1, 1923, 4; Forbes, "Development of a Native American Intelligentsia."

9. Forbes, "Development of a Native American Intelligentsia," 78.

10. Jack D. Forbes to Drew Pearson, April 8, 1961, box 228—Native Higher Education and Colleges, Forbes Collection, UC Davis; Forbes, "Proposal to Create," Forbes Collection; Forbes, "American Tribal Higher Education: A Proposal," 1965, Forbes Collection.

11. Henry Roe Cloud to Mrs. Walter C. Roe, October 4, 1922, reel 1, records of AII.

12. H. Cloud to Mrs. Roe, October 4, 1922.

13. Henry Roe Cloud to Mrs. J. F. Schermerhorn, March 7, 1923, reel 2, records of AII; see also Henry Roe Cloud to Mrs. Walter C. Roe, March 5, 1923, reel 1, records of AII.

14. Forbes, "American Tribal Higher Education: A Proposal," 1965, Forbes Collection. See also Rodriguez, *Our Sacred Maiz*, 85–86.

15. Forbes, "Proposal to Create," Forbes Collection; Forbes, "American Tribal Higher Education: A Proposal," 1965, Forbes Collection, 52.

16. Forbes, "American Tribal Higher Education: A Proposal," 1965, Forbes Collection, 52.

17. Forbes, "American Tribal Higher Education: A Proposal," 1965, Forbes Collection, 49–53; Lutz, *D-Q University*, 9.

18. See for example Henry Roe Cloud to E. C. Sage, April 24, 1918, reel 2, records of AII; *Indian Outlook*, October–November 1925; *Indian Outlook*, December 1925; and Mary A. Steer to Henry Roe Cloud, March 20, 1928, reel 1, records of AII.

19. Forbes, "American Tribal Higher Education: A Proposal," 1965, Forbes Collection, 51.

20. Forbes, "American Tribal Higher Education: A Proposal," 1965, Forbes Collection, 50, 53.

21. Forbes, "American Tribal Higher Education: A Proposal," 1965, Forbes Collection, 52.

22. Forbes, "American Tribal Higher Education: A Proposal," 1965, Forbes Collection, 53.

23. Jack D. Forbes, "American Tribal Higher Education," 1968, box 228—Native Higher Education and Colleges, Forbes Collection, UC Davis.

24. Forbes, "American Tribal Higher Education: A Proposal," 1965, Forbes Collection, 68.

25. Forbes, "American Tribal Higher Education: A Proposal," 1965, Forbes Collection, 53; see also H. Cloud, "Education of the American Indian."

26. Forbes, "American Tribal Higher Education," 1968, Forbes Collection, 67.

27. Quote is from Lutz, *D-Q University*, 13; see also Forbes to D. Pearson, April 8, 1961.

28. Lutz, *D-Q University*, 14.

29. Lutz, *D-Q University*, 15. UC Davis was among the first of schools to form a Native American studies program in the late 1960s, along with UC Berkeley and UCLA.

30. Barbara Risling, "Lifetime Achievement: Jack D. Forbes," box 1—Chronology and Biography, Forbes Collection, UC Davis.

31. Lutz, *D-Q University*, 22.

32. Jack D. Forbes, "My Elder Brother Walks On," 2005, https://nas.ucdavis.edu/sites/g/files/dgvnsk7031/files/files/page/risling_tributebyjackforbes.pdf; see also "Past Contributors," UC Davis Native American Studies website, accessed February 27, 2017, https://nas.ucdavis.edu/past-conributors.

33. Forbes, "My Elder Brother."

34. Forbes, "My Elder Brother."

35. "Council Approves Community College Board of Regents," *Navajo Times*, July 25, 1968; Forbes, "Brief Proposal for D-Q University," Forbes Collection, 115; Lutz, *D-Q University*, 21–22.

36. "About William H. Donner," William H. Donner Foundation, accessed February 25, 2017, https://www.donner.online/about.aspx; "The William H. Donner Foundation," Foundation Directory Online, accessed February 25, 2017, https://fconline.foundationcenter.org/grantmaker-profile?collection=grantmakers&key=DONN004; Sedelta Oosahwee, "50th Anniversary Legacy," American Indian Graduate Center, accessed June 16, 2021, https://www.aigcs.org/news/50-year-legacy/.

37. Forbes, "Brief Proposal for D-Q University," Forbes Collection, 115.

38. Lutz, *D-Q University*, 22.

39. Lutz, *D-Q University*.

40. Forbes, "American Tribal Higher Education," 1968, Forbes Collection.

41. Lutz, *D-Q University*, 22–24. For more information on the Alcatraz occupation and its relationship with other Native activism of the time see Smith and Warrior, *Like a Hurricane*; Fortunate Eagle, *Heart of the Rock*; and Banks, *Ojibwa Warrior*.

42. Indians of All Tribes, "Proclamation: To the Great White Father and All His People" (San Francisco, 1969), https://digilab.libs.uga.edu/exhibits/exhibits/show/civil-rights-digital-history-p/item/474.

43. Larry Spears, "Indians, Chicanos Get Their University," *Oakland Tribune*, February 14, 1971.

44. Muñoz, *Youth, Identity, Power*, 193–95; Rosales, *Chicano!*, 174.

45. Lutz, *D-Q University*, 1, 26.

46. Jack D. Forbes quoted in Lutz, *D-Q University*, 26. See also "Deganawidah-Quetzalcoatl University," 1971, box 252—D-Q University: Chronology, Correspondence, Clippings, Forbes Collection, UC Davis.

47. Larry Spears, "Indians, Chicanos Get Their University," *Oakland Tribune*, February 14, 1971.

48. "Key to Transcript," box 252—D-Q University: Chronology, Correspondence, Clippings, Forbes Collection, UC Davis. See also "Deganawidah-Quetzalcoatl University," Forbes Collection.

49. Forbes, "Brief Proposal for D-Q University," Forbes Collection, 116.

50. Forbes, "American Tribal Higher Education," 1968, Forbes Collection, 69.

51. Forbes, "American Tribal Higher Education," 1968, Forbes Collection, 62–64; "Deganawidah-Quetzalcoatl University," Forbes Collection.

52. Forbes, "Brief Proposal for D-Q University," Forbes Collection, 114–19.

53. Lutz, *D-Q University*, 22–24.

54. Forbes, Martin, and Risling, "Establishment of D-Q University."

55. Forbes, Martin, and Risling, "Establishment of D-Q University," 23.

56. Lutz, *D-Q University*, 24.

57. Forbes, "American Tribal Higher Education," 1968, Forbes Collection.

58. Forbes, Martin, and Risling, "Internal Problems," 95–99.

59. Forbes, Martin, and Risling, "Internal Problems," 96.

60. Forbes, Martin, and Risling, "Internal Problems," 98–99.

61. Forbes, "American Tribal Higher Education," 1968, Forbes Collection.

62. Lutz, *D-Q University*, 37–38.

63. Lutz, *D-Q University*, 35–37.

64. Lutz, *D-Q University*, 31.

65. Banks, *Ojibwa Warrior*.

66. Banks, *Ojibwa Warrior*, 321–22.

67. Lutz, *D-Q University*, 34, 37, 45–48. See also Forbes, "Development of a Native American Intelligentsia."

68. Lutz, *D-Q University*, 39.

69. Jack D. Forbes, "Dear Friends," n.d. (ca. 1972), box 252—D-Q University: Chronology, Correspondence, Clippings, Forbes Collection, UC Davis.

70. "Deganawidah-Quetzalcoatl University," Forbes Collection.

71. "Deganawidah-Quetzalcoatl University," Forbes Collection; Lutz, D-Q University, 28.

72. Forbes, "Development of a Native American Intelligentsia."

73. "Graduate Committee Minutes, February 25, 1974," box 252—D-Q University: Chronology, Correspondence, Clippings, Forbes Collection, UC Davis; "A Preliminary Presentation on Ph.D. Degree," box 252—D-Q University: Chronology, Correspondence, Clippings, Forbes Collection, UC Davis; "Key to Transcript," Forbes Collection.

74. Forbes, "Development of a Native American Intelligentsia," 75–88.

75. Forbes, "Development of a Native American Intelligentsia," 79.

76. Larry Belgarde, Turtle Mountain Community College Statement, 1974, quoted in Stein, Tribally Controlled Colleges, 88.

77. For the TCCCA Act, see "Tribally Controlled Community College Assistance Act of 1978," Public Law 95-471, U.S. Statutes at Large 92 (1978), 1325–31. For the effort by DQU to obtain TCCCA Act funds, see Lutz, D-Q University, 29–30.

78. Forbes, "Development of a Native American Intelligentsia," 83.

79. Forbes, "Development of a Native American Intelligentsia," 78.

80. Lutz, D-Q University.

81. Forbes, "Development of a Native American Intelligentsia," 79.

82. Banks, Ojibwa Warrior, 322–24.

83. Banks, Ojibwa Warrior, 41.

84. Jack D. Forbes, "Suggestions for Improving Our Indian Program," 1960, box 2—Jack Forbes: Correspondence, Forbes Collection, UC Davis. For Haskell vocational focus see "The Haskell Story," 1967, box 4, folder 31, Galluzzi Collection, KU; Mrs. Louise L. Baker, "Haskell Alumni News Letter," 1970–75, box 4, folder 26, Galluzzi Collection, KU; and Haskell Indian Nations University, "School History," accessed December 12, 2016, http://www.haskell.edu/about/history.

85. "Haskell Institute Bulletin of Information," 1964, quoted in Goodner, Woods, and. Harkins, Characteristics and Attitudes, 3–4. For Haskell alumni updates regarding the 1960s vocational training, see Baker, "Haskell Alumni," Galluzzi Collection.

86. Baker, "Haskell Alumni," Galluzzi Collection.

87. For Henry Roe Cloud on leadership at Haskell, see "Haskell Needed for Future Work: Commissioner Silences Rumors," Indian Leader, November 23, 1934, 17–18. See also Annette M. Lingelbach, "Indian Leadership: Reading Past History," Indian Leader, November 17, 1933, 9; and Annette M. Lingelbach, "Indian Leadership: Personal Contacts," Indian Leader, January 26, 1934, 5.

88. Forbes, "Suggestions for Improving," Forbes Collection; Thom, "For a Greater Indian America."

89. Schultz, Haynie, McCulloch, and Aoki, Encyclopedia of Minorities, 592; Fixico, Bureau of Indian Affairs, 168.

90. Schultz, Haynie, McCulloch, and Aoki, Encyclopedia of Minorities, 592; "Chronological History," American Indian Graduate Center, accessed February 25, 2017, https://www.aigcs.org/news/50-year-legacy/.

91. "Resume of Wallace E. Galluzzi," box 4, folder 20, Galluzzi Collection, KU.

92. For example, see Jack D. Forbes to Secretary of the Interior, June 28, 1957, box 2—Jack Forbes: Correspondence, Forbes Collection, UC Davis; see also Parker, *Singing an Indian Song*, 132–36, 176.

93. "Resume of Wallace E. Galluzzi," Galluzzi Collection.

94. "Resume of Wallace E. Galluzzi," Galluzzi Collection.

95. Wallace E. Galluzzi to Superintendent, Haskell Institute, April 15, 1968, box 1, folder 13, Galluzzi Collection, KU.

96. Galluzzi to Superintendent, Haskell Institute, April 15, 1968.

97. "Resume of Wallace E. Galluzzi," Galluzzi Collection; "Haskell Bids Farewell," *Indian Leader*, Commencement Issue, 1969, 6.

98. "Evaluation Team," 1969, folder A, RH MS P202, Glinka Collection, KU; see also "Administrators, Staff Lead," *Indian Leader*, Commencement Issue, 1970, 10.

99. "Resume of Wallace E. Galluzzi," Galluzzi Collection; "Administrators, Staff Lead," *Indian Leader*, Commencement Issue, 1970, 10.

100. "Administrators, Staff Lead," *Indian Leader*, 10; Lew Ferguson, "Indian School's New Name Signals Change," *Aberdeen (SD) American-News*, September 24, 1970; "Spring Semester 1972," 1971, box 1, folder 12, Galluzzi Collection, KU.

101. Ferguson, "Indian School's New Name Signals Change"; "Resume of Wallace E. Galluzzi," Galluzzi Collection, KU. The school would soon after be known by the shorter "Haskell Indian Junior College."

102. Johnson, "Special Message."

103. Nixon, "Special Message."

104. Jane Lee, "Self-Leadership, Education Cited as Vital to Indians," *Lawrence (KS) Journal-World*, October 25, 1971.

105. Office of Indian Education, Bureau of Indian Affairs, *Higher Education*, 10.

106. Wallace E. Galluzzi, "Projection for the Future Development of Haskell Indian Junior College," in *Haskell Indian Junior College, Lawrence Kansas: Self-Study Report*, 1973, box 4, folder 35, Galluzzi Collection, KU, i–ii.

107. Galluzzi, "Projection for the Future," Galluzzi Collection, i.

108. Galluzzi, "Projection for the Future," Galluzzi Collection.

109. "Outreach," *Indian Leader*, Yearbook Issue, 1976, 180.

110. Galluzzi, "Projection for the Future," Galluzzi Collection, i.

111. Galluzzi, "Projection for the Future," Galluzzi Collection, ii.

112. Galluzzi, "Projection for the Future," Galluzzi Collection, ii.

113. *Haskell Indian Junior College*, Galluzzi Collection, 4.

114. *Haskell Indian Junior College*, Galluzzi Collection, 6–7.

115. Baker, "Haskell Alumni," Galluzzi Collection, no. 5, p. 10.

116. Forbes, "American Tribal Higher Education: A Proposal," 1965, Forbes Collection; Forbes, "American Tribal Higher Education," 1968, Forbes Collection; Forbes, "Brief Proposal for D-Q University," Forbes Collection.

117. Office of Indian Education, Bureau of Indian Affairs, *Higher Education*, 9; Esther Harjo, "Tribes Compiled Categorically," *Indian Leader*, Yearbook Issue, 1976, 20–21.

118. "Story of Haskell," 162.

119. "Story of Haskell," 164.

120. "Story of Haskell," 162.

121. Cyndy Bell, "North Central Lists Strengths, Weaknesses," *Indian Leader*, February 23, 1979.

122. "Miss Indian America Opens Pow Wow," *Indian Leader*, May 19, 1978.

123. Fred Rednest, "Right to Be Indian Conference Held at Haskell," *Indian Leader*, May 19, 1978.

124. Rednest, "Right to Be Indian."

125. Forbes, "Development of a Native American Intelligentsia," 84.

126. Rednest, "Right to Be Indian."

127. Galluzzi, "Projection for the Future," Galluzzi Collection.

128. U.S. Government Accountability Office to the Honorable James B. Pearson, United States Senate, April 11, 1975 (GAO-B-114868). U.S. Government Accountability Office, https://www.gao.gov/products/b-114868-6. For the legislation, see "Vocational Education Act of 1963," Public Law 88-210, *U.S. Statutes at Large* 77 (1963), 403–19; and "Higher Education Act of 1965," Public Law 89-329, *U.S. Statutes at Large* 79 (1965), 1219–70.

129. U.S. Government Accountability Office to the Honorable James B. Pearson, April 11, 1975.

130. Bell, "North Central Lists Strengths."

131. Bureau of Indian Education, *Budget Justifications*. See also Sara Shepherd, "Haskell Formally Resolves to Gain More Autonomy from Federal Government, Create Endowment Association," *Lawrence (KS) Journal-World*, October 8, 2015; "Haskell Indian Nations University Funding Falls Flat," *Native Times*, October 11, 2015, http://www.nativetimes.com/index.php/life/education/12229-haskell-indian-nations-university-funding-falls-flat.

Conclusion

1. Cobb, *Native Activism*, 194.

2. Henry Roe Cloud, "Foreword," *Indian Leader*, September 7, 1934, 1.

3. Henry Roe Cloud to Mrs. J. F. Schermerhorn, March 7, 1923, reel 2, records of AII; Mrs. S. Thornton Hollinshead, "The American Indian, Life, Morals, Characteristics, Art and Traditions, Why We Should Conserve and Preserve Them," *Indian Outlook*, February 10, 1924, 6; "Indians Played Alto Flutes Long before Inventions by Whites," *Indian Outlook*, September–October, 1924, 6; "Indians Give Corn to the Western Hemisphere," *Indian Outlook*, January 1925, 4; Rev. Richard H. Harper, "Some Indian Leaders, Past and Present," *Indian Outlook*, October–November, 1925, 1, 3.

4. Henry Roe Cloud to Mrs. Walter C. Roe, March 25, 1927, reel 1, records of AII.

5. Elizabeth Roe Cloud, "New Frontiers for the American Indian," 1952, box 68—Roe Cloud, Elizabeth, NCAI records, NMAI; D'Arcy McNickle and Elizabeth Roe Cloud, "American Indian Development—A Project Sponsored by the National Congress of American Indians: First Annual Report," 1952, reel 54, 1922–68 (microfilm), Collier Papers, ASU.

6. Elizabeth Roe Cloud, "Indian Affairs Newsletter," July 1952, box 68—Roe Cloud, Elizabeth, NCAI records, NMAI, 2.

7. E. Cloud, "New Frontiers," NCAI records, 1.

8. McNickle and E. Cloud, "American Indian Development"; Parker, *Singing an Indian Song*, 127–29, 132–36.

9. McNickle, "Four Years of Indian Reorganization"; McNickle, "What Do the Old Men Say?," 24–26; McNickle, "Toward Understanding"; McNickle, "We Go On from Here"; McNickle, *They Came Here First*.

10. Rosalie H. Wax, "A Brief History and Analysis of the Workshops on American Indian Affairs Conducted for American Indian College Students, 1956–1960, together with a Study of Current Attitudes and Activities of Those Students," 1961, box 144—American Indian Development, 1961–66, NCAI records, NMAI; AID, "Education for Leadership: The Indian People See the Future in Their Children," 1961, box 1, folder 12, records of NIYC.

11. Gerald T. Wilkinson to John Carlson, April 5, 1971, box 3, folder 35, records of NIYC.

12. Sol Tax to Dr. Jack D. Forbes, January 3, 1965, box 2—Jack Forbes: Correspondence, Forbes Collection, UC Davis; Melvin D. Thom to Dr. Jack Forbes, September 14, 1965, box 2—Jack Forbes: Correspondence, Forbes Collection, UC Davis; Jack D. Forbes to Robert Roessel, June 26, 1967, box 4—Jack Forbes: Correspondence, Forbes Collection, UC Davis. See also Frank-Cardenas, "Rise and Fall of D-Q University."

13. For examples of reservation-based discourse see Iverson, *"For Our Navajo People."* For urban context see Fixico, *Urban Indian Experience.*

14. Higher Learning Commission, *Distinctive and Connected.* See also AIHEC.org, the website of the American Indian Higher Education Consortium.

15. Bay Mills Community College, *Bay Mills Community College 1994–1996 Catalog*, 2.

16. Sisseton Wahpeton Community College, *Sisseton Wahpeton Community College Catalog 1994–96*, 2.

17. Cajete, Sachs, and Gagnier, "Spiral of Renewal," 323.

18. Pavel, Inglebret, and Banks, "Tribal Colleges and Universities," 60.

19. Pavel, Inglebret, and Banks, "Tribal Colleges and Universities," 60.

20. Gonzales, "Tribal Colleges Offer."

21. Cajete, Sachs, and Gagnier, "Spiral of Renewal." See also University of Kansas, "Exchange Program," Haskell/KU Partnership, accessed June 1, 2020, https://haskellpartnership.ku.edu/exchange-programs.

22. "Preserving the Wisdom: The Navajo Oral History Project," *Tribal College Journal*, February 6, 2014, https://tribalcollegejournal.org/preserving-wisdom-navajo-oral-history-project/.

23. Harris, Sachs, and Morris, *Re-Creating the Circle*, vii.

24. Gallup and American Indian College Fund, *Alumni of Tribal Colleges*, 8.

25. Gallup and American Indian College Fund, *Alumni of Tribal Colleges*, 11.

26. Gallup and American Indian College Fund, *Alumni of Tribal Colleges*, 10–11.

27. Gallup and American Indian College Fund, *Alumni of Tribal Colleges*, 12 (emphasis mine).

28. For example see HeavyRunner and DeCelles, "Family Education Model"; Guillory and Wolverton, "It's about Family"; and Ginger Stull, Demetrios Spyridakis, Marybeth Gasman, Andres Samayoa, and Yvette Booker, "Redefining Success: How Tribal Colleges and Universities Build Nations, Strengthen Sovereignty, and Persevere through

Challenges," Center for Minority Serving Institutions, 2015, https://repository.upenn
.edu/cgi/viewcontent.cgi?article=1386&context=gse_pubs.

29. Gallup and American Indian College Fund, *Alumni of Tribal Colleges*, 4.

30. Tom Burnett, "The Tragedy of Tribal Colleges," James G. Martin Center for Academic Renewal, June 9, 2013, https://www.jamesgmartin.center/2013/06/the-tragedy
-of-tribal-colleges/#.U84JZ-NdXJD.

31. Burnett, "Tragedy of Tribal Colleges."

32. Gallup and American Indian College Fund, *Alumni of Tribal Colleges*; Higher Learning Commission, *Distinctive and Connected*, 9–13.

33. Diné College, *Empowered*.

34. Wichita State University, *Annual Operating Budget for Fiscal Year 2020*, accessed June 10, 2020, https://www.wichita.edu/administration/budget/BudgetBookOnlineFinal
.pdf, 2.

35. Wichita State University, *Student Enrollment Factbook for Fall Census Day*, October 1, 2019, https://www.wichita.edu/services/planning_and_analysis/documents/Enrollment
_Fall_Census_OPAweb.pdf, 2.

36. Diné College, *Empowered*, 2, 10.

37. Higher Learning Commission, *Distinctive and Connected*, 9.

38. Gallup and American Indian College Fund, *Alumni of Tribal Colleges*, 19.

39. Bureau of Indian Education, *Budget Justifications*, 6.

40. Bureau of Indian Education, *Budget Justifications*, 18.

41. "Haskell Needs a Champion," editorial, *Lawrence Journal-World*, May 23, 2017, https://www2.ljworld.com/news/2017/may/23/editorial-haskell-needs-champion/.

42. S. Deloria quoted in Fred Rednest, "Right to Be Indian Conference Held at Haskell," *Indian Leader*, May 19, 1978, 2.

43. Henry Roe Cloud to E. E. Olcott, January 10, 1923, reel 1, records of AII; Henry Roe Cloud to Mary S. E. Baker, April 17, 1923, reel 2, records of AII.

44. Forbes, "Development of a Native American Intelligentsia," 83.

45. Maddox, *Citizen Indians*, 166.

46. Joan Noble to Herb Blatchford, July 30, 1961, box 1, folder 11, records of NIYC.

BIBLIOGRAPHY

Unpublished Sources

Collier, John. Papers. Ross-Blakely Law Library, Arizona State University, Phoenix. Microfilm.

Forbes Collection, Jack. University Library Special Collections, University of California, Davis.

Galluzzi Collection, Wallace. Kansas Collection. Kenneth Spencer Research Library, University of Kansas, Lawrence.

Glinka Collection, John L. Kansas Collection. Kenneth Spencer Research Library, University of Kansas, Lawrence.

National Congress of American Indians (NCAI) Records. National Museum of the American Indian Cultural Resources Center (NMAI), Suitland, Maryland.

Records of the American Indian Institute (AII). Presbyterian Historical Society, National Archives of the Presbyterian Church (USA), Philadelphia. Microfilm.

Records of the Bureau of Indian Affairs. Record Group 75. National Archives and Records Administration, Kansas City (NARA KC).

Records of the Bureau of Indian Affairs. Record Group 75. National Archives and Records Administration, Washington DC (NARA DC).

Records of the National Indian Youth Council (NIYC). Center for Southwest Research, University of New Mexico, Albuquerque.

Witt, Shirley Hill. Papers. Center for Southwest Research, University of New Mexico, Albuquerque.

Published Sources

Ablon, Joan. "The American Indian Chicago Conference." *Journal of American Indian Education* 1, no. 2 (January 1962): 17–23.

Adams, David. "A Case Study: Self-Determination and Indian Education." *Journal of American Indian Education* 13, no. 2 (January 1974): 21–27.

Adams, David Wallace. *Education for Extinction: American Indians and the Boarding School Experience, 1875–1928.* Lawrence: University Press of Kansas, 1995.

Allen, Chadwick. "Introduction: Locating the Society of American Indians." Special Issue, *American Indian Quarterly* 37, no. 3, and *Studies in American Indian Literatures* 25, no. 2 (Summer 2013): 1–22.

Allen, Chadwick, and Beth Piatote, eds. "The Society of American Indians and Its Legacies." Special Issue, *American Indian Quarterly* 37, no. 3, and *Studies in American Indian Literatures* 25, no. 2 (Summer 2013).

American Indian Higher Education Consortium and the Institute for Higher Education Policy. *Tribal College Contributions to Local Economic Development*. Alexandria VA: American Indian Higher Education Consortium, 2000.

Aronilth, Wilson, Jr. *Foundation of Navajo Culture*. Tsaile AZ: Navajo Community College Press, 1991.

Ashe, Robert W. *Survey Report: Navajo Community College*. Tempe AZ: Bureau of Educational Research and Services, College of Education, Arizona State University, 1966.

Banks, Dennis, with Richard Erdoes. *Ojibwa Warrior: Dennis Banks and the Rise of the American Indian Movement*. Norman: University of Oklahoma Press, 2004.

Barden, Jack, ed. *Self-Study: Standing Rock Community College*. Fort Yates ND: Standing Rock Community College, 1984.

Bay Mills Community College. *Bay Mills Community College 1994–1996 Catalog*. Brimley MI: Bay Mills Indian Community, 1994.

Bederman, Gail. *Manliness and Civilization: A Cultural History of Gender and Race in the United States, 1880–1917*. Chicago: University of Chicago Press, 1995.

Begay, Manley A., Jr., Stephen Cornell, Miriam Jorgensen, and Joseph P. Kalt. "Development, Governance, Culture: What Are They and What Do They Have to Do with Rebuilding Native Nations?" In Jorgensen, *Rebuilding Native Nations*, 34–54.

Benham, Maenette K. P., and Wayne J. Stein. *The Renaissance of American Indian Higher Education: Capturing the Dream*. Mahwah NJ: Lawrence Erlbaum, 2003.

Bhabha, Homi K. *The Location of Culture*. New York: Routledge, 1994.

Blackhawk, Ned. *Violence over the Land: Indians and Empires in the Early American West*. Cambridge MA: Harvard University Press, 2006.

Boas, Franz. *Anthropology and Modern Life*. Reprinted with an introduction by Ruth Bunzel. New York: Norton, 1962.

Bourdieu, Pierre. *Outline of a Theory of Practice*. New York: Cambridge University Press, 1977.

Boyer, Paul. *Capturing Education: Envisioning and Building the First Tribal Colleges*. Pablo MT: Salish Kootenai College Press, 2015.

Brayboy, Bryan McKinley Jones, Amy J. Fann, Angelina E. Castagno, and Jessica A. Solyom, eds. *Postsecondary Education for American Indian and Alaska Natives: Higher Education for Nation Building and Self-Determination*. San Francisco: Wiley Subscription Services, 2012.

Bureau of Indian Education. *Budget Justifications and Performance Information, Fiscal Year 2020*. Washington DC: U.S. Department of the Interior, 2019. https://www.bie.edu/sites/default/files/documents/idc2-092115.pdf.

Cajete, Gregory A., Stephen M. Sachs, and Phyllis M. Gagnier. "The Spiral of Renewal: Appropriate Indian Education." In Harris, Sachs, and Morris, *Re-Creating the Circle*, 317–78.

Calloway, Colin. *First Peoples: A Documentary History of American Indians*. 6th ed. New York: MacMillan, 2019.

Castile, George Pierre. *Taking Charge: Native American Self-Determination and Federal Indian Policy, 1975–1993*. Tucson: University of Arizona Press, 2006.

———. *To Show Heart: Native American Self-Determination and Federal Indian Policy, 1960–1975*. Tucson: University of Arizona Press, 1998.

Champagne, Duane, and Jay Stauss, eds. *Native American Studies in Higher Education: Models for Collaboration between Universities and Indigenous Nations*. Walnut Creek CA: AltaMira Press, 2002.

Charles, C. M. "A Tutoring-Counseling Program for Indian Students at the University of New Mexico." *Journal of American Indian Education* 1, no. 3 (May 1962): 10–12.

Child, Brenda. *Boarding School Seasons: American Indian Families, 1900–1940*. Lincoln: University of Nebraska Press, 1998.

Clark, Ferlin. "In Becoming Sa'ah Naaghai Bik'eh Hozhoon: The Historical Challenges and Triumphs of Diné College." PhD diss., University of Arizona, 2009.

Cloud, Henry Roe. "Education of the American Indian." *Quarterly Journal of the Society of American Indians* 2, no. 3 (July–September 1914): 203–9.

———. "From Wigwam to Pulpit." *Missionary Review of the World* 38 (1915): 329–39.

Cobb, Daniel M. *Native Activism in Cold War America: The Struggle for Sovereignty*. Lawrence: University Press of Kansas, 2008.

Cobb, Daniel M., and Loretta Fowler, eds. *Beyond Red Power: American Indian Politics and Activism since 1900*. Santa Fe NM: School for Advanced Research, 2007.

Coulthard, Glen S. *Red Skin, White Masks: Rejecting the Colonial Politics of Recognition*. Minneapolis: University of Minnesota Press, 2014.

Cowger, Thomas W. *The National Congress of American Indians: The Founding Years*. Lincoln: University of Nebraska Press, 1999.

Crum, Steven. "Henry Roe Cloud, a Winnebago Indian Reformer: His Quest for American Indian Higher Education." *Kansas History* 11, no. 3 (Autumn 1988): 171–84.

Danver, Steven L., ed. *Encyclopedia of Politics in the American West*. Los Angeles: Sage Reference, 2013.

DeJong, David H. *Promises of the Past: A History of Indian Education in the United States*. Golden CO: North American Press, 1993.

Deloria, Philip J. *Playing Indian*. New Haven CT: Yale University Press, 1998.

Deloria, Vine, Jr. *Custer Died for Your Sins: An Indian Manifesto*. 2nd ed. Norman: University of Oklahoma Press, 1988.

Deloria, Vine, Jr., and Daniel Wildcat. *Power and Place: Indian Education in America*. Golden CO: Fulcrum, 2001.

Denetdale, Jennifer Nez. *Reclaiming Diné History: The Legacies of Navajo Chief Manuelito and Juanita*. Tucson: University of Arizona Press, 2007.

Diné College. *Empowered into the Next 50 Years: FY 2017–18 Annual Report*. Tsaile AZ: Diné College Marketing and Communications, 2018. https://www.dinecollege.edu/wp-content/uploads/2018/04/2018-1920V17-compressed.pdf.

Drinnon, Richard. *Keeper of Concentration Camps*. Berkeley: University of California Press, 1987.

Dumont, Robert V., Jr. "Education and the Community," *Americans before Columbus* 2, no. 3 (July 1964), 3.

———. "Oglala Community School Program." *Americans before Columbus* 2, no. 4 (December 1964), 6.

Edmo, Se-ah-dom, Jessie Young, and Alan Parker. *American Indian Identity: Citizenship, Membership, and Blood.* Santa Barbara CA: ABC-CLIO, 2016.

Fear-Segal, Jacqueline. *White Man's Club: Schools, Race, and the Struggle of Indian Acculturation.* Lincoln: University of Nebraska Press, 2007.

Fixico, Donald L. *The American Indian Mind in a Linear World: American Indian Studies and Traditional Knowledge.* New York: Routledge, 2003.

———. *Bureau of Indian Affairs.* Santa Barbara CA: Greenwood, 2012.

———. *Indian Resilience and Rebuilding: Indigenous Nations in the Modern American West.* Tucson: University of Arizona Press, 2013.

———. *Termination and Relocation: Federal Indian Policy, 1945–1960.* Albuquerque: University of New Mexico Press, 1986.

———. *The Urban Indian Experience in America.* Albuquerque: University of New Mexico Press, 2000.

Fletcher, Matthew L. M. *American Indian Education: Counternarratives in Racism, Struggle, and the Law.* New York: Routledge, 2008.

Forbes, Jack D. "An American Indian University: A Proposal for Survival." *Journal of American Indian Education* 5, no. 2 (January 1966): 1–7.

———. "The Development of a Native American Intelligentsia and the Creation of D-Q University." In Lutz, *D-Q University*, 75–88.

———. *Native Americans and Nixon: Presidential Politics and Minority Self-Determination 1969–1972.* Los Angeles: American Indian Studies Center, UCLA, 1981.

Forbes, Jack D., Kenneth R. Martin, and David Risling Jr. "The Establishment of D-Q University: An Example of Successful Indian-Chicano Community Development," 1972. In Lutz, *D-Q University*, 22–23.

———. "Internal Problems Faced by the D-Q Movement," 1972. In Lutz, *D-Q University*, 95–99.

Fortunate Eagle, Adam, with Tim Findley. *Heart of the Rock: The Indian Invasion of Alcatraz.* Norman: University of Oklahoma Press, 2002.

Frank-Cardenas, Joshua. "The Rise and Fall of D-Q University: Foundations." *Tribal College: Journal of American Indian Higher Education* 31, no. 2 (Winter 2019). Web exclusive. https://tribalcollegejournal.org/the-rise-and-fall-of-d-q-university-foundations/.

Gallup and American Indian College Fund. *Alumni of Tribal Colleges Better Their Communities.* Washington DC: Gallup, 2019.

Garroutte, Eva. *Real Indians: Identity and the Survival of Native America.* Berkeley: University of California Press, 2003.

Gonzales, Jennifer. "Tribal Colleges Offer Basic Education to Students 'Not Prepared for College.'" *Chronicle of Higher Education* 58, no. 32 (2012): A25–A26.

Good, Harry G., and James D. Teller. *A History of American Education.* 3rd ed. New York: Macmillan, 1973.

Goodner, James, Richard G. Woods, and Arthur M. Harkins. *Characteristics and Attitudes of 1968 Haskell Institute Students.* Minneapolis: University of Minnesota, 1970.

Griffin-Pierce, Trudy. *Earth Is My Mother, Sky Is My Father: Space, Time, and Astronomy in Navajo Sandpainting.* Albuquerque: University of New Mexico Press, 1995.

Guillory, Raphael M., and Mimi Wolverton. "It's about Family: Native American Student Persistence in Higher Education." *Journal of American Indian Education* 79, no. 1 (2008): 58–87.

Hafen, P. Jane. "'Help Indians Help Themselves': Gertrude Bonnin, the SAI, and the NCAI." Special Issue, *American Indian Quarterly* 37, no. 3, and *Studies in American Indian Literatures*, 25, no. 2 (Summer 2013): 199–218.

Harris, LaDonna, Stephen Sachs, and Barbara Morris, eds. *Re-Creating the Circle: The Renewal of American Indian Self-Determination.* Albuquerque: University of New Mexico Press, 2011.

Harvard Project on American Indian Economic Development. *The State of the Native Nations: Conditions under U.S. Policies of Self-Determination.* New York: Oxford University Press, 2008.

Hatathli, Ned. "Position Paper, 1970." In House "Historical Development," 112–16.

HeavyRunner, Iris, and Richard DeCelles. "Family Education Model: Meeting the Student Retention Challenge." *Journal of American Indian Education* 41, no. 2 (2002): 29–37.

Hertzberg, Hazel W. *The Search for an American Indian Identity: Modern Pan-Indian Movements.* Syracuse NY: Syracuse University Press, 1971.

Hetherington, Penelope. *Settlers, Servants, & Slaves: Aboriginal and European Children in Nineteenth-Century Western Australia.* Crawley: University of Western Australia Press, 2002.

Higher Learning Commission. *Distinctive and Connected: Tribal Colleges and Universities and HLC Accreditation—Considerations for HLC Peer Reviewers.* Chicago: Higher Learning Commission, 2013.

History and Semi-Annual Report by the Office of Navajo Economic Opportunity to the Advisory Committee of the Navajo Tribal Council. Fort Defiance AZ: Office of Navajo Economic Opportunity, 1968.

Horne, Esther Burnett, and Sally McBeth. *Essie's Story: The Life and Legacy of a Shoshone Teacher.* Lincoln: University of Nebraska Press, 1998.

House, Lloyd L. "The Historical Development of Navajo Community College." PhD diss., Arizona State University, 1974.

Hoxie, Frederick E. *A Final Promise: The Campaign to Assimilate the Indians, 1880–1920.* Lincoln: University of Nebraska Press, 1984.

———. *Parading through History: The Making of the Crow Nation in America, 1805–1935.* New York: Cambridge University Press, 1995.

———. *This Indian Country: American Indian Political Activists and the Place They Made.* New York: Penguin, 2012.

Iverson, Peter, ed. *"For Our Navajo People": Diné Letters, Speeches & Petitions, 1900–1960.* Albuquerque: University of New Mexico Press, 2002.

Jacobs, Margaret. *White Mother to a Dark Race: Settler Colonialism, Maternalism, and the Removal of Indigenous Children in the American West and Australia, 1880–1940.* Lincoln: University of Nebraska Press, 2009.

Jacoby, Karl. *Shadows at Dawn: An Apache Massacre and the Violence of History*. New York: Penguin, 2009.

Johansen, Bruce Elliot. *Encyclopedia of the American Indian Movement*. Santa Barbara CA: ABC-CLIO, 2013.

Johnson, Troy R. *The Occupation of Alcatraz Island: Indian Self-Determination and the Rise of Indian Activism*. Urbana: University of Illinois Press, 1996.

Johnson, Troy R., Joane Nagel, and Duane Champagne. *American Indian Activism: Alcatraz to the Longest Walk*. Urbana: University of Illinois Press, 1997.

Johnston, Basil H. *Indian School Days*. Norman: University of Oklahoma Press, 1989.

Jorgensen, Miriam, ed. *Rebuilding Native Nations: Strategies for Governance and Development*. Tucson: University of Arizona Press, 2007.

Josephy, Alvin M., Jr., ed. *Red Power: The American Indians' Fight for Freedom*. New York: American Heritage Press, 1971.

Juhnke, William E., ed. *President Truman's Committee on Civil Rights*. Frederick MD: University Publications of America, 1984.

Kutsche, Paul. "Cherokee High School Dropouts." *Journal of American Indian Education* 3, no. 2 (January 1964): 22–30.

Link, Martin A., ed. *Navajo: A Century of Progress, 1868–1968*. Window Rock AZ: Navajo Tribe, 1968.

Lomawaima, K. Tsianina. "The Mutuality of Citizenship and Sovereignty: The Society of American Indians and the Battle to Inherit America." In Allen and Piatote, "Society of American Indians and Its Legacies," 333–51.

———. *They Called It Prairie Light: The Story of Chilocco Indian School*. Lincoln: University of Nebraska Press, 1995.

Lomawaima, K. Tsianina, and Teresa L. McCarty. *"To Remain an Indian": Lessons in Democracy from a Century of Native American Education*. New York: Teachers College Press, 2006.

Lose, Nelson. "Why We Need Our Education." *Journal of American Indian Education* 1, no. 3 (May 1962): 22–25.

Lowery, Melinda Maynor. *Lumbee Indians in the Jim Crow South: Race, Identity, and the Making of a Nation*. Chapel Hill: University of North Carolina Press, 2010.

Lutz, Hartmut. *D-Q University: Native American Self-Determination in Higher Education*. Davis: Native American Studies Tecumseh Center, University of California–Davis, 1980.

Maddox, Lucy. *Citizen Indians: Native American Intellectuals, Race, and Reform*. Ithaca NY: Cornell University Press, 2006.

Maroukis, Thomas C. "The Peyote Controversy and the Demise of the Society of American Indians." In Allen and Piatote, "Society of American Indians and Its Legacies," 158–80.

Martinez, David, ed. *The American Indian Intellectual Tradition: An Anthology of Writings from 1772 to 1972*. Ithaca NY: Cornell University Press, 2011.

———. *Life of the Indigenous Mind: Vine Deloria Jr. and the Birth of the Red Power Movement*. Lincoln: University of Nebraska Press, 2019.

McCarty, Teresa L. *A Place to Be Navajo: Rough Rock and the Struggle for Self-Determination in Indigenous Schooling*. New York: Routledge, 2002.

McDade, Jeffrey R. *The Birth of the American Indian Manual Labor Boarding School: Social Control through Culture Destruction, 1820–1850.* Lewiston NY: Edwin Mellen Press, 2008.

McKenzie-Jones, Paul. "Evolving Voices of Dissent: The Workshops on American Indian Affairs, 1956–1972." *American Indian Quarterly* 38, no. 2 (Spring 2014): 207–36.

McNickle, D'Arcy. "Alaska: Getting Acquainted." *Indians at Work* 4, no. 7 (November 15, 1936): 5–7.

———. "Four Years of Indian Reorganization." *Indians at Work* 5, no. 11 (July 1, 1938): 4–11.

———. "Hill 57." *Indians at Work* 4, no. 12 (February 1, 1937): 19–21.

———. "The Straddle between Cultures." *Indians at Work* 5, no. 4 (December 1, 1937): 29–30.

———. *The Surrounded.* Albuquerque: University of New Mexico Press, 1978. Originally published 1936.

———. *They Came Here First: The Epic of the American Indian.* Philadelphia: J. B. Lippincott Company, 1949.

———. "Toward Understanding." *Indians at Work* 9, no. 9 (May–June, 1942): 4–7.

———. "We Go On from Here." *Indians at Work* 11, no. 4 (November–December, 1943): 14–21.

———. "What Do the Old Men Say?" *Indians at Work* 9, no. 4 (December 1, 1941): 24–26.

Meador, Bruce. "The Pupil as a Person." *Journal of American Indian Education* 4, no. 2 (January 1965): 17–22.

Meriam, Lewis. *The Problem of Indian Administration.* Baltimore: Johns Hopkins Press, 1928.

Messer, David W. *Henry Roe Cloud: A Biography.* Lanham MD: Hamilton Books, 2010.

Mihesuah, Devon A. *Cultivating the Rosebuds: The Education of Women at the Cherokee Female Seminary, 1851–1909.* Urbana: University of Illinois Press, 1997.

Miller, J. R. *Shingwauk's Vision: A History of Native Residential Schools.* Toronto: University of Toronto Press, 1996.

Miller, Susan A. "Seminoles and Africans under Seminole Law: Sources and Discourses of Tribal Sovereignty and 'Black Indian' Entitlement." In *Native Historians Write Back: Decolonizing American Indian History,* edited by Susan A. Miller and James Riding In, 187–206. Lubbock: Texas Tech University Press, 2011.

Minton, Charles E. "The Place of the Indian Youth Council in Higher Education." *Journal of American Indian Education* 1, no. 1 (June 1961): 29–32.

Moquin, Wayne, ed. *Great Documents in American Indian History.* New York: Praeger, 1973.

Morgan, Thomas J. "Supplemental Report on Indian Education, December 1, 1889." In *Documents of United States Indian Policy,* edited by Francis Paul Prucha, 176–79. 3rd ed. Lincoln: University of Nebraska Press, 2000.

Muñoz, Carlos. *Youth, Identity, Power: The Chicano Movement.* 2nd ed. Brooklyn: Verso, 2007.

Nash, Philleo. "The Education Mission of the Bureau of Indian Affairs." *Journal of American Indian Education* 3, no. 2 (January 1964): 1–4.

"National Indian Youth Council Named New Sponsor of United Scholarship Service." *Americans before Columbus* 2, no. 5 (June 1965): 4.

The Navajo Culture Center Purpose and Plans: A Shrine and Living Symbol for the Navajo. Tsaile AZ: Navajo Community College Press, 1972.

North, Woesha Cloud. "Informal Education in Winnebago Tribal Society with Implications for Formal Education." PhD diss., University of Nebraska, 1978.

Office of Indian Education. Bureau of Indian Affairs. *Higher Education Opportunities for American Indians.* Washington DC: U.S. Department of the Interior, 1971.

"Oglala Sioux Educational Survey." *Americans before Columbus* 1, no. 1 (October 1963): 9.

Oppelt, Norman T. *The Tribally Controlled Indian Colleges: The Beginnings of Self-Determination in American Indian Education.* Tsaile AZ: Navajo Community College Press, 1990.

Parker, Dorothy R. "D'Arcy McNickle: An Annotated Bibliography of His Published Articles and Book Reviews in a Biographical Context." In *The Legacy of D'Arcy McNickle: Writer, Historian, Activist*, edited by John Lloyd Purdy, 3. Norman: University of Oklahoma Press, 1996.

———. *Singing an Indian Song: A Biography of D'Arcy McNickle.* Lincoln: University of Nebraska Press, 1992.

Parman, Donald L. *The Navajos and the New Deal.* New Haven CT: Yale University Press, 1976.

Pavel, D. Michael, Ella Inglebret, and Susan Rae Banks. "Tribal Colleges and Universities in an Era of Dynamic Development." *Peabody Journal of Education* 76, no. 1 (2001): 50–72.

Pfister, Joel. *The Yale Indian: The Education of Henry Roe Cloud.* Durham NC: Duke University Press, 2009.

Philp, Kenneth. *John Collier's Crusade for Indian Reform, 1920–1954.* Tucson: University of Arizona Press, 1977.

Pratt, Richard H. "The Advantages of Mingling Indians with Whites." In *Americanizing the American Indians: Writings by the "Friends of the Indian," 1880–1900*, edited by Francis Paul Prucha, 260–71. Cambridge MA: Harvard University Press, 1973.

"Proposed Articles of the National Indian Youth Council." *Aborigine* 1, no. 1 (1962): 21.

Prucha, Francis Paul. *Documents of United States Indian Policy*, 3rd ed. Lincoln: University of Nebraska Press, 2000.

———. *The Great Father: The United States Government and the American Indians.* Lincoln: University of Nebraska Press, 1995.

Raibmon, Paige. *Authentic Indians: Episodes of Encounter from the Late-Nineteenth-Century Northwest Coast.* Durham NC: Duke University Press, 2005.

Ramirez, Renya K. "Ho-Chunk Warrior, Intellectual, and Activist: Henry Roe Cloud Fights for the Apaches." Special Issue, *American Indian Quarterly* 37, no. 3, and *Studies in American Indian Literatures*, 25, no. 2 (Summer 2013): 291–309.

———. *Native Hubs: Culture, Community, and Belonging in Silicon Valley and Beyond.* Durham NC: Duke University Press, 2007.

———. *Standing Up to Colonial Power: The Lives of Henry Roe and Elizabeth Bender Cloud.* Lincoln: University of Nebraska Press; and American Philosophical Society, 2018.

Reno, Thomas R. "A Demonstration in Navaho Education." *Journal of American Indian Education* 6, no. 3 (May 1967): 1–5.

Report to the Navajo Tribal Council for Navajo Community College. Many Farms AZ: Navajo Community College Press, 1972.

Reyhner, Jon, and Jeanne Eder. *American Indian Education: A History*. Norman: University of Oklahoma Press, 2004.

Rodriguez, Roberto Cintli. *Our Sacred Maiz Is Our Mother: Indigeneity and Belonging in the Americas*. Tucson: University of Arizona Press, 2014.

Roessel, Robert A., Jr. "A Light in the Night." *Journal of American Indian Education* 11, no. 3 (May 1972): 26–29.

———. *Navajo Education, 1948–1978: Its Progress and Its Problems*. Rough Rock AZ: Navajo Curriculum Center, Rough Rock Demonstration School, 1979.

———. "The Right to Be Wrong and the Right to Be Right." *Journal of American Indian Education* 7, no. 2 (January 1968): 1–6.

Roessel, Ruth, ed. *Navajo Stories of the Long Walk Period*. Tsaile AZ: Navajo Community College Press, 1973.

———, ed. *Navajo Studies at Navajo Community College*. Many Farms AZ: Navajo Community College Press, 1971.

———, ed. *Papers on Navajo Life and Culture*. Many Farms AZ: Navajo Community College Press, 1970.

———. *The Role of Indian Studies in American Education*. Chinle AZ: Navajo Community College Press, 1974.

Roessel, Ruth, and Broderick H. Johnson. *Navajo Livestock Reduction: A National Disgrace*. Chinle AZ: Navajo Community College Press, 1974.

Rosales, F. Arturo. *Chicano! The History of the Mexican American Civil Rights Movement*. Rev. ed. Houston: Arte Publico Press, 1997.

Ryser, Rudolph C. "American Indian Policy Review Commission." In *Native America in the Twentieth Century: An Encyclopedia*, 38–39. Rev. ed. New York: Routledge, 2014.

Sakiestewa Gilbert, Matthew. *Education beyond the Mesas: Hopi Students at Sherman Institute, 1902–1929*. Lincoln: University of Nebraska Press, 2010.

Schmidtke, Carsten, ed. *American Indian Workforce Education: Trends and Issues*. New York: Routledge, 2016.

Schultz, Jeffrey D., Kerry L. Haynie, Anne M. McCulloch, and Andrew Aoki, eds. *Encyclopedia of Minorities in American Politics: Hispanic Americans and Native Americans*. Phoenix: Oryx, 2000.

Scott, James C. *Weapons of the Weak: Everyday Forms of Peasant Resistance*. New Haven: Yale University Press, 1985.

Shreve, Bradley G. *Red Power Rising: The National Indian Youth Council and the Origins of Native Activism*. Norman: University of Oklahoma, 2011.

Sisseton Wahpeton Community College. *Sisseton Wahpeton Community College Catalog 1994-96*. Sisseton SD: Sisseton Wahpeton Sioux Tribe, 1994.

Smith, Paul Chaat. *Everything You Know about Indians Is Wrong*. Minneapolis: University of Minnesota Press, 2009.

Smith, Paul Chaat, and Robert Allen Warrior. *Like a Hurricane: The Indian Movement from Alcatraz to Wounded Knee*. New York: New Press, 1996.

Smith, Sherry L. *Hippies, Indians, and the Fight for Red Power*. New York: Oxford University Press, 2012.

Smithers, Gregory D. "The Soul of Unity: The Quarterly Journal of the Society of American Indians, 1913–1915." In Allen and Piatote, "Society of American Indians and Its Legacies," 263–89.

Stein, Wayne J. *Tribally Controlled Colleges: Making Good Medicine*. New York: Peter Lang, 1992.

Swisher, Karen Gayton, and John Tippeconnic III, eds. *Next Steps: Research and Practice to Advance Indian Education*. Charleston WV: ERIC Clearinghouse, 1999.

Szasz, Margaret Connell. *Education and the American Indian: The Road to Self-Determination since 1928*. 3rd ed. Albuquerque: University of New Mexico Press, 1999.

Tetzloff, Jason. "To Do Some Good among the Indians: Henry Roe Cloud and Twentieth Century Native American Advocacy." PhD diss., Purdue University, 1996.

Tetzloff, Lisa. "Elizabeth Bender Cloud: 'Working for and with Our Indian People.'" *Frontiers: A Journal of Women Studies* 30, no. 3 (2009): 77–115.

Thelin, John R. *A History of American Higher Education*. Baltimore: Johns Hopkins University Press, 2004.

Thom, Mel. "For a Greater Indian America." *Americans before Columbus* 2, no. 1 (March 1964): 1–2.

———. "Statement of the National Indian Youth Council," *Aborigine* 1, no. 1 (1962): 1.

Thompson, Hildegard. "You and Your Future: A Message to Indian Youth." *Journal of American Indian Education* 1, no. 3 (May 1962): 1–4.

Tippeconnic, John W., III. "Tribal Control of American Indian Education: Observations since the 1960s with Implications for the Future." In Swisher and Tippeconnic, *Next Steps*, 33–52.

Townsend, Irving D. "Reading Achievement of Eleventh and Twelfth Grade Indian Students." *Journal of American Indian Education* 3, no. 1 (October 1963): 9–10.

Trafzer, Clifford E., Jean A. Keller, and Lorene Sisquoc, eds. *Boarding School Blues: Revisiting American Indian Educational Experiences*. Lincoln: University of Nebraska Press, 2006.

Trahant, Mark N. *The Last Great Battle of the Indian Wars: Henry M. Jackson, Forrest J. Gerard, and the Campaign for Self-Determination of America's Indian Tribes*. Fort Hall ID: Cedars Group, 2010.

Ulrich, Roberta. *American Indian Nations from Termination to Restoration, 1953–2006*. Lincoln: University of Nebraska Press, 2010.

U.S. Senate Subcommittee on Indian Education. *Indian Education: A National Tragedy—A National Challenge*. Washington DC: U.S. Government Printing Office, 1969.

Vicenti Carpio, Myla. *Indigenous Albuquerque*. Lubbock: Texas Tech University Press, 2011.

Warner, Linda Sue. "The Emergence of American Indian Higher Education." *Thought and Action* 8, no. 1 (1992): 61–72.

Warner, Linda Sue, and Gerald E. Gipp, eds. *Tradition and Culture in the Millennium: Tribal Colleges and Universities*. Charlotte: Information Age Publishing, 2009.

Warren, Kim Cary. *The Quest for Citizenship: African American and Native American Education in Kansas, 1880–1935*. Chapel Hill: University of North Carolina Press, 2010.

Warrior, Robert. "The SAI and the End(s) of Intellectual History." Special Issue, *American Indian Quarterly* 37, no. 3, and *Studies in American Indian Literatures*, 25, no. 2 (Summer 2013): 219–35.

———. *Tribal Secrets: Recovering American Indian Intellectual Traditions.* Minneapolis: University of Minnesota Press, 1995.

Wax, Murray, and Rosalie Wax. "Cultural Deprivation as an Educational Ideology." *Journal of American Indian Education* 3, no. 2 (January 1964): 15–18.

Wesley, Clarence. "Indian Education." *Journal of American Indian Education* 1, no. 1 (June 1961): 4–7.

Wilkins, David E. *American Indian Politics and the American Political System.* Lanham MD: Rowman and Littlefield, 2011.

———, ed. *The Hank Adams Reader: An Exemplary Native Activist and the Unleashing of Indigenous Sovereignty.* Golden CO: Fulcrum, 2011.

———. *The Navajo Political Experience.* Rev. ed. Lanham MD: Rowman and Littlefield, 2003.

Wilkinson, Charles. *Blood Struggle: The Rise of Modern Indian Nations.* New York: Norton, 2005.

Wolfe, Patrick. "Settler Colonialism and the Elimination of the Native." *Journal of Genocide Research* 8, no. 4 (December 2006): 387–409.

Zaglauer, Hans P. "The Role of a Tribal College in the Academic Performance of American Indian Students." Master's thesis, University of Montana, 1993.

INDEX

Index

Assimilation, Resilience, and Survival: A History of the Stewart Indian School, 1890–2020
Samantha M. Williams

This Benevolent Experiment: Indigenous Boarding Schools, Genocide, and Redress in Canada and the United States
Andrew Woolford

To order or obtain more information on these or other University of Nebraska Press titles, visit nebraskapress.unl.edu.

www.ingramcontent.com/pod-product-compliance
Lightning Source LLC
Chambersburg PA
CBHW030735280326
41926CB00086B/1655